Watching the world

Manchester University Press

For Guy and Noah

Watching the world

Screen documentary and audiences

Thomas Austin

Manchester University Press
Manchester and New York
distributed exclusively in the USA by Palgrave

Published by Manchester University Press
Oxford Road, Manchester M13 9NR, UK
and Room 400, 175 Fifth Avenue, New York, NY 10010, USA
www.manchesteruniversitypress.co.uk

Distributed exclusively in the USA by
Palgrave, 175 Fifth Avenue, New York,
NY 10010, USA

Distributed exclusively in Canada by
UBC Press, University of British Columbia, 2029 West Mall, Vancouver, BC, Canada V6T 1Z2

British Library Cataloguing-in-Publication Data
A catalogue record for this book is available from the British Library

Library of Congress Cataloging-in-Publication Data applied for

ISBN 978 0 7190 7689 3 *hardback*

First published 2007

16 15 14 13 12 11 10 09 08 07   10 9 8 7 6 5 4 3 2 1

Typeset
by Frances Hackeson Freelance Publishing Services, Brinscall, Lancs
Printed in Great Britain
by Cromwell Press Ltd, Trowbridge, Wiltshire

Contents

Acknowledgements	*page* vi	
Introduction	1	
1	Continuity and change: the documentary 'boom'	12
2	Seeing, feeling, knowing: *Etre et avoir*	34
3	'Suspense, fright, emotion, happy ending': documentary form and audience response to *Touching the Void*	60
4	'The most confusing tears': home video, sex crime and indeterminacy in *Capturing the Friedmans*	84
5	Approaching the invisible centre: middle-class identity and documentary film	109
6	'Our planet reveals its secrets': wildlife documentaries on television	122
7	Conclusion: documentary world views	178
	Methodological appendix	184
	Select bibliography	205
	Index	215

Acknowledgements

Special thanks to Charlotte Adcock, as always, for critical insight, advice, love and support; Matthew Frost at MUP for believing in this book; Mike Stones for doing a great job very quickly; Lee Grieveson for 15 years of friendship, and for making me go the extra mile: your questions and suggestions improved this book immeasurably.

Thanks also to Margaret Adcock, Guy Austin, Roger Austin, Sue Austin, Helen Branwood, Rachel Davies (for introducing me to the book of *Touching the Void*), Eric Faden, Ian Huffer, Geoff King, Peter Krämer, Joanne Lacey, Hannah Lowe, Ernest Mathijs, Andy Medhurst, Sean Mendez, James Montgomery (for your friendship and cuttings service, and for taking me to see *Grizzly Man*), Anna Nathanson, Mick O'Malley, Paul Petit, Sue Thornham, Dolores Tierney, Ana Vicente, Paul Ward, Brian Winston, and to Dorothy Sheridan, Sandra Koa Wing, Karen Watson and Simon Homer at the Mass Observation Archive, University of Sussex.

Research undertaken via the Mass Observation Archive, and a research trip to the Sheffield International Documentary Festival in October 2005, were funded by the Research Fund of the School of Humanities, University of Sussex.

Finally, thanks to all those who participated in audience research projects for this book.

An earlier version of Chapter 2 appeared as 'Seeing, feeling, knowing: a case study of audience perspectives on screen documentary', published online in *Participations*, 2:1, August 2005.

Introduction

Anglophone screen documentary has experienced a marked rise in visibility and popularity since the late 1990s. This book is both a response to these developments and a contribution to them, insofar as it attempts to extend the reach of documentary studies. It does so by pursuing a critical inquiry into some recent instances of screen documentary, and the uses and possibilities that they offer audiences. What can such an analysis discover about how viewers engage with documentary?

I consider documentaries viewed at cinemas and on home video and DVD, as well as television programming.[1] The primary focus of the book is on mainstream British and American screen material, although it does also offer a case study of British viewers watching a French film. My intention has been to explore not only documentary texts, but also some of the commercial, discursive and social contexts in which they circulate and are watched, and the expectations and responses of some of their audiences. *Watching the World* proceeds by putting all these objects of study side by side, and analysing points of contact between them, rather than by isolating each as discrete and entirely separate from the others. Case studies focus on the interfaces between textual mechanisms, promotional tactics and audiences' viewing strategies. In the process, I investigate topics such as film and televisual form; the cognitive, sensory and emotional rewards of watching documentary; truth claims and issues of trust; and documentary ethics.

Of the three fields raised above – texts, contexts, and audiences for documentary – it is, rather predictably, the latter that has had the least academic attention. Since the early 1990s, screen scholarship has been energised by a renewed interest in documentary.

Important work by Bill Nichols, Brian Winston, John Corner, Stella Bruzzi and Michael Renov, to name but a few, has considered textual form, audience address, ethical concerns and industrial contexts, in productive and stimulating ways.[2] Despite this welcome blossoming of interest – and despite the odd exception[3] – audience perspectives on screen documentary remain significantly under-researched. Perhaps this should not be such a surprise, given the halting pace at which qualitative audience studies have been taken up within media and film scholarship in general. (The *idea* of doing audience research has become well established, and has been rehearsed in a number of overviews and review essays, but new empirical work still remains relatively thin on the ground.)[4] Audiences for screen documentary have been given even less attention than audiences for fiction film, or, more recently, for factual programming and 'reality television'.[5] For instance, a major collection of 27 essays on screen documentary, which announces itself as 'employing a wide range of critical and theoretical perspectives', has no room for any work on audiences.[6] This is fairly typical of the lack of academic interest in viewers' responses to, and uses of, documentary.

Screen documentary is generally organised around the expansive promise of delivering what Bill Nichols has called 'views of the world'.[7] It seems odd, then, that scholarly work on this mode has for so long ignored one crucial way in which documentaries exist in the world – via audiences' engagements with them. Hopefully, this book will provide an example of some of the insights that can be achieved by turning attention to this unaccountably neglected object of study. Investigations like this are long overdue if viewers of documentary are to be treated with the seriousness with which audiences for screen fictions are now being addressed.

The politics of location

Ideas of location, both literal and figurative, are central to my analysis. If documentary is about gaining mediated access to 'the world', where exactly is this world in relation to the audience? How is it framed and represented, and how is it to be apprehended from the standpoint of viewers, both presumed and actual? How might notions of the near and the faraway, of the familiar and the 'other' (be it exoticised or abject) operate via the discursive positioning and textual proposals of documentary, and in the responses of particular socially situated audiences? How might the binaries that I have just adumbrated become (re-)installed, queried or complicated? What are the political and ethical dimensions of such issues of proximity and distance, similarity and difference, whether constituted in geographical, social or cultural terms?[8]

These abiding concerns connect the case studies developed in this book. For instance, an unthreatening geographical distance contributes to the pastoral appeal of rural France for some British viewers of *Etre et avoir* (France, 2002), whose Francophilia can be considered as a classed disposition. Class is also central to my discussion of the 'white trash' representations deployed in the *Paradise Lost* films (US, 1996 and 2000), which attends to classed locations (including my own) and disjunctions, as well as issues of spatial separation. The chapter on *Touching the Void* (UK, 2003) examines how a geographically remote mountain-top adventure of risk and survival can be appropriated as a source of inspiration for the more quotidian demands of everyday life. In the case of *Capturing the Friedmans* (US, 2003) the family home, the mythical *locus classicus* of security and comfort, is construed as a site of endangerment and awful secrets, and subjected to criminal investigation and public scrutiny, with audiences invited to judge for themselves 'what really happened'. Finally, my analysis of audiences for wildlife programming considers constructions of the familiar and the exotic, and investigates respondents' attitudes towards first-hand and mediated encounters with the natural world.

Debates about the politics of speaking positions and the impossibility of standing beyond them emerged as part of the major epistemological shift associated with the post-structuralist turn in humanities and (some areas of) the social sciences. As touched on in Chapters 2 and 4, the form and purpose of documentary has itself been rethought in the light of these developments. (Brian Winston, for example, has noted the 'crisis of legitimation' threatening Griersonian documentary that stemmed from a combination of anti-realist critiques and more wholesale 'postmodernist' challenges to any attempts at truth-telling.)[9] They have also led to an interrogation of academic research as another way of making sense of, and producing knowledge about, the world. As the anthropologist Kirsten Hastrup has observed:

There is no way of speaking from nowhere in particular ... not
even for transculturated anthropologists ... In anthropology, as
in linguistics and philosophy, we have come to the end of 'the
dream of a description of a physical reality as it is apart from
observers, a description which is objective in the sense of being
"from no particular point of view"'.[10]

A swing towards radical relativism is not the best response to
this state of affairs, however.[11] Sensitivity to issues of location should
not lead to the abandonment of attempts to find out and 'report
back' about 'the world', near or far, via either documentary or, in
this instance, audience research. Certainly, the truth claims that
attach to both these discursive forms should not be taken at face
value. The knowledges that they offer must be considered as partial, enmeshed with power relations, and deriving from the contingencies of particular contexts and situations. However, that does
not invalidate either form, nor does it render it impossible to dis-
tinguish between examples of good and bad practice in each case.[12]

Defining documentary

John Corner has suggested that 'the term *documentary* is always
much safer when used as an adjective rather than a noun'. He
writes, 'to ask "is this a documentary project" is more useful than
to ask "is this film a documentary?" with its inflection toward firm
definitional criteria and the sense of something being more object
than practice'.[13] Corner argues that this is particularly true of what
he terms 'the "postdocumentary" culture of television',[14] where
documentary elements have increasingly been combined with
components from fictional, light entertainment and popular factual formats to produce a wide range of textual hybrids. (For more
on such combinations see Chapter 6.) As he notes, despite its commercial fragility, documentary in cinema 'still has the strong contrast with its dominant Other – feature film – against which it can
be simply defined as "nonfiction"'. On the other hand, nonfiction
on television 'describes half the schedule and so the question of
generic identifiers becomes immediately more troublesome'.[15]

Clearly, in the case of both cinema and television, individual
viewers will have their own preconceptions and expectations of
material labelled 'documentary' (either by themselves or by others), and these may or may not accord with more established

definitions.[16] However, such understandings will always be socially shaped by a host of factors – which may include advertising
hype, and trade and journalistic discourses about documentary –
in addition to the textual organisation of any screened material.
Paul Arthur gives a summary of some factors shaping the slippery notion of film documentary when he writes:

> Some theorists assert that doc [sic] itself is a genre, although a
> more sensible approach would describe it as a mode of production,
> a network of funding, filming, postproduction and exhibition
> tendencies common to work normally indexed as 'documentary'.[17]

Crucially, however, Arthur omits commonly proposed or deployed audience assumptions, orientations and viewing strategies
from his list. As Dai Vaughan has argued: 'What makes a film
"documentary" is the way we look at it; and the history of documentary has been the succession of strategies by which film-makers
have tried to make viewers look at films this way.' Vaughan continues, 'To see a film as documentary is to see its meaning as
pertinent to the events and objects which passed before the camera; to see it, in a word, as signifying what it appears to record.'[18]
Of course, as Vaughan is aware, such a response can never be
entirely 'guaranteed' on the part of any viewer, even allowing for
the significant discursive interventions made via marketing and
reviewing in demarcating a territory called 'documentary'.

In addition, the indexing of which Arthur writes cannot be
taken for granted. Some marketing campaigns deliberately avoid
the label 'documentary' when it is considered to be off-putting to
potential audiences. Such decisions may inform, but do not automatically predetermine, viewers' responses. Thus, ambiguously
marked material may on occasions still be viewed and made use
of by audiences as a 'documentary experience'.[19] This has been
the case, to varying degrees, with all three of my case-study films.
I consider viewer expectations of, and dispositions towards, documentary in more detail in Chapter 2.

The method and shape of this book

This book proceeds via a number of case studies, each of which
synthesises examinations of texts, contexts and audiences. The first
three, in Chapters 2, 3 and 4, focus on documentaries that enjoyed

commercial and critical success as cinema releases, before appearing in other release windows, including DVD and television broadcasts. The final study in Chapter 6 focuses on wildlife documentaries on television. Sandwiched between the films and the television study is Chapter 5, where I consider my own, classed, subjectivity, via a critical examination of my personal responses to two documentary films watched on video. Both my choice of case studies and my empirical audience samples constitute necessarily partial and selective investigations into a complicated and extensive object of inquiry. My arguments are often more suggestive than comprehensive. But I hope that, in addition to the particularities pursued in each chapter, some of my propositions will also aid critical thinking about screen documentary and its audiences more generally.

My research methods combine close analysis of documentary texts with contextual investigations into some of the commercial practices shaping these texts and their promotion, and qualitative audience studies aimed at finding more about viewers' encounters and engagements with the films and programmes. The exact balance between these three critical approaches, and the specific points of interface located among them, varies from chapter to chapter, but my overarching goal is to integrate these methods in order to achieve a kind of triangulation of readings brought to bear on some recent instances of screen documentary.[20] (For a further consideration of the specific audience research strategies that I employed, including examples of questionnaire design, see the methodological appendix.)

Chapter 2 draws on research among British arthouse cinemagoers watching the French documentary hit *Etre et avoir*, which recounts a year in a tiny rural school. Vectors of inquiry include viewers' operative generic assumptions about documentary (which *Etre et avoir* was seen to either fulfil or refuse), and their perspectives on issues of veracity and the essential truth claims of the genre. The study also explores distinctions made between notions of the 'authentic' and the 'inauthentic', the 'honest' and the 'contrived', and between ideas of documentary and reality television as good and bad objects respectively.

Chapter 3 uses research among audiences for *Touching the Void*, the highest grossing British documentary in history, adapted from a best-selling climbing memoir. It examines the film's form (which intercuts interviews and reconstructions), and interrogates a mode of engagement that treated the film as an 'inspirational' story of (male) suffering and survival. The chapter explores the appeal of the endangerment/survival scenario at the centre of the film, encapsulated in the promotional tagline: 'What would you do to survive?' and traces viewers' responses, both pleasurable and pained.

Chapter 4 centres on *Capturing the Friedmans*, the controversial and award-winning film about allegations of child abuse in a middle-class American family. The chapter makes use of close analysis of the film text, along with entries posted over a period of 18 months by viewers on the film's official website forum. It raises questions such as: what are the consequences of the extensive use of home movie and video footage in the film? How does *Capturing the Friedmans* make claims to authenticity by deploying this material, and how do editing strategies render it into a suspenseful 'thriller' narrative? The study also considers interfaces in the film between the public and the private, the personal and the political.

In Chapter 5 I briefly turn to some of my own responses to documentary films, and explore how my identity, particularly its middle-class aspect, has shaped these reactions. My argument here is influenced by work within both audience studies and feminist traditions that has focused on 'speaking positions' in order to avoid the universalising assumptions of supposedly 'objective' research. But my particular critical concern with middle-class identity is one that remains under-examined in much work on culture and the media. The chapter is intended to clarify the position from which I have conducted the research in this book, and act as a spur towards more critical thinking about class, in all its manifestations and complexities, within film and media studies.

Chapter 6 examines recent commercial and formal developments in the popular and enduring genre of the wildlife documentary on television. It draws on three original qualitative audience studies to look at the responses of viewers to a range of wildlife programming, from high budget 'blue-chip' series to hybrids borrowing celebrity presenters and formats from 'reality television' and other popular genres.

The reader will notice further connections as well as points of difference between the chosen texts. All three case study films (*Etre et avoir, Touching the Void* and *Capturing the Friedmans*), and most of the television programmes discussed here, are, to varying degrees, what might loosely be termed 'realist' documentaries. (As

Brian Winston has observed, 'the realist documentary makes the greatest "truth claims" for itself. [It] constitute[s] the dominant tradition, not just in the United Kingdom and North America but also in the rest of Western Europe ... Finally, the contemporary realist documentary dominates word-wide because it is the preferred variant of the form on television.')[21] One could also argue that the films, at least, fit the rubric of what Mark Cousins has called 'a new phase of classicism' in documentary.[22] Certainly, each has a clear focus on a limited number of human characters, and a dramatically effective narrative shape.

But there are also clear contrasts between the texts, in terms of form as well as subject matter. As such, this selection reflects something of the diversity to be found in recent screen documentary. *Etre et avoir* is an example of observational documentary, *Touching the Void* combines talking head interviews with dramatised reconstructions, and *Capturing The Friedmans* intercuts retrospective interviews with 'found footage' in the form of home movies and videos. Equally, the television documentaries analysed are drawn from a wide spectrum, ranging from 'traditional' prestige series like *Life in the Undergrowth* to new hybrid formats such as *Animal Crime Scene*.

In Chapter 7 I draw together some strands of the book by considering the social and political potential of documentaries to inform and galvanise audiences, to prompt new engagements with the world via the 'world views' that are screened for them. What are the possibilities and limitations of the mode in fostering new perspectives and understandings?

The ideas for *Watching the World* were slowly developing before the so-called 'documentary boom' of 2002 onwards, but that phenomenon gave a new impetus to the project, and provided some particular lines of inquiry. Three of my case studies are critically and commercially successful films from this period: *Etre et avoir, Touching the Void*, and *Capturing the Friedmans*.[23] It is easy to get overexcited about the revival of documentaries in cinemas, however, and to stress recent changes at the expense of continuities from earlier periods. It is also important not to overlook the presence of documentaries on television, particularly in the current multi-channel era. So the book includes an extended study taken from the wide range of documentary output carried on British television. This is a terrain less scrutinised than that of the cinematic boom, but one that also deserves inquiry, in terms of its popularity, recent and ongoing shifts in its commercial and textual organisation, and the meanings and pleasures that audiences derive from it. Before turning to my case studies I will, in Chapter 1, examine the contexts for documentary in cinemas and on television in more detail.

Notes

1 A more extensive study of documentary formats might encompass important developments in reality television, webcasting and blogging. However, while trying to remain aware of the reach and complexity of documentary as a cross-media phenomenon, I have sacrificed some breadth in order to concentrate on a handful of case studies in depth. For more on blogging and other forms of autobiographical documentary on the web, see Michael Renov, *The Subject of Documentary* (Minneapolis, University of Minnesota Press, 2004).

2 Bill Nichols, *Representing Reality: Issues and Concepts in Documentary* (Bloomington, Indiana University Press, 1991); Brian Winston, *Claiming the Real: The Documentary Film Revisited* (London, British Film Institute, 1995); John Corner, *The Art of Record: A Critical Introduction to Documentary* (Manchester, Manchester University Press, 1996); Stella Bruzzi, *New Documentary: A Critical Introduction* (London, Routledge, 2000); Renov, *The Subject of Documentary*.

3 For example, John Corner, Kay Richardson and Natalie Fenton, *Nuclear Reactions: Form and Response in Public Issue Television* (Academia Research Monograph 4) (Luton, John Libbey, 1990).

4 For excellent overviews of key issues facing the field in the 1990s, which are still relevant today, see for instance John Corner, 'Meaning, genre and context: the problematics of "public knowledge" in the new audience studies', in James Curran and Michael Gurevitch (eds), *Mass Media and Society* (London, Edward Arnold, 1991), pp. 267-84; Ann Gray, 'Audience and reception research in retrospect: the trouble with audiences', in Pertti Alasuutari (ed.), *Rethinking the Media Audience* (London, Sage, 1999), pp. 22-37; Sonia Livingstone, 'Audience research at the crossroads: the "implied audience" in media and cultural theory', *European Journal of Cultural Studies*, 1:2 (1998), pp. 193-217.

5 See for instance Annette Hill, '*Big Brother*: the real audience', *Television and New Media*, 3:3 (2002), pp. 323-40, and *Reality TV: Audiences and Popular Factual Television* (Abingdon, Routledge, 2005); Ernest Mathijs and Janet Jones (eds), *Big Brother International: Format, Critics and Publics* (London, Wallflower Press, 2004).

6 B.K. Grant and J. Sloniowski (eds), *Documenting the Documentary: Close*

Readings of Documentary Film and Video (Wayne State University Press, 1998), p. 20.

7   Nichols, *Representing Reality*, p. ix.

8   Of course, such questions may also be pertinent to screen fiction, but they seem particularly significant in making sense of documentary.

9   Winston, *Claiming the Real*, pp. 242-7. Winston quotes Christopher Norris's convincing refutation of Jean Baudrillard on this matter: 'It just does not follow from the fact that we are living through an age of widespread illusion and disinformation that *therefore* all questions of truth drop out of the picture'. Norris, *What's Wrong with Postmodernism: Critical Theory and the Ends of Philosophy* (Baltimore, MD, Johns Hopkins University Press, 1990), p. 182, italics in original, cited in Winston, *Claiming the Real*, p. 247. In an excellent discussion of subjectivity and autobiography in the field of documentary, Michael Renov argues that the 'repression of subjectivity has been a persistent, ideologically driven fact of documentary history' and that the study of documentary needs to take account of the 'waning of objectivity as a compelling social narrative'. Renov, *The Subject of Documentary*, pp. xviii, xvii.

10 Kirsten Hastrup, *A Passage to Anthropology: Between Experience and Theory* (London and New York, Routledge, 1995), pp. 13, 163, citing Hilary Putnam, *Realism With a Human Face* (Cambridge, Mass, Harvard University Press, 1990), p. 11.

11 Grappling with this issue, Start Hall, for instance, cannot ultimately do without some notion of an extradiscursive reality. He argues: 'I regard the extradiscursive as a kind of wager. It's a kind of bet that the world exists, which cannot be proven in a philosophical sense. I don't know how one would prove it. [...] I suppose, nevertheless, I simply can't think "practice" without touching ground, with each practice always touching ground as the necessary but not sufficient element – its materiality, its material registration. Somewhere. What that, however, pushes me to is what I would call the historically real, which is not philosophically real but has a good deal of determinacy in it.' 'Reflections upon the encoding / decoding model: an interview with Stuart Hall', in Jon Cruz and Justin Lewis (eds), *Viewing, Reading, Listening: Audiences and Cultural Reception* (Boulder, Westview Press, 1994), p. 268.

12 In a discussion of power relations and research practice that could also be applied to the politics of documentary, Beverley Skeggs argues that: 'unless researchers [...] make subaltern stories available how would most people know about the subaltern at all? If subaltern groups have no access to the mechanisms and circuits for telling and distributing their knowledge, how do others even know they exist? It is surely a mater of how we do the research rather than abdicate responsibility entirely.' Beverley Skeggs, *Class, Self, Culture* (London,

Routledge, 2004), p. 130. Of course, such an awareness should not indemnify either audience research or documentary against valid criticism, but it is an important counter to more sweeping and ultimately nihilistic critiques of both practices. Skeggs adds: 'there is a risk of assuming that epistemological authority [...] must necessarily entail a social / moral inequality of worth between the researcher and the researched. [... But] [m]ost of us do empirical research to learn from others, not to exploit and use them.' *Ibid.*, p. 131. In quoting Skeggs I am well aware that the situations of those people I have researched, and consequently the associated power relations, have varied from one instance to another.

13   John Corner, 'Performing the real: documentary diversions', *Television and New Media*, 3:3 (2002), p. 258.

14   *Ibid.*, p. 257.

15   *Ibid.*, p. 258.

16   There is no automatic consensus over such definitions. On processes of constructing genres within fiction film, including disputes over definitions and borders, see Thomas Austin, *Hollywood, Hype and Audiences: Selling and Watching Popular Film in the 1990s* (Manchester, Manchester University Press, 2002), chapter 4, and Rick Altman, *Film/Genre* (London, British Film Institute, 1999).

17   Paul Arthur, 'Extreme makeover: the changing face of documentary', *Cineaste*, 30:3 (2005), p. 20. As Arthur notes, it is also possible to locate generic types with 'family resemblances' — such as musical or natural history material — within the category of documentary.

18   Dai Vaughan, *For Documentary: Twelve Essays* (Berkeley, University of California Press, 1999), pp. 84-5.

19   For more on this debate, see Dai Vaughan, 'The aesthetics of ambiguity', in *For Documentary*, pp. 54-83; Winston, *Claiming the Real*, pp. 252-8; Paul Ward, *Documentary: The Margins of Reality* (London, Wallflower Press, 2005), pp. 28-30.

20   For a more detailed commentary on the implications of this kind of multi-dimensional approach, see Austin, *Hollywood, Hype and Audiences*, especially, pp. 1-10, 27-31, 195-8.

21   Winston, *Claiming the Real*, p. 7.

22   Mark Cousins, 'What's up doc?', *Sight and Sound* (NS), 14:2 (2004), p. 5.

23   How long will the boom last? What will be its consequences? When viewed in retrospect, will it be understood as a significant, lasting shift, or a temporary phenomenon? These questions are beyond the scope of this book, but will be very much worth asking at a later moment.

1

Continuity and change: the documentary 'boom'

In the period from late 2002 to early 2004, trade and popular film publications and websites in the United States and Britain began to identify a 'boom' in documentary cinema.[1] Such commentaries were based initially on the commercial success of a handful of documentary features, most notably Michael Moore's *Bowling for Columbine* (US, released October 2002, grossed $21 million in the US); the sleeper hit *Winged Migration* (France, a dubbed version of *Le Peuple Migrateur*, released April 2003, grossed $11 million); spelling contest film *Spellbound* (US, released April 2003, grossed nearly $6 million); and Errol Morris's *Fog of War* (US, released December 2003, grossed $4 million).[2] While music-related documentaries have occasionally done well over the years,[3] the subject matter of these films covered a much wider range.[4] So what were the factors behind this phenomenon?

There is no doubt that in 2003 and 2004 cinema audiences for documentary were growing, in both the US and the UK. More money than previously was being spent on watching documentaries – and this was not just due to the ticket price inflation that allows Hollywood to perennially hype every year as better than the one before. For instance, at the start of 2005, of the 20 biggest-grossing documentary films in US history, 11 were released in 2003 and 2004, and seven of these were in the top ten (eight if *Bowling for Columbine* is also included).[5] Unusually, some documentaries outperformed high profile arthouse and 'independent' fiction films. For example, as the *Los Angeles Times* noted, *Bowling For Columbine* 'out-grossed a host of more costly star-studded adult-oriented films, including *Far From Heaven*, *Antwone Fisher*, *Adaptation*, *Punch-Drunk Love* and *Confessions of a Dangerous Mind*'.[6] Equally, in the UK, mountaineering documentary *Touching the Void* grossed more than £2 million to become the second highest earning British film released in 2003. And in the same year subtitled French documentary *Etre et avoir*, already a hit in France, ranked ninth in the UK box office chart for foreign language films.[7]

In addition to these relatively big earners, less spectacular successes also gained more exposure than might have been expected. For example, *Ceský Sen/Czech Dream* (Czech Republic, 2004), a provocative hoax film involving the launch of a non-existent hypermarket, secured small but significant distribution deals in ten countries, a record for a documentary from Eastern Europe. Moreover, the total number of documentaries gaining theatrical release in the US climbed significantly, from an average of 15 in the late 1990s to around 40 in 2003 and 50 in 2004.[8] As Paul Arthur notes, this figure accounted for 'roughly ten percent of total film releases but more than one-fourth of the rosters for smaller, nonstudio distributors.'[9]

Four important points need to be borne in mind here. The first is that the commercial achievements of documentaries at the cinema have to be kept in proportion. While some have crossed over to the multiplex sector, the majority remain very much a niche taste, and deliver a fraction of the revenues earned by successful fiction films. As one professional observer of the US film industry put it: 'In the world of blockbusters, the [box office] mark to hit is $100 million, but in the world of documentaries, it's $1 million.'[10]

Another issue to consider is that most of the strong financial performers in the boom have been American. A handful of French films – *Etre et avoir*, *Le Peuple Migrateur/Winged Migration*, and *La Marche de l'empereur/March of the Penguins* (2005) – have done very well both at home and overseas, and *Touching the Void* became an unprecedented documentary hit in both the UK and the US, but these are very much the exceptions to the trend of American dominance. (The highly uneven but relatively healthy documentary sector in the US benefits from economies of scale in the home market, while UK filmmakers face the twin problems of sharing a language with American competitors, and the reluctance of 'risk averse'[11] distributors and exhibitors to handle home-grown products, two issues that have dogged UK fiction film producers for decades.)[12]

The third point is that some significant antecedents of the so-called boom appeared in the late 1980s and 1990s. Work in these decades by Nick Broomfield, Errol Morris and Michael Moore, among others, won both critical attention and audiences. Eric Faden identifies five influential films that paved the way for the documentary boom in the US: Morris's *The Thin Blue Line* (US, 1988, grossed over $1 million in the US), Moore's *Roger and Me* (US, 1989, grossed more than $6 million); basketball story *Hoop Dreams* (US, 1994, grossed nearly $8 million); low-budget fiction success *The Blair Witch Project* (US, 1999, grossed $140 million), and finally, Moore's *Bowling for Columbine*.[13]

According to Faden, *The Thin Blue Line* was significant not just in terms of the stylised reconstructions and film noir aesthetics praised by many commentators, but also because of the successful exploitation of its thriller narrative in the marketing campaign run by distributor Miramax.[14] Faden also notes the fit between Moore's emerging persona in *Roger and Me* – later apparent in his television appearances, books and the film *Bowling for Columbine* – and the 'journalist as star' tendency in American television in the 1990s. Finally, he stresses the importance of form (digital video blown up to 35 mm) and content (suspenseful narrative) in *Hoop Dreams*, and the role of *The Blair Witch Project* in apeing documentary style and so acclimatising audiences to a particular aesthetic involving hand-held (video) camera, location shooting, and the use of available light.[15]

The fourth point to note is that the boom was in part a discursive phenomenon, constructed in the output of film magazines, websites and newspapers.[16] It is therefore instructive to analyse some of them to get a measure of how they characterised this development and its significance for potential audiences.

For example, in May 2004 the British film monthly *Empire*, a forum not usually interested in documentary cinema, ran a five-page feature on 'modern cinema's most resurgent art form'.[17] The article differentiated between recent, successful films and earlier, unsuccessful ones, by deploying a combination of negative and positive discourses about documentary as a distinct mode of film-making. It described films such as *Fog of War, Touching the Void, Capturing the Friedmans* and *Onibus 174/Bus 174* (Brazil, 2002) as surprising additions to 'one of cinema's least popular genres, the dreaded documentary'.[18] Filmmakers were at last moving away from didactic documentaries 'that lectured their audiences – offering all the gripping drama of an introduction to differential calculus delivered in an airing cupboard'.[19] Documentary's status as what Bill Nichols has called a 'discourse of sobriety' emerges as a problem here, but, crucially, the evidential status of the mode, the claim to veracity, retains its pull.[20] According to *Empire*, the new films told 'quirky and often moving stories which have the ultimate gimmick: they're true'. Thus authenticity and human-centred stories are cast as the touchstones of successful documentary, encapsulated in the headline 'Reel life drama'.

The article quoted several documentary practitioners who positively compared recent films to a range of competing media forms. Andrew Jarecki, director of *Capturing the Friedmans*, located audience appetite for screen documentary in a disappointment with television news: 'News is so pared down. There's a hunger for more complete versions of stories'. Similarly, veteran filmmaker Nick Broomfield contrasted documentary cinema with the omnipresence of reality television: 'I've been really upset to see [UK] Channel 4 which is really the home of documentaries, switching to things like *Wife Swap* or *Big Brother* to try and desperately keep their ratings up. A lot of people who used to turn to Channel 4 have been alienated, so this audience goes to the cinema more because those documentaries they used to watch simply aren't on television anymore'. Kevin Macdonald, director of *Touching the Void*, pointed to documentary's advantages over Hollywood blockbusters: 'because mainstream movies have become so detached from reality – and in a fiction film these days *anything* is possible because of digital effects – I think that a real sense of surprise and wonder is easier to find in documentaries'.[21] The feature concluded:

> The paradox is obvious: the cinemas, the places where previous generations hunkered down, suspended their disbelief and engaged in a communal dream, are to some extent becoming refuges from the relentless artifice, places where we can go to wake up, to find out what's really going on. Or at least to engage with stories and experiences in which we can believe.[22]

The stress placed on the significance of character and story in new documentaries was also evident in a commentary by writer and filmmaker Mark Cousins in *Sight and Sound* magazine. For Cousins, reality television was not necessarily pushing audiences towards cinema documentary through its own failings, but was encouraging viewers to seek further involvement in real people's stories: 'Reality TV convinced viewers that those attributes they

craved – character, narrative, suspense, conflict and romance –
were present in rawer, more engaging states when real people
submitted themselves to the lens.'[23] Building on this list of audience demands, Cousins argued that documentary was entering 'a
new phase of classicism', centred unashamedly on character and
story. He cited *Touching the Void*, directed by Kevin Macdonald, and
Etre et avoir, directed by Nicholas Philibert, as key examples of this
trend: 'Macdonald and Philibert's work is at least as penetrating as
the [social problem] films inspired by Grierson, but is more linear
and proportioned, less straining for effect.'[24]

So, were new documentaries succeeding because of their differences from, or similarities to, Hollywood films? There was no
clear critical consensus at the time. Many films were seen to place
particular emphasis on conventions of story-telling and character
development familiar from fiction film. But documentaries still remained sufficiently different from much Hollywood output in this
period to be reviewed – if not always marketed – as a distinct com-
modity and experience. (For more on the ambiguous labelling of
documentaries in advertising campaigns, see Chapters 2, 3 and 4.)

There are important insights on offer in the commentaries discussed so far. But any investigation of the changing fortunes of
documentary needs to look beyond individual films and filmmakers in order to situate them in the larger setting of commercial
logics and industrial practices. For instance, it is clear that low-
cost digital technology has brought down some barriers to entry by
allowing documentaries to be shot and edited relatively cheaply.[25]
(The most celebrated example of this trend is Jonathan Caouette's
autobiographical *Tarnation* (US, 2003), famously made for $218.)[26]
However, without distribution and exhibition deals, any film will
remain largely unnoticed. The documentary sector, much like that
for fiction films, remains a buyer's market: 'Doug Hawes-Davis, a
filmmaker who recently founded a documentary film festival [says]
"Most of the distributors won't look at anything that comes unso-
licited".'[27] Tom Grievson, marketing manager, theatrical, at UK
distributor Metrodome, which handled *Spellbound* and *Mad Hot
Ballroom* (US, 2005), warned in October 2005 that the documentary market was nearing saturation. He estimated that 40 per cent
of the films sent to Metrodome's acquisitions department were
documentaries. Of these, just two per year would actually be picked
up by the company.[28]

Distribution and exhibition strategies are crucial in connecting filmmakers and audiences, and they have to be scrutinised in
order to gain a clearer picture of the boom. As Faden has noted, in
the US in particular, conditions for documentaries have been radically changed by shifts in the ecology of the so-called 'independent' sector.[29] The well-documented expansion of media
conglomerates (via takeovers and the creation of new in-house
divisions) into territory previously left to the independents has
impacted on documentaries just as much as on fiction films. These
developments have led to, among other things, the increasing use
of aggressive promotion methods pioneered by Miramax, which,
as Justin Wyatt puts it: 'has thrived due to its marketing savvy,
particularly the ability to apply "exploitation" techniques to art
house product'.[30] The kind of story- and character-centred documentaries celebrated in *Empire* and *Sight and Sound* clearly lend
themselves to this kind of marketing, and have proved attractive
and profitable to distributors of varying sizes.[31]

Elsewhere, Wyatt has written of 'high concept' Hollywood fiction films in terms of three major selling points: 'the hook, the
look and the book'.[32] While most documentaries lack the last two
elements (easily commodified visuals or production design, and
reliance on 'pre-sold' properties adapted for the screen),[33] many
recent hits have been hyped on the basis of an appealing, reso-
nant or controversial selling point – the narrative 'hook'.

For instance, controversial but humorous political content,
supplemented by the established 'gonzo' persona of Michael Moore
as star-director, was used to sell both *Bowling for Columbine* and his
subsequent, even bigger hit, *Fahrenheit 9/11* (US, 2004). Lacking
the presence of Moore as a documentary auteur, but influenced by
the format of his films, *Super Size Me* (US, 2004) landed the fifth
highest documentary gross at the US box office ($11 million) by
also courting controversy and combining it with humour.[34] Director Morgan Spurlock had a high profile target in McDonald's, and
his critique of junk food, along with the veracity of his argument,
was grounded in the onscreen endangerment of his own body,
whose involuntary responses (vomiting, alarming medical signs,
waning sex drive) provided an index of his declining health while
on a month-long burger binge.[35]

As will become clear, images of childhood, and a rural setting, were key to the promotion of *Etre et avoir*, a huge hit in France,

which grossed a respectable $777,000 in the US, despite being sub-titled (see Chapter 2). Similarly, footage of children, along with the suspense of a dramatic contest, provided much of the appeal for *Spellbound*, which placed tenth on the US all-time chart for documentaries, with a box office of nearly $6 million.[36] *Touching the Void* (see Chapter 3) grossed more than $4 million and ranks one place below *Spellbound*. It was marketed not as a documen-tary but as a mountain-top thriller centred on characters, action and scenery, along with the added attraction of being an adapta-tion of a best-selling book. *Capturing the Friedmans* (Chapter 4) grossed $3 million after being promoted as a family melodrama and an unresolved controversy about which viewers had to make up their own minds.

Following the surprise success of *Le Peuple Migrateur/Winged Migration*, another French wildlife film, *La Marche de l'empereur*, was picked up by Warner Independent Pictures, who targeted it at both arthouse and family audiences in the summer of 2005.[37] WIP changed the title to *The March of the Penguins*, added a new score and a voiceover from Hollywood star Morgan Freeman, and worked with the spectacular footage and extensive anthropomorphism al-ready present in the original film, summing them up with the tagline 'In the harshest place on Earth, love finds a way.' Branded activity guides, colouring sheets, and iron-on transfers were of-fered via the film's website. US exhibitor Greg Laemmle, presi-dent of Laemmle Theatres, commented, 'You've got that rarest of commodities – an arthouse film that also appeals to families. Just as we saw with *Spellbound* and *Winged Migration*, you've got some-thing where people are coming with kids and people who have no kids are coming.'[38] *The March of the Penguins* won an Oscar for best documentary and to date has grossed $77 million at the US box office, making it the second highest grossing documentary in US history.[39]

Good reviews and positive word of mouth tend to be more important for documentaries than for heavily advertised and 'front-loaded' big-budget fiction films. But advertising and publicity cam-paigns have certainly played a significant part in bringing documentaries to the attention of audiences. And there are signs that both exhibitors and distributors are increasingly demanding 'fast burn' ticket sales from documentaries, much as from fiction films. Tom Grievson, of distributor Metrodome, has noted the increasing pressure for documentaries to deliver quick returns at the box office:

> The days of opening a documentary and letting it tick over [in cinemas] have disappeared now. It's all about the opening weekend and keeping your film in the cinema. It's pretty brutal really ... You are ultimately battling against the other 12 [fiction films] that are released that week.[40]

While small distributors struggle to secure a decent theatrical run for their releases, both documentary and fiction, others have more clout in the marketplace. In the US, new marketing methods have been accompanied by a shift in power relations, such that some distributors have been able to demand longer runs in cinemas and better rental terms from exhibitors for selected documentaries. For example, Faden has shown how Michael Moore's *Fahrenheit 9/11* (released in 2004 by Fellowship Adventure Group, with Lions Gate Films and IFC Films)[41] was only made available to exhibitors on its initial run for bookings of four weeks or more. It peaked at a total of 2,011 screens in the US – comparable to the exposure of a mainstream fiction film – and earned $119 million at the box office, a record for a documentary.[42] Moore's previous hit, *Bowling for Columbine* (distributed by United Artists) had a minimum booking period of one week, peaked at a maximum of just 248 screens, and grossed $21 million, still the third highest US gross for a documentary.[43] Clearly, other contributory factors also shaped the relative earning power of these two films – including Moore's widely publicised attempt to intervene in the US presidential election campaign of 2004 with *Fahrenheit 9/11*. But it is also the case, as Faden argues, that one important reason why some documentaries have earned more at the box office than their predecessors is that they appeared on more screens and stayed around for longer.

While recent hits like those discussed so far have shown the viability of documentaries in the marketplace, the genre can also appear attractive to distributors because of acquisition costs that are still relatively low compared to fiction films. For example, Sony Pictures Classics paid $600,000 for the theatrical rights to release *Winged Migration* in all English-speaking territories.[44] As noted above, the film grossed $11 million at the US box office alone. Furthermore, marketing and publicity costs are usually lower than those incurred with fiction films. Commenting on the vogue for documentaries, one trade publication remarked: 'Publicity costs are lower because the films have no stars.' The report quoted Mark Urman, head of distribution for ThinkFilm, which released *Spellbound* in the US, contrasting the relatively cheap media campaign for the documentary with that for a Jodie Foster film also handled by ThinkFilm: 'Of the $6 million I'm grossing with *Spellbound*, a lot more of it goes into my pocket.'[45]

With distributors facing rising marketing costs in the cinema sector, post-theatrical markets such as DVD have become increasingly important. Much as in the case of many arthouse and 'independent' fiction films, cinema is being treated as a loss leader prior to DVD release. Tom Grievson, of UK distributor Metrodome explains, 'It's very, very hard [in the theatrical market] it's the ancillary markets where you make the money.' For example, Metrodome released *The Corporation* (Canada, 2003) on 20 prints in the UK. Prints and advertising cost £95,000 and the film earned £300,000 at the box office, of which the distributor received about 30 per cent. So, although the film did reasonably well, Metrodome barely broke even in the theatrical market, and Grievson was hoping that DVD sales would make the film profitable.[46]

Some documentaries have flourished in the DVD market. As Pat Aufderheide notes, 'sales of documentaries on DVD tripled between 2001 and 2004 … to nearly $4 million in the US. Online purchases, often through big name sites like amazon.com and Best Buy, have boosted DVD figures, while smaller scale web campaigns and viral marketing via email have encouraged the "house party" trend of group viewings, particularly for political documentaries.'[47] Some filmmakers choose to bypass the theatrical sector – and established distributors – entirely. For instance, in 2006 UK independent filmmakers' network Shooting People launched Word of Mouth, its own distribution label and online DVD sales outlet.

Documentaries can also provide a relatively cheap source of programming for proliferating cable and satellite television channels, many of them owned by media corporations involved in theatrical distribution and exhibition. Several of these – and other – television companies have supported and co-financed documentaries in recent years, including big earners like *Touching the Void* (Film Four, UK), *Capturing the Friedmans* (HBO Documentary, US) and *Etre et avoir* (Canal+, France), as well as many lower profile films. In addition to such supply side factors, Faden, like Cousins, suggests that some audience demand for such material on both big and small screens follows on from the popularity of reality television.[48] The next section looks in more detail at the spaces made available for documentaries on television.

Multi-channel television: new opportunities and new ghettoes?

In the field of television, much like the cinema sector, contexts of production, distribution and exhibition for documentaries have been undergoing significant shifts in recent years. As Simon Cottle has pointed out, 'New technologies of production and delivery, heightened competitiveness, industrial centralization, fragmenting audiences and internationalizing markets have all dramatically impacted on the "production ecology"'.[49] Cottle is discussing the environment for natural history programmes (see also Chapter 6 below), but there are few if any areas of television, either in Britain or the US, that remain untouched by these ongoing developments.

One key change in the television landscapes of many developed countries over the past decade or so is the continuing proliferation of, and growing audience shares won by, cable and satellite channels beyond the major networks. Whether this has led to better opportunities for documentaries to find (significant) audiences remains open to debate.

Writing on television documentary in the US, Brian Winston argues:

> As a corollary of technicist hype, it is also sometimes argued that the 'New Cabled World', augmented by satellite, has more than compensated for the disappearance of the documentary from the US broadcast networks with whole channels now devoted to such output. The truth is that these outlets command very small audiences, just as documentary and other serious programming did on the old nets. The Discovery Channel, for example, had a cumulative rating of 1.1, that is around a mere million homes, at the point when the networks were killing off their documentaries [following the 1984 removal of the Federal Communications Commission's requirements for them to carry public service programming] ... However, as with all upscale programming on

other equally comparatively unwatched cable channels ... Discovery works for cable just as documentary had originally worked for the networks – a 'duty channel' as opposed to a 'duty-genre'. They supply programming of a perceived 'quality' which could be used to legitimate the entire multi-channel output. It provided, in effect, the 'public service' legitimisation cable needed.[50]

Since Winston wrote these remarks, Discovery Communications Inc has continued to diversify beyond the so-called 'quality' documentaries niche, and now operates 13 channels in the US, including health, lifestyle, travel and children's programming.[51] If anything, the continuing proliferation of lifestyle and 'reality television' shows on both cable and the networks confirms Winston's critique of documentaries' limited foothold on US television.

In Britain terrestrial television 'brands' such as the BBC, ITV and Channel 4 have recently diversified into digital spinoff channels. For instance, in addition to its two terrestrial channels available via analogue and digital signals, publicly funded broadcaster the BBC operates a portfolio of digital-only windows, delivered via terrestrial, cable and satellite systems. These include the youth-targeted BBC 3 and the arts and factual-centred BBC4 (previously BBC Knowledge), as well as news, parliament and children's channels. Commercial operator ITV runs ITV2, ITV3 and ITV4 as digital-only channels, in addition to its core outlet ITV1. Meanwhile Channel 4 operates E4, a youth entertainment channel, and in 2005 launched both More4 – marketed as a new type of 'adult entertainment' channel combining drama, current affairs and documentary strands – and Fourdocs, a website running four-minute documentaries via broadband.[52] Danny Cohen, head of documentaries at Channel 4, has said of these developments:

> [FourDocs is] a place for new talent in particular to publish their work, to experiment with the form, and to learn craft skills from top British directors. And the launch of More4 is ... an additional creative space for factual programmes. A way of using the digital landscape to provide more blue-chip factual for viewers and more room for producers to experiment.[53]

In the context of this ongoing segmentation of audiences and markets, commissioners and schedulers have the option to place some documentary programming on smaller, specialist channels, in addition to that carried on mainstream outlets. Decisions about what material goes where and when have become very significant.

For some commentators and practitioners, this development has been a positive step, opening up spaces and bringing new opportunities for documentaries to be screened, sometimes with related footage spread across other channels. For others, the proliferation of niche markets simply allows many documentaries deemed too 'challenging' or 'unattractive' for a mainstream audience to be cordoned off into television ghettoes.

The more positive view is expressed by Cohen and by Martin Davidson, executive producer, specialist factual, at the BBC. He emphasises the 'sharply accentuated' colour palette available to documentary makers across the range of BBC outlets. This means that 'The BBC can offer specialist factual producers a range of settings for their work.'[54] Alastair Fothergill, former head of the BBC's Natural History Unit, is also optimistic about the proliferation of windows. Writing in the *Guardian* newspaper, media critic Ros Coward quoted Fothergill on this topic:

> At the last Wildscreen festival, one judge criticised Fothergill's *Blue Planet* [screened in 2001] as 'eight hours of programming about pristine oceans with nothing about the damage being done to the environment.' Fothergill thinks that the answer lies in channel diversification. 'It is understandable that at primetime you don't dwell on environmental issues, but on BBC4, for example, you can cover them. Alongside [then forthcoming] *Planet Earth* we are planning accompanying programmes on other channels, pan-programming. Now we view a production not as destined for one channel but as a portfolio.'[55]

This strategy effectively ghettoises environmental issues, however. For instance, just before the launch of *Planet Earth* on BBC1 in March 2006, a short 'climate change season' ran on BBC4, two programmes from which were repeated on BBC2. The season was in fact a disparate collection of one-off programmes with neither the prestige, the budget, nor the media profile granted to *Planet Earth*. The presence of such 'difficult' content on BBC4 allowed *Planet Earth* to remain effectively insulated from the issue of global warming, which was notably absent from the wildlife series. In this respect, BBC4 functions as the BBC's 'duty channel', to borrow Winston's phrase, both enabling and providing an alibi for the broadcaster's decision to restrict the coverage of climate change to a narrow window.[56] It is no coincidence that BBC4 captures only a tiny share of television audiences in multi-channel homes, measured at 0.2 per cent for 2003 and the first half of 2004 – compared to 19 per cent each for ITV (now ITV1) and BBC1.[57]

A critique of scheduling in the context of multiple channels is offered by Sean Mendez, second director of *Bang!Bang! in Da Manor* (UK, 2004), a documentary which traces connections between materialism, drug dealing and violent crime within some black communities in London.[58] The film was screened at over one hundred cinemas, community centres and schools around the country, and pirate copies circulated on DVD before it was picked up by the BBC's youth-oriented digital channel BBC3.

Bang!Bang! interviews an underground arms dealer, shows a drugs gang preparing its goods for the streets, and takes viewers inside an active crack house. It introduces critiques of consumerism into the debate, arguing that this is a major contributory factor shaping problems of drug dealing, gun violence and anti-social behaviour among black and working-class people. Mendez was pleased to have the film shown on television, but questioned the timing and positioning of the broadcast, on a niche channel at 11p.m. mid-week. He argued that the film's unique approach led to its relative marginalisation on the periphery of the schedule:

> I am unaware of any other film ever broadcast in the UK [on this topic] which [blames] capitalist culture for the breakdown of social, moral and spiritual values. I do not believe the mainstream channels would dare criticize capitalism and this blinkered view rules out [understanding] the current wave of anti-social behaviour as one of the side effects of capitalism.[59]

Mendez suggested that many supporters of the film 'considered the screening to be the BBC bowing to the public's demand, but burying the film in their digital schedule. Many comments reflected the view that the film … should have been broadcast on terrestrial television at a reasonable hour and advertised with a panel and public debate following the screening.' [60]

Whichever view seems more persuasive, that of Fothergill or Mendez, it is hard to disagree with John Ellis when he writes about television scheduling: 'This little studied but crucial aspect of broadcast management is central in determining the nature of any television service and any national televisual universe.'[61]

Other factors within the UK television industry are also the source of concern for some. For example, practitioners speaking at the Sheffield International Documentary Festival in October 2005 and at the Brighton Documentary Film Festival the following month expressed concern about the difficulty of making a reasonable living from television documentary in a climate of intensifying competition and contracting budgets, and suggested that documentary makers risked undercutting each other to win commissions at unsustainably low rates.

Luke Holland, director of the five-part Storyville series *A Very English Village* which 'breaks a number of rules' by exploring topics at some length, commented:

> It's a buyer's market. One of the problems which bedevils the film-making community is that to succeed we need to calibrate between a marketplace that is characterised by competition and our creativity ... there is an unhealthy paradox. One can enjoy critical success without enjoying commercial success. These are problems endemic to the industry.[62]

But others in the UK industry appear more optimistic about what they see as a growing appetite for documentary on mainstream television, and in cinemas. Such differences in opinion about the health of the industry may depend in part on which sector the speaker is working in. For instance, Nick Fraser, the man who commissioned Holland's films as series editor of the Storyville documentary strand (which originated with eight films on BBC2 in 2003 and has now expanded to around 50 national and overseas documentaries a year, spread across BBC2 and BBC4) gave this upbeat assessment at the British Documentary Awards in November 2005:

> I would like to advance three simple propositions. Firstly ... docs are the new rock and roll. They are really the only truly original cultural form in an era that appears addicted to retreads and knockoffs, tyrannised by formats. I know this is a sweeping generalisation, but here goes. Docs are also the ultimate one-offs, and docs right now are better than feature films. Why? Because they tell us about the world. So I am grateful that I was there, or here, at the great doc moment ... Proposition number two: docs are truly global ... The third proposition: docs are still hot on TV. So much is talked about cinemas and documentaries but let's be real for a moment. Documentaries cannot survive without television. When television loses interest film makers starve or do something else.[63]

Fraser's comments about the primacy of television as the key exhibition window for documentary are worth paying attention to in the midst of hype about documentaries succeeding in cinemas. There is also undoubtedly a trace of moral superiority in his remarks, however, which may appear as yet another instance of distinctions being made between documentary and the more 'irresponsible' attractions of fictional or entertainment-driven film and television. As Bill Nichols has noted, similar claims have been made repeatedly by practitioners and commentators over the course of the twentieth century. However, this 'belief in redemption through an avowed social purpose has come under siege' recently from theorists who posit that documentary is simply a construct, 'a fiction like any other'.[64]

I shall return to this debate in the later chapters that follow, particularly the conclusion. For now, Fraser's speech shows that the notion of documentary as a distinct mode of telling audiences 'about the world' remains influential within the UK industry. This is perhaps unsurprising, given that it potentially gives documentary projects a unique selling point, so differentiating them from other programmes. Thus, without being cynical about the motives of Fraser or certain filmmakers, the question may appear to some in the business to be as much about product differentiation as about political or moral imperatives. Finally, it is essential that documentary should not be granted a kind of moral exceptionalism in the cultural sphere which fireproofs it against properly critical scrutiny, so obviating all criticism of the mode. I hope that the last point is put into practice in this book.

Notes

1   See for instance Robert Koehler, 'Fest loads up on nonfiction cinema: the doc is in, with a nod to H'wood', www.variety.com/toc-archive/2002/20020514.html, posted 15 May 2002; Patrick Goldstein, 'No longer "dull", documentaries rev up art houses', 15 July 2003, *Los Angeles Times*, pp. E1, E4; M. Kreinin Souccar, 'Film companies wake to reality', Crain's New York Business, www.findarticles.com/p/articles/mi_go1577/is_200310/ai_n9427169, posted 20 October 2003; 'Film Reporter', Hollywood Reporter online at Hollywoodreporter.com, posted 22 August 2003; Nick Poppy, 'Truth in Entertainment; Five Hot Documentaries', www.indiewire.com/movies/movies_031117docs.html, posted 17 November 2003; Steve

Winn, 'Michael Moore is not alone. These are heady days for documentary filmmakers with something to say (or spin). But is the trend here to stay?', San Francisco Chronicle online, www.sfgate.com/cgi-bin/article.cgi?f=/c/a/2004/08/06/DDGIP82QTJ1.DTL, posted 6 August 2004 . All sites accessed June 2005. For examples from the British press, see discussion later in this chapter. For a French perspective, see Juliette Cerf and Olivier Joyard, 'Le Reel est entre dans les salles', *Cahiers du Cinema* (November 2002), pp. 12–19. Thanks to Guy Austin for providing me with this article.

2   All figures are for US box office, taken from boxofficemojo.com, accessed April 2005. UK grosses are as follows: *Bowling for Columbine*, £1.7 million; *Spellbound*, £480,000. Charles Gant, 'Does truth pay?', *Sight and Sound*, 15:9 (September 2005), p. 8.

3   For instance, *Madonna: Truth or Dare* (US, 1991) grossed $15 million in the US, and £1.2 million in the UK; *Buena Vista Social Club* (Germany, 1999) grossed $7 million and just shy of £1 million. Figures from www.imdb.com and Gant, 'Does truth pay?'

4   Hip-hop biopic *Tupac: Resurrection* (US, released November 2003, grossed $7 million) was rarely if ever mentioned in these articles.

5   *La Marche de l'empereur/March of the Penguins*, released in the US in June 2005, rose to second place in the all-time box office chart.

6   Goldstein, 'No longer "dull", documentaries rev up art houses'.

7   Eddie Dyja (ed.), *BFI Film Handbook 2005* (London, British Film Institute, 2004), pp. 43–6.

8   Arthur, 'Extreme makeover', p.18. Arthur's figures exclude IMAX releases and non-commercial venues.

9   *Ibid.*

10 Paul Dergarabedian, president of film industry monitor Exhibitor Relations, quoted in Carla Meyer, 'In a summer of blockbuster attractions full of blondes, pirates and machines, discerning Bay Area movie audiences are flocking to three documentaries', San Francisco Chronicle online, posted 15 July 2003, at www.sfgate.com, accessed 16 June 2005. Thanks to Ana Vicente for pointing me to this article.

11 The phrase comes from Jess Search, co-founder of Shooting People, an independent film makers' network, and chief executive of the Channel 4 British Documentary Film Foundation, talking at 'The rise of the cinema documentary' panel held at Sheffield International Documentary Festival, 14 October 2005.

12 One recent attempt to support and develop documentary film making in the UK, including solving the perennial problems of gaining distribution and exhibition deals, is the Channel 4 British Documentary Film Foundation. This initiative was launched in autumn 2005 with a budget of £2.6 million over three years to 'develop, fund and distribute the work of the most innovative UK documentary film-

makers'. The foundation is 'looking to back short films, particularly by new filmmakers, feature-length projects with the potential to break through, [and] experimental films'. 'We want the foundation's work to help maintain the UK's world-class reputation as the home of documentary, as well as finding new avenues for films to be seen both in the UK and on the international film circuit.' www.britdoc.org, accessed November 2005.

13 Eric Faden, *Media Stylo 4: The Documentary's New Politics*, premiered at Society for Cinema and Media Studies conference, London, 31 March 2005. Thanks to Eric Faden for giving me a copy of his film.

14 Faden quotes a letter from Harvey Weinstein of Miramax to director Errol Morris, in which the latter is urged to be less 'boring' in media interviews about the film. Weinstein writes: 'If you continue to be boring I will hire an actor in New York to pretend he's Errol Morris … keep it short and keep selling it.'

15 A similar point about film form is made by Mark Cousins, who points to the use of digital video in other recent fiction films: 'Where most filmgoers used to expect grainless and transparent imagery, the palpable attractions of *Festen* and *28 Days Later* … seem to have introduced an openness to a less slick aesthetic.' Cousins, 'What's up doc?'.

16 An interesting example of the recuperation of 'documentary' as a valid and marketable label occurred in the autumn of 2005 when British broadcaster Channel 4 screened 'The top 50 documentaries'. This was a compilation show made up of clips, interviews and commentaries, centred on both film and television documentaries. The selection could be criticised for excluding foreign language material, and for including reality television hits like *Faking It* and *Wife Swap*. But the very existence of such a programme on a commercial channel at peak time on a Sunday night shows that by 2005 television viewers were not considered to be antipathetic or indifferent to the notion of documentary as a recognisable category. Channel 4, 9 October 2005.

17 Adam Smith, 'Reel life drama', *Empire* (May 2004), pp. 117–22. Thanks to Ian Huffer for pointing me to this piece.

18 *Ibid.*, p. 117.

19 *Ibid.*, pp. 118–19.

20 Nichols, *Representing Reality*, p. 3. The formulation of the mode as a 'discourse of sobriety' seems rather rigid and outdated when confronted with a host of formal innovations and new hybrids, such as formatted documentaries, celebrity vehicles and 'mockumentaries'. But to argue that no documentaries mobilise or engage with such a discourse would be overstated and inaccurate, even in this new landscape.

21 Smith, 'Reel life drama', pp. 118–19, italics in original. As will become apparent in my case studies, some of the distinctions made in the

Empire piece, particularly between documentary and reality television, were similarly deployed by respondents in my audience research samples.

22 *Ibid.*, p. 122.

23 Cousins, 'What's up doc?'. See similar comments by Mark Urman, of ThinkFilm, quoted in Souccar, 'Film companies wake to reality': 'Even though *Temptation Island* and these fine [documentary] films that go into theaters have little in common, it is still significant that millions of Americans are sitting home on their couches and watching something that doesn't have stars and fancy sets and costumes.'

24 Cousins, 'What's up doc?'.

25 Nick Fraser, series editor of the long running BBC documentary strand Storyville, commented in a 2004 interview: '[one] reason why documentaries have exploded is the steadily lowering cost of equipment. It's a transformation. People can now afford to make documentaries. There's no equivalent form of journalism, or writing or entertainment that's been changed so totally as the documentary.' Fraser also suggested that documentaries 'have become fashionable because there's been a reaction against the platitudes and stereotypes of television. It's no coincidence that this movement has got furthest where the platitudes of television are strongest – ie America.' www.bbc.co.uk/bbcfour/documentaries/storyville/nick-fraser-interview.shtml, accessed March 2006.

26 The figure of $218 has been widely quoted, and is listed, for example, on imdb.com as the budget for the film. It has also been disputed, however, as it excludes several important costs. These include the cost of acquiring the i-Mac on which the film was edited (lent to Cauoette by his partner), cost of the cameras used, transfers of Super 8 and other footage to i-Mac compatibility, and, most significantly, an estimated $500,000 in fees paid for music and samples clearance rights. One estimate gives the film's 'real' budget as $510,000. See Mike Ashcroft, 'Low-fi futures', letter in *Sight and Sound* (NS), 15:6 (2005), p. 88. Paul Arthur has noted the increasing costs of buying rights to music and archival materials, which may hit makers of historical documentaries particularly hard: 'the popularity spurt over the past several years, in combination with greater emphasis on intellectual property rights, has created obstacles for continued easy access to archival materials and music ... ballooning clearance costs represent a looming crisis'. Arthur, 'Extreme makeover', p. 22.

27 Souccar, 'Film companies wake to reality'.

28 Tom Grievson, 'The rise of the cinema documentary', panel at Sheffield International Documentary Festival, 14 October 2005.

29 Faden, *Media Stylo 4*.

30 Justin Wyatt, 'The formation of the "major independent": Miramax,

New Line and the New Hollywood', in Steve Neale and Murray Smith (eds), *Contemporary Hollywood Cinema* (London, Routledge, 1998), p. 83.

31 There have also been some examples of creative programming on the part of exhibitors. For instance, at some American cinemas, the fiction film *Cidade de Deus/City of God* and the hijack documentary *Onibus 174/Bus 174* ran as a double bill. Each film was handled by a different distributor (respectively, Miramax and ThinkFilm), but they were linked via shared settings in the slums of Rio de Janeiro, as well as their positioning in the marketplace, targeted, in this instance at least, at an audience that was expected to watch them both. Thanks to Eric Faden for this example.

32 Justin Wyatt, *High Concept: Movies and Marketing in Hollywood* (Austin, University of Texas Press, 1994), pp. 20–2.

33 Nevertheless, some documentaries have been effectively pre-sold on the basis of their stars and/or subject matter. These include various music documentaries and, in the latter category, films based on already mediated news events, including the previously televised bus hijack retold in *Bus 174*, and Michael Moore's reworking of September 11th and the Columbine shooting in *Fahrenheit 9/11* and *Bowling for Columbine*.

34 *Super Size Me* grossed £1 million in the UK, placing it fourth on the all-time chart for documentaries in summer 2005. Gant, 'Does truth pay?', p. 8.

35 By comparison, *The Corporation* (Canada, 2003), a much wider-ranging critique of business practices which shared some similar targets such as the blizzard of advertising aimed at children, lacked the focus on a single issue, narrative economy and deadline, all condensed around first-person experience, that made *Super Size Me* particularly attractive to audiences. *The Corporation*'s marketing hook was to put on trial the 'crimes' of big business as if it were a person, but the film, while commercially successful, remained harder to market than *Super Size Me*. *The Corporation* grossed just under $2 million in the US, around one sixth of the figure for *Super Size Me*. www.imdb.com, accessed November 2005.

36 Director Jeff Blitz was reportedly influenced by watching Rene Clair's 1945 adaptation of Agatha Christie's *And Then There Were None*: 'My generation is a lot more comfortable borrowing ideas from older Hollywood films. Seeing *And Then There Were None* offered a great lesson in the shorthand of creating characters and building suspense.' Quoted in Goldstein, 'No longer "dull"', p. E4.

37 The production budget was provided by a number of backers, including Canal+, Buena Vista France and National Geographic.

38 Roshan McArthur, 'Super fluffy animals', *Guardian*, 15 July 2005, G2, p. 7.

39 www.imdb.com, accessed November 2005.

40 Tom Grievson speaking at 'The rise of the cinema documentary' panel.

41 Fellowship Adventure Group was formed by the Weinstein brothers after corporate parent Disney objected to plans for Miramax to distribute *Fahrenheit 9/11*, due to its political content. Following its own successful involvement in the release of the film, Lions Gate Entertainment established a documentary unit 'to develop feature-length single-subject documentary projects in partnership with broadcasters that are suitable for television, theatrical and home entertainment distribution'. An early result of this strategy was Werner Herzog's *Grizzly Man* (US, 2005), which was produced by Discovery Docs for theatrical release and subsequent television screening on the Discovery Channel, and was distributed theatrically in the US by Lions Gate. www.grizzlyman.com.production.html; http://dsc.discovery.com/convergence/grizzlyman/about/discoverydocs.html, both accessed September 2005.

42 The film is also the all-time top grossing documentary in the UK, with a gross of nearly £7 million. Gant, 'Does truth pay?', p. 8.

43 Faden, *Media Stylo 4*.

44 Souccar, 'Film companies wake to reality', cited in Ana Vicente, 'Exhibition of Documentary Films in Europe', 2004, unpublished paper. Thanks to Ana Vicente for making her paper available to me.

45 Souccar, 'Film companies wake to reality'.

46 Grievson, 'The rise of the cinema documentary'.

47 Pat Aufderheide, 'The changing documentary marketplace', *Cineaste*, 30:3 (2005), p. 26.

48 Faden also notes that the initial US reality TV boom – which took place a few years after that in the UK – was itself spurred in part by the threatened writers' and actors' strikes of 2000. Faden, *Media Stylo 4*.

49 Simon Cottle, 'Producing nature(s): on the changing production ecology of natural history TV', *Media, Culture and Society*, 26:1 (2004), p. 82.

50 Brian Winston, *Lies, Damn Lies and Documentaries* (London, British Film Institute, 2000), p. 48. In a discussion of the 'quality television debate' in Britain, Helen Wheatley also points to the symbolic role played by 'flagship' programming: 'those people using the BBC Natural History Unit's *The Blue Planet* throughout 2001–02 to argue for the continued vigour of a public service broadcasting ethos within British television (including Greg Dyke, then Director General of the BBC, Tessa Jowell, Culture Secretary, and Patricia Hodgson, Head of the Independent Television Commission) inadvertently announced the state of disrepair that the rest of British public service broadcasting was in.' Helen Wheatley, 'The limits of television? Natural history programming and the transformation of public service broadcasting', *European Journal of Cultural Studies*, 7:3 (2004), p. 326.

51 www.discovery.com, accessed November 2005.

52 See www.channel4.com/fourdocs. The site is conceived of as both an educational resource (including a growing archive of documentaries from 1906 to the early 2000s, along with technical and legal guides for filmmakers), and a venue where new works can be uploaded and seen. It thus chimes with Channel 4's public service remit but also constitutes an extension of the 'talent ladder' whereby the channel can attract material and filmmakers for possible television screenings and future projects. In mid-2006, an average of 15 films a month were being uploaded on to the site, which was receiving around 70,000 hits a month, some 60 per cent of which were from outside the UK. At this time plans were being developed to supplement the site's four-minute format with 59-second 'microdocs' and 30-minute films. Information from Emily Renshaw Smith, Fourdocs producer, and Patrick Uden, executive editor, presentation at University of Sussex, 23 May 2006.

53 Danny Cohen, 'Exploring new territory', *Broadcast* (7 October 2005), p. 14. Cohen added, 'It feels like ideas emerging from the world of factual entertainment have been much better so far at making new technology integral to their form and success. Web viewing and telephone and text interactivity are playing huge roles in this area. Documentary seems much further behind when it comes to thinking about new media at the genesis of an idea rather than as a bolt-on to be worked out at a later stage.'

54 Martin Davidson, speaking at 'Science or art: commissioning specialist factual' panel, Sheffield International Documentary Festival, 13 October 2005.

55 Ros Coward, 'Back to Nature', *Guardian*, 9 May 2005, G2, p. 6.

56 Some of this programming was repeated on BBC4 as part of a subsequent 'Climate Chaos' season. This included a more sustained engagement with environmental issues on BBC1, centred on two hour-long prime time documentaries presented by David Attenborough: 'Are we changing planet earth?', 24 May 2006; 'Can we save planet earth?', 1 June 2006.

57 Alistair D. McGown (ed.), *BFI Television Handbook 2005* (London, British Film Institute, 2004), p. 26.

58 Thanks to Anna Nathanson for introducing me to this film, and to Sean Mendez.

59 Mendez also questioned the motives of the BBC in buying the rights to the film: 'Executives from the BBC acknowledge that it would have been extremely difficult for a BBC journalist to be granted the access we had. However, although we believe the BBC recognised the authenticity and value of the film, we believe their decision had more to do with the BBC wanting to be seen to support and promote "black"

independent production companies. Past experience determines for us the mainstream media's enthusiasm to be recognised as diverse and multi-cultural, and unfortunately all too often this becomes the factor which determines the interest of the mainstream broadcasters.' BBC3 acquired the rights to broadcast the film 12 times over 5 years.

60 Sean Mendez, email corespondence with author, 8 July 2005.

61 John Ellis, *Seeing Things: Television in the Age of Uncertainty* (London and New York, I.B.Tauris, 2000), p. 2. New technologies such as personal video recorders and digital video recorders, including Sky Plus, have the capability to override centralised scheduling, however. As Peter Bazalgette, chairman of Endemol, has suggested, 'Allowing people to watch programmes whenever they want and in any order they want is the beginning of the death of scheduling.' Quoted in *Guardian*, 30 December 2005, G2, p. 7.

62 Luke Holland speaking at the Brighton Documentary Film Festival, 20 November 2005.

63 Nick Fraser speaking at The British Documentary Awards, broadcast on BBC4, 29 November 2005. Fraser was collecting a Trustees Award from the Grierson Trust for his outstanding contribution to documentary film making. A more pessimistic assessment was made by Alan Hayling shortly after resigning as head of television documentaries at the BBC in summer 2006. Hayling blamed his decision on cost cutting and staff reductions, and warned that plans to open up more projects to independent producers under Director General Mark Thompson's 'Window of Creative Competition' initiative would erode the BBC's long-standing role as a training house for the whole sector in the ethos of public service broadcasting. James Silver, 'The radical who fled the revolution', *Guardian*, 12 June 2006, Media section, p. 5.

64 Nichols, *Representing Reality*, p. 108. Nichols argues against both the extremes outlined here.

2
Seeing, feeling, knowing: *Etre et avoir*

This chapter draws on a small study conducted in July 2003, using questionnaires submitted by self-selected and largely middle-class cinemagoers who watched the French documentary *Etre et avoir* (2003) at an arthouse cinema in Brighton, England. My initial vectors of inquiry were cinemagoers' operative generic assumptions about documentary (which *Etre et avoir* was seen to either fulfil or to refuse), and their perspectives on issues of veracity and the so-called crisis over trust and the essential truth claims of the mode. Other issues raised by audience response to the film included a series of distinctions made between notions of the 'authentic' and the inauthentic, the 'honest' and the contrived, and between ideas of documentary and reality television as good and bad objects respectively. Towards the end of the chapter I turn to questions of ethics, shaped in part by a legal action pursued by one of the film's subjects.

The choice of film, cinema and, ultimately, audience also facilitated some insights into the cultural tastes and practices of that nebulous category, the English middle classes, and in particular what Mike Savage et al. have called the 'professional middle class'. (Savage et al. divide the British middle classes into three categories: entrepreneurial, managerial and professional. These are 'differentiated mainly by their respective command of property, organizational and cultural assets'.)[1] Middle-class identity as it relates to cultural and media practices is all too often naturalised, rendered almost 'invisible' and excused from proper scrutiny in fields of study which have typically excavated other dimensions of identity (like race, gender and sexuality) much more energetically. This relative lack of attention is apparent not just in otherwise highly self-conscious modes of semi-autobiographical academic writing. As Ann Gray has recently argued, it is also evident in the area of audience research. Gray points out that this neglect has been linked to an understandable critical enthusiasm for listening to the voices of 'ordinary people', and, often, for validating popular culture in the face of inherited cultural canons. However, its consequences can be problematic:

> The emphasis of cultural studies thus far on popular forms ... ignores crucially important groups – cultural producers, consumers of middle or so-called 'high' culture, policy-makers – who in different ways shape and form the cultural landscape.[2]

Two further points are relevant here. First, I would argue that many studies of fans, viewers and audiences, *have* actually focused on members of the middle classes, but that this classed dimension has not been addressed explicitly. Class still seems to be a critical lens used most frequently, if at all, to think about the other – usually the working classes – rather than those closer to home – the middle classes. Second, I want to avoid any simplistic notion that middle-class people only consume 'high culture' objects like opera, foreign films and certain documentaries. Equally, I am not suggesting that the audiences for these genres are always exclusively middle-class.[3] Nevertheless, as will become clear, the particular audience sample upon which this study is based is very much a middle-class one.

To return to my case study: *Etre et avoir* centres on a year in the life of a dozen pupils aged from 3 to 11 and their teacher in a one-class rural school in the tiny community of Saint-Etienne-sur-Usson in the Auvergne region of France. Given chronic problems in the French education system, along with radical social changes taking place in rural France, the film was often taken as emblematic of wider issues beyond the particular school in question. According to the teacher, Georges Lopez, the film was intended to be about a boy learning to read. 'But he got camera-shy and it wasn't working. So it became a film about the death of a certain kind of life in France.'[4] A magazine feature noted:

> As the nature of France's countryside changes, with 60,000 hectares of agricultural land disappearing annually, so the 'petite ecole en milieu rural' is under threat. Saint-Etienne-sur-Usson is typical of this trend: it consists of 18 hamlets with clusters of houses

and 234 inhabitants – no shops, no high street, no village. According to France's Association of Rural Councils, there were 19,000 of these schools in 1960. Now there are fewer than 5,000.[5]

The French scholar Guy Gauthier placed *Etre et avoir* in a tradition of documentaries examining education in France, including *Alertez les Bébés* (Jean-Michel Carre, 1978), *Recreations* (Claire Simon, 1992), *Grands Comme Le Monde* (Denis Gheerbrant, 1998) and *Grandir au Collège* (Andre Van In, 2004). He wrote: 'Some have seen in this film nostalgia for a paradise lost, the little rural school, surrounded by nature and sheltered from the currents of contemporary society.'[6] A feature in the film magazine *Positif* drew connections between the school building and its teacher's methods and the secular republicanism of early twentieth-century French schooling: 'It could only belong to the third republic: this school is emblematic of the secular ABC [l'etre et l'avoir] ... In its near perfection, it appears as a unique case'. The article warned, 'It would be depressing if a conservative gambit used the argument of *Etre et avoir* to put on trial for the umpteenth time the failings of the educational system, saying that the old ways were so good!'[7]

The film was a big hit in France, where it attracted 1.8 million cinemagoers and earned the equivalent of $10 million.[8] *Etre et avoir* occupied a much narrower cultural niche in Britain, however. As not only a documentary, but also a subtitled French film, and one predictably exhibited at a small number of specialist and arthouse cinemas, it was clearly not an example of popular cinema as the term is commonly understood. Six months after its release the film had earned just over £670,000 at the UK box office.[9]

The audience sample

The audience research for this chapter is based on 36 questionnaires returned from a total of 123 given out at the Duke of York's Picturehouse in Brighton.[10] The sample was entirely white, and very much middle-class (insofar as the majority of respondents were professionals, usually working in teaching or related fields) with relatively high levels of cultural capital. All bar three were educated to degree level, many to MA level. Some had been to private school. Many were middle-aged or older. The average age of respondents was 44. (As the film was screened in July, this may have led to fewer students watching it than would have been the case during term time.) In gender terms, the sample was split evenly, comprising 18 women and 18 men.[11]

Because of its self-selected nature, and the absence of comparable class or gender breakdowns for the film's British audience, the sample cannot be taken as statistically representative of a larger audience. However, the research material is suggestive of some viewing strategies and modes of response to documentary in general, and to this film in particular.

Generic labelling

When tracking audience perspectives on a topic such as screen documentary, which has already had its fair share of scholarly attention, it is important not to take for granted the concept's existence in cinemagoers' viewing repertoires. There is a danger that the researcher will effectively constitute the object (here the mode or genre of documentary) which he or she claims to find, by deploying an *a priori* analytical and experiential category which may not be a valid term for audiences.[12] How valid among respondents was the term 'documentary' as a label for screened material, and if so, what were the associations and expectations carried by such a category? Was *Etre et avoir* approached and viewed as a documentary or not?

In the event, for many (but not necessarily all) respondents, 'documentary' appeared to be a legitimate category. For some, it was considered to be a mode or genre that crossed the formats of film and television. Of these respondents, some complained that few documentaries made it to cinema screens. But others characterised documentary as essentially televisual. For instance:

> Q6: *How important to your enjoyment was the fact that the film is a documentary?*
> I rarely see docs at the cinema. Are they best suited to TV? Few seem to be worth a trip – *When We Were Kings* an exception.
> (Tim, British, white, male, teacher, age 46)

As it happened, the British poster and press ad images for *Etre et avoir* (later reproduced in video and DVD cover art) gave no indication that this was actually a documentary, and six respondents reported that they did not know that it was one until they saw the film. Others went to see *Etre et avoir* more or less despite the fact that it was a documentary. For example:

> Q13: *Are you a regular consumer of documentary films?*
>
> No – not usually interested – I expect the format/content to be dull.
>
> (Lynne, British, white, female teacher, age 51)

This viewer likened *Etre et avoir* to other French films, which appear to include, by implication, screen fiction of a particular, 'scenic' kind as well as documentary. While the film's Frenchness was seen as an asset, its status as a documentary was potentially offputting:

> Q2: *Why did you go to see the film?*
>
> Well reviewed – like pace and scenic qualities of many French films.
>
> Q6: *How important to your enjoyment was the fact that the film is a documentary?*
>
> Not – I don't usually watch them.

Another respondent commented similarly:

> Q2: *Why did you go to see the film?*
>
> Read a good comment about it in *The Guardian*, and I was curious. In general, I like French films.
>
> Q6: *How important to your enjoyment was the fact that the film is a documentary?*
>
> Not much, I did not feel like watching a documentary.
>
> (Mar, Spanish, white, female research fellow in physics, age 36)

The (albeit unquantified) success of the film with cinemagoers such as these two who appear suspicious or agnostic about documentary, and are keener on some French fiction films, appears to vindicate the marketing decision not to label the film as a documentary in adverts and trailers. The next section will discuss in more detail exactly what expectations and assumptions the documentary category carried with it for members of the sample.

Seeing, feeling, knowing

Feeling and knowing are two axes of possible viewer engagement, two sets of pleasures, two currencies of value, potentially available to documentary audiences. These modes of experience are best approached analytically as co-present: they can and do overlap for viewers.[13] Their exact balance will of course depend on the specificities of the particular documentary text, and on the perspectives of individuals, who may value each quality differently. Nevertheless, some commonsensical assumptions about documentary suggest that the form is largely (or even wholly) concerned with delivering information and knowledge, to the exclusion of emotional engagement. In this section I will consider some viewer responses which suggest that feeling and knowing are mutually exclusive, and others which attest to their coexistence. In the process, such statements reveal respondents' assumptions and expectations about documentary and what – if anything – makes it distinctive from other screened material.

The three examples below suggest that *Etre et avoir*'s informational content is relatively limited compared to other examples of the mode or genre, but the respondents cite this as a strength of the film, a quality which distinguishes it from their preconceptions about screen documentary:

> *Q6: How important to your enjoyment was the fact that the film is a documentary?*
>
> I do not usually go to the cinema to see documentary films but this film did not have a documentary 'feel': this was important as I felt part of the film – the emotions were stronger than the 'facts'.
>
> (Anon. (9), British, white, female, teacher, age 45)
>
> *Q1: What were your responses to* Etre et avoir?
>
> Overall very impressed. It didn't try to explain itself with voiceovers, the pace of the film was quite slow at times, in line with the learning of some of the children. It made me think about a lot of things I hadn't for a long time.
>
> (Anon. (4), British, white, male, entertainment news editor, age 38)
>
> *Q1: What were your responses to* Etre et avoir?
>
> Good documentary, it was also a very touching, real and sincere film.
>
> *Q16: How would you describe the differences between documentary film (in general) and fiction film (in general)?*
>
> Excepting *Etre et avoir*, documentary is rather objective and doesn't show feelings or emotions as being important, just facts.
>
> (Anon. (10), British, white, male, student, age 30)

Bill Nichols, among others, has described the will to knowledge as a desire central to the appeal of documentary. He writes: 'Documentary convention spawns an epistephilia. It posits an organizing agency that possesses information and knowledge, a text that conveys it, and a subject who will gain it.'[14] Certainly in the three cases above, the generic promise of documentary, and its proposed viewing strategy, is assumed to be epistephiliac. However, in these instances (and unlike other examples below) *Etre et avoir* is seen to succeed in a large part by refusing some of the expected informational content of the mode or genre, and by offering instead a degree of emotional engagement more likely to be associated with fiction film.

Similarly, for the following respondent, the film's deviance from an expected documentary template was a bonus – here in terms of its deployment of humour:

> *Q6: How important to your enjoyment was the fact that the film is a documentary?*
>
> Quite important, in that I forgave it some 'unfinishedness' and was pleasantly surprised at how funny it was – I wasn't expecting from a doc.
>
> *Q13: Are you a regular consumer of documentary films?*
>
> No – there aren't many available, and there is a sense that documentary will be terribly worthy, earnest and dry.
>
> (Paul, British, white, male, teacher, age 31)

Other respondents appear to have expected, and valued, some kind of balance between the informational dimension and mechanisms of engagement operating via emotion and character. For instance:

> *Q15: How would you define a good documentary film?*
>
> A story that transcends a factual account. Thought provoking, moving and maybe progressive.
>
> (Chris, British, white, male, teacher, age 44)
>
> One that shows facts *and* emotions.
>
> (Sophie, British, white, female, teacher, age 23) (her emphasis)

Emotional and informational qualities were valued differently by the following respondents, however. While popular among some viewers the film's formal simplicity and slow pace were problematic here, in so far as they were perceived as corrolaries of a disappointing lack of information:

> *Q5: What did you like least about the film?*
> Not being able to seek more information – more understanding.
> We only saw a selection of images etc.
> (Anon. (11), British, white, female, learning and development
facilitator, age 50)

> Its length, pretty but unnecessary countryside shots and I found
> the structure slightly odd – ie no informative voice-over, occa-
> sional talking straight to camera and no text to give extra info.
> (Caroline, British, white, female, student, age 34)

The second respondent, Caroline, also took the opportunity offered
by the questionnaire to compare *Etre et avoir* with fiction film, and
again found it wanting, this time not so much because of limited
informational content, but due to a relatively weak narrative drive.
Thus, for this viewer, the film suffers from not only an informational lack as a less than successful documentary, but also from
the absence of mechanisms of narrative momentum and viewer
engagement expected in fiction film. These deficits appear to out-
weigh (for her) the film's surplus of 'authenticity':

> *Q6: How important to your enjoyment was the fact that the film is a
> documentary?*
> I would probably have enjoyed it more had it been fictional with
> more of a narrative.

> *Q7: How would you describe the differences between this particular film
> and a typical fiction film?*
> Less narrative, less forward motion, less to engage the viewer.
> More authenticity making it totally believable and real as opposed
> to fiction.

> *Q12: Did you notice anything about the film's form (over and above its
> content?)*
> I like more info from a documentary. This one washed over me in
> a pleasant way but I wanted to know more about the children,
> their backgrounds, the area, their expectations, etc etc. It was like
> a magnifying glass over an area that didn't move – very frustrat-
> ing after a while.
> (Caroline, British, white, female, student, age 34)

In their book on documentary depictions of nuclear power,
John Corner et al. noted the existence among some viewers of a
'civic frame' of understanding, which was 'concerned with

propriety in addressing a national audience on a controversial topic', and which often prioritised the evaluation of 'balance' between contrasting standpoints.[15] *Etre et avoir* has a rather less controversial topic, and such a framework was not deployed by any respondents in the sample. But the issue of informational content, cast in more general terms, was still a source of concern for some. The viewers quoted above had expected this (missing) content to be delivered via expositional techniques such as voice-over and graphics. In these examples, informational values are seen as central to documentary, a part of a generic promise which *Etre et avoir* fails to fulfil.

Slow pacing and 'authenticity'

Among those who enjoyed *Etre et avoir*, the film's relatively slow pace – in terms of both form and content – was a commonly mentioned aspect of its appeal. For example:

> Q4: *What did you like best about the film?*
> Well shot, stories gently told.
> > (Mark, British, white, male, book editor, age 39)
>
> Q1: *What were your responses to* Etre et avoir?
> I thought that it was wonderful. I liked the 'slowness' of it, a pace of life that seems to elude us. Our own young orientated culture seems so fast, everything must be 'now' and extremely quick. Whereas this film showed that learning and caring is a slow process of growth.
> > (John, English, white, male, instructor, age 60)
>
> I loved the beginning of the film – the long slow shots of the countryside, the dancing trees … and the tortoises creeping across the schoolroom floor. At once I knew this film was different. I was encouraged to slow down, observe and find meanings in the detail. In other words, to work with the director in making the film. I was encouraged in this way from the start and became part of the experience rather than a casual passenger.
> > (Anon. (1) British, white, female, school counsellor, age 51)
>
> Slow, moving, peaceful
> > (Anon. (8), British, white, female, nurse, age 52)

It is tempting to draw on Bill Nichols' concept of excess in documentary when approaching these responses. According to

Nichols: 'If excess tends to be that which is beyond narrative in fiction films, excess in documentary is that which stands beyond the reach of both narrative and exposition … It stands outside the web of significance spun to capture it.'[16] Can the slow, repeated landscape shots, the trees in the wind, the tortoises creeping across the floor, be addressed by this concept? Perhaps, but on closer inspection it becomes clear that, for some viewers at least, the qualities of slow pacing, long takes, landscape, and a sense of time anchored to the seasons, are *not* beyond the film's argument. Instead, they are very much bound up with its key propositions (and pleasures). These are: a sense of the rarity, for a contemporary urban audience, of this rural setting and way of life, condensed in many ways into the representation of the school and its pupils. Thus, for some viewers, the appeal of *Etre et avoir* was based on the relative uniqueness of both the subject matter – the school – and its form of representation.

In addition to its slow pacing and rural location, the sincerity and honesty of the film was valued by several respondents. For instance:

> *Q1: What were your responses to* Etre et avoir?
>
> A wonderfully human film which touched forgotten memories of childhood. Its sincerity was 100% and left me with an image of a kind dedicated man who would be the backbone of any educational system …
>
> (Kenneth, British, white, male, retired telecomms engineer, age 82)
>
> Good documentary, it was also a very touching, real and sincere film.
>
> (Anon. (10), British, white, male, student, age 30)

Despite the so-called crisis in the evidential status of documentary and its central truth claims, which has been much debated in Anglophone scholarship,[17] a notion of gaining access to 'the real' was a major element of the film's popularity and authority among the sample. As well as the statements above, see for example:

> *Q1: What were your responses to* Etre et avoir?
>
> I really enjoyed, it was just something different from other films, and real.
>
> (Mar, Spanish, white, female, research fellow in physics, age 36)

In addition, and often underpinning expressions of the appeal of 'the real', the use of a discourse of authenticity frequently revealed taste markers and a set of cultural distinctions deployed by these cinemagoers, notably between the veracity and 'honesty' of *Etre et avoir*, and the contrasting 'fakery' and 'inauthenticity' of reality television. For instance:

> Q4: What did you like best about the film?
>
> The way it showed *real* life with all its ups and downs, hard work and difficulties, moments of success and joy, its ordinariness without resorting to 'reality TV' type tricks. Such close observation.
>
> (John, English, white, male, instructor, age 60)

What concerned several respondents in the sample was not so much the critically scrutinised indexical guarantee of documentary, but rather a less well defined and nebulous sense of qualities such as the 'human[ity]', 'honesty', 'sincerity', and specialness of the film. The notion of 'honesty' in these accounts can be approached in two ways. The first is in relation to the truth claims and epistephiliac pleasures of the documentary mode – introduced above and discussed further below. The second is via a notion of a 'simpler' kind of film-making, which contrasts with omnipresent media clamour.[18]

Jim Collins's argument about developments in Hollywood fiction film during the 1980s and 1990s can be usefully imported here. Collins locates what he calls a 'new sincerity' in film-making of this period – a trend exemplified in *Dances With Wolves* (US, 1990) – which he sees as a particular response to the background noise of the media array that surrounds us. (Another response is a playful engagement with the media-saturated landscape of everyday life, found in highly intertextual films like *Back to The Future III* (US, 1990).) Collins writes of the 'new sincerity':

> Rather than trying to master the array through ironic manipulation, these films attempt to reject it altogether, purposefully evading the media-saturated terrain of the present in pursuit of an almost forgotten authenticity, attainable only through a sincerity that avoids any sort of irony or eclecticism.[19]

Collins's proposal fits with elements present in the following responses:

> Q4: what did you like best about the film?

The simplicity of it, yet it was a very touching and intelligent film.
(Anon. (10), assume British, white, male, student, age 30)

Gentle build-up of a picture of rural education. Revelation of 'characters' unfolded as if naturally.
(Anon. (13), British, white, male, teacher and psychotherapist, age 52)

Sincerity
(Kenneth, British, white, male, retired telecomms engineer, age 82)

The last respondent also commented:

Q12: Did you notice anything about the film's form (over and above its content)?

Simplicity. Both in and out of the classroom, no clever tricks were employed.

I am certainly not proposing here that Collins's argument is applicable to documentary as a whole. Indeed, for some respondents, *Etre et avoir* was significant and pleasurable in part because of its difference from other documentaries – including the proliferation of hybrids and 'formatted documentaries' currently found on television – formats which might have more in common with Collins's notion of eclectic irony and playful intertextuality than with a new sincerity. For instance:

Q1: What were your responses to Etre et avoir?

It was a lovely film, I can't think of a film to compare it with. The long (time) shots and very relaxed editing gave it the feel of being barely edited.

Q28: Is there anything else you would like to say …?

I think that documentaries have less gravitas now. Why? I'm not sure – perhaps through the sheer number available, perhaps because of the frequent mixing of the modes of representation.
(David, British, white, male, teacher, age 36)

This is not to suggest that viewers of *Etre et avoir* have a facile notion of truth (a view also suggested by Annette Hill's work on audiences for reality television).[20] Notions of sincerity and authenticity do not simply equate to a naive acceptance of transparency or self-evident truths in documentary. This became clear after the sample was asked explicitly whether they trusted documentary to tell the truth. The question produced a wide range of responses, and of interpretations of its wording – linking 'truth' to notions of honesty or formal transparency. Some of those who had enjoyed the film's sincerity and honesty replied:

Q21: Do you trust documentary films to tell the truth?

In principle, yes, but I always try to question the point of view of what is shown and said. Showing some facts but not all can lead to a different conclusion.

(Mar, Spanish, white, female, research fellow in physics, age 36)

Yes. I think, generally speaking, that there is a long history of honesty in documentary film making.

(John, English, white, male, instructor, age 60)

No I don't trust them, but nevertheless I expect it. Was it Cousteau the French underwater film maker who later was accused of manipulating the truth? How we all enjoyed Cousteau originally.

(Kenneth, British, white, male, retired telecomms engineer, age 82)

Others wrote:

Q21: Do you trust documentary films to tell the truth?

No. Any film will involve a process of selection.

(Chris, white, British, male, teacher, age 44)

No. The truth is usually boring.

(Bernard, British, white, male, chartered surveyor, age 52)

Not 100% – everything is partial/open to interpretation.

(Anon. (7), British, white, female, teacher/lecturer, age not given)

No of course not – we don't even show everything of ourselves to our friends why would someone show the world every little bit of all their daily life or issues?

(Sophie, British, white, female, teacher, age 23)

No, it depends on the bias of the director. The director can choose the source material which fits their visual interpretation and edit together accordingly.

(Victoria, British, white, female teacher, age 29)

Other respondents were more willing to accept some of documentary's implicit truth claims:

Q21: Do you trust documentary films to tell the truth?

Yes – you expect them to educate and inform, that they tell the truth is implicit.

> (Anon. (8), British, white, female, nurse, age 52)

In as far as one trusts essays to 'tell the truth'. Clearly there will be bias but one expects the filmmakers to act in good faith.

> (Paul, British, white, male, teacher, age 31)

Finally, two examples of the coexistence of different knowledges and viewing strategies, mobilised by audience members at differing moments:

> *Q21: Do you trust documentary films to tell the truth?*
>
> When thinking about the question I would be aware of the possibility of a film maker being able to present events in a certain light. However, when watching documentaries I probably accept a lot as the truth.

> (Haydn, British, white, male, Access student, age 29)

> A version of the truth.

> (Cas, British, white, female, teacher, age 51)

The last respondent, Cas, replied to *Q1: What were your responses to* Etre et avoir?

> Loved it! Could have happily sat through another year in the life of the school. I recognised that an editing agenda had allowed the development of some characters at the expense of others – but accepted the version presented quite happily.

This respondent draws on two viewing strategies – one of scepticism and the other a willing abandonment to the film, and chooses to deploy them at different moments during the events of watching the film and responding to the research inquiry.

In this sample at least, viewers expected to find elements of authority (along with some dullness perhaps) in the documentary genre. But this does not mean that they assumed that documentary could offer unmediated access to 'the truth'. The general coexistence of a degree of trust with a degree of scepticism is significant because it refutes some problematic claims made by scholars about the gullibility of spectators, who are often assumed to approach documentary as a transparent rendering of 'real life'.[21]

Reality tv as bad object

Considerations of viewing habits invited by the questionnaire often put into play some binary oppositions between good/bad; 'authentic'/fake or fabricated; genuine emotional impact/cheap sensationalism; information and insight/trivia and exploitation. The operative distinction here is between documentary and reality television, two modes that tend to be arranged on opposing sides of these polarities.[22]

For example:

Q13: Are you a regular consumer of documentary films?
Yes – if the subject interests me – human interest stories biographies …

Q18: Are you a regular consumer of 'reality television'?
No. It holds little interest for me. There are enough interesting things happening without having to manufacture them.
(Anon. (4), British, white, male, entertainment news editor,
age 38)

No. Manipulative, exploitative, cheap, nasty.
(Anon. (1) British, white, female, school counsellor, age 51)

No if you mean *Big Brother*, etc. Exploitation of people for entertainment? Not relevant to me.
(Anon. (11), British, white, female, learning and development
facilitator, age 50)

No – I think they are exploitative and often degrading. I dislike the pleasure we seem to enjoy watching others expose themselves.
(Anon. (9), British, white, female, teacher, age 45)

No because there is no content beyond – it's stage and performance with no story
(Anon. (3), French, white, female, senior lecturer, age 44)

The last statement focusing on stage and performance provides an interesting point of contrast with Annette Hill's research into viewers of *Big Brother*, which suggests that one of the pleasures in watching the show was precisely in the often *inadvertent* revelation of emotional truths that could play havoc with attempted performance.[23]

Thus, among *Etre et avoir*'s middle-class audience sample at the Duke of York's, distinctions were made between the film (embodying relatively rare qualities of honesty and sincerity) and reality television (represented most commonly by *Big Brother*) as emblematic of mindless television and a debasement of the documentary project. At times this taste opposition *may* have had a classed dimension – although this was actually not very clear. Inevitably, classed distinctions are not often openly or simply stated as such. And, in the case of my research, middle-class people tended to discuss and relate their own tastes without much attention to the classed nature of this activity.[24] Furthermore, class may not necessarily be a relevant factor, despite the suspicions of the analyst.[25] For example, in the next instance, the key taste difference was generational:

> Q19: *Please list the last three 'reality television' programmes you watched.*
>
> Not sure I've seen any, apart from walking in to see my middle child following a very tedious *Big Brother* – and a bit of something about a traffic warden some time ago.
>
> (Jon, British, white, teacher and psychotherapist, age 52)

Francophilia

Given its subject matter – the lives of largely working-class children in a remote and relatively deprived area of France – *Etre et avoir* could have been organised around the voyeuristic paternalism of what Brian Winston has called the 'victim-documentary'.[26] However, it was commonly reviewed as a positive, life affirming experience, in both Britain and France.[27] In the sample, many respondents enjoyed it as a 'feelgood film' (Anon. (6), British, white, female, teacher, age 29).

Etre et avoir's director, Nicolas Philibert, has stated that:

> The theme is universal – how teachers give children confidence – and how they learn is the same throughout the world, in the city or the countryside. So you're not in the Auvergne in this school, but in a timeless no-man's land, which lends the film the aspect of a fable.[28]

However, for the British audience under analysis here, as well as the French commentators and viewers discussed earlier, the particularity of *Etre et avoir*'s setting in rural France was highly significant. The location of the film in 'La France profonde' contributed to the 'feelgood' factor for many respondents. Francophilia was an important element in shaping the pleasures that they derived from the film, and a love of the French countryside, and of holidays in France, was often mentioned. Several of the sample had an additional professional investment in the country, working as teachers of French.

In the next accounts, *Etre et avoir* is enjoyed for, among other things, its Frenchness and the pleasures of nostalgia which it offers; a chance to recall a slower, less hectic pace of life. Two points are worth making here. First, that this notion of slow pace, attractive to several respondents, is due to the film's form as much as its content. Second, that the Frenchness of the film is, for the second viewer quoted at least, significant in both contributing to and allowing for, the pleasures of a pastoral idyll:

> *Q4: What did you like best about the film?*
> Characterisation
> Naturalness
> Photography
> 'Old fashioned' values and atmosphere
> FRANCE!
> > (Anne, British, white, female, home tutor, age 55)
>
> *Q1: What were your responses to* Etre et avoir?
> I was completely absorbed, though at times I wondered why. I felt a nostalgia for a way of life that has disappeared in England. The film always felt realistic however.
>
> *Q6: How important to your enjoyment was the fact that the film is a documentary?*
> It gave permission to accept it as real, not pure nostalgia or another *Year in Provence*.
>
> *Q7: How important to your enjoyment was the fact that the film is French?*
> It also made it easy to accept a simple pastoral world, if it had been in England it would've needed more of a Ken Loach kind of social realism, poverty and economic problems, etc.
> > (Graham, British, white, male, teacher, age 57)

Note that the film's representation of rural French life is, for the above respondent, crucially different to (and more 'real' than) another representation of rural France popular with a middle-class British audience. *Etre et avoir* is praised in part via an explicit rejection of *A Year in Provence*, the best-selling book by Peter Mayle, which recounts the move he and his wife made to a farmhouse in the Luberon region of France, and which was later adapted as a television series. *A Year in Provence* stands here for a notion of an *unacceptably* nostalgic, touristic and perhaps middle-brow approach to finding a rural retreat in France. The documentary status of *Etre et avoir* is important in distinguishing it from the 'bad pleasures' of *A Year in Provence*.[29]

For Graham, the respondent quoted above, the French identity of the film also operates to allay concerns and preclude objections that would attend watching, and complicate enjoyment of, a British version of the same topic. Contrast his account with the following statement, where the film is seen to fail precisely because it lacks an explicit engagement with social problems and political issues, which are again associated with the work of Ken Loach:

> *Q1: What were your responses to* Etre et avoir?
>
> Rather disappointing. A missed opportunity. Not enough about the background to the school or the kids. The piece to camera with M Lopez [the teacher] jarred slightly because it was the only interview. Ken Loach would have done a far better job.
>
> (Tim, British, white, male, teacher, age 46)

Here the notion of an informational deficit is again evident, notably focused around the larger social and political contexts in which the school and the community might be located.

The Francophilia evident in the sample should not be thought of as inevitable, universal, or naturally occurring. Instead, it is best seen as a particular example of a middle-class taste for, and uses derived from, the culture of others. As Beverley Skeggs points out, such attitudes and practices should be thought of as classed, in terms of both the sense of entitlement and the resources (social, cultural and economic) that they require. She writes: 'The disposition of entitlement is one of the most obvious ways that class is written on the body, as it can be read as rights, privilege, access to resources, cultural capital, self-authorization and propriety.'[30] In this specific instance, some respondents already had an appetite for (particular notions of) French culture and 'lifestyle', which were both depicted and instantiated by *Etre et avoir*. While allowances must be made for individual differences, these viewers' dispositions had in general been shaped by factors including education (especially in language and culture), tourism, and professional experience, and to this extent can be read as manifestations of class privilege.

Ethics, law, performance

Ethical issues around screen documentary tend to arise in two distinguishable but overlapping fields: (i) the processes and procedures of film-making and (ii) the form and address of the finished film, its propositions to viewers and implicit orientations towards its subjects. In terms of film form, the semiotic approach to issues of signification that has been so influential in studies of fiction film needs to be revised and widened in scope once the referent becomes a 'real world' person or event. As Bill Nichols has suggested, semiotics is an inadequate tool with which to confront the various impacts of documentary on 'those who have their image "taken"'. He notes that issues of privacy, libel and slander are never simply semiotic phenomena.[31]

In the case of *Etre et avoir*, moral and legal notions of exploitation were raised most directly by the decision of its key adult protagonist, the teacher Lopez, to sue the film's director, producers, distributor and even the composer of its music, for at least 250,000 euros for 'counterfeiting' his class.[32] Whatever the merits or otherwise of Lopez' claim – which was announced a few months after my audience research was carried out, and which was ultimately rejected by a Paris court[33] – it was not entirely surprising, given the film's reliance on his teaching performance in front of the class.

A *Screen International* report on the case and its possible implications for documentary film-making carried this comment from the head of France's Association of Directors and Producers: 'What shocks me in Lopez' claim is his pretension to be recognised as the co-author of a work in which he was only a model. Mona Lisa didn't paint the Mona Lisa.'[34] Philibert, the film's director, has said: 'To have paid someone for their presence on the screen – it would have meant the death of the documentary. From the moment you pay someone to appear in a documentary, the people you are filming become your subordinates. They no longer have the freedom to say "No, stop filming".'[35] These lines of thinking are persuasive, but they do overlook documentary filmmakers' well established predilection for focusing on professional performers, from entertainers and politicians to less showy individuals like Lopez.[36]

Furthermore, as Nichols suggests, screen documentary has become dependent upon a more general casting of individuals who can behave in an engaging yet unselfconscious fashion in front of the camera. He calls this way of appearing 'virtual performance', and notes:

> Like trained actors, social actors who convey a sense of psychological depth by means of their looks, gestures, tone, inflection, pacing, movement and so on become favored subjects. The impulse is toward social actors who can 'be themselves' before a camera in an emotionally revealing manner.[37]

Nichols's concept of virtual performance is applicable to Lopez' appearance in *Etre et avoir*, as well as to that of some of the pupils, especially JoJo, the boy featured on the film's poster image.[38] (Indeed, since Lopez' case, the parents of seven of his 11 pupils are now going to court to seek payment of 20,000 euros each for their children's parts in the film.)[39]

This is not to support the reductive logic of Lopez' legal claim, but rather to point to a common feature of a certain style of documentary film-making, and a crucial element of its appeal – the use of sympathetic characters. Thus, for several members of the audience sample, Lopez' quiet charisma was a key element in the success of *Etre et avoir*. For instance:

> *Q1: what were your responses to* Etre et avoir?
>
> A wonderfully human film which touched forgotten memories of childhood. Its sincerity was 100% and left me with an image of a kind dedicated man who would be the backbone of any educational system ...
>
> (Kenneth, British, white, male, retired telecomms engineer, age 82)
>
> LOVED IT! Inspiring teacher who never raises his voice – *this* is what teaching is all about. Wonderful rapport with pupils – brings out the best in even the reluctant ones.
>
> (Anne, British, white, female, home tutor, age 55, her emphasis)

In Anne's account above, Lopez' performance and the film's depiction of a notably pre-bureaucratic version of school teaching allow *Etre et avoir* to be enjoyed as, among other things, a validation of the profession.

As the court case did not take place until after the British release of *Etre et avoir*, the particular issues of exploitation and ownership which it raised were not directly considered by members of the sample. However, concerns about voyeurism, intrusion, and possible exploitation of the schoolchildren were raised by some respondents. For instance:

> Q1: what were your responses to Etre et avoir?
>
> Wonderful bit of filmmaking – I felt there were so many layers to it. Two things concerned me though. One was that I was very aware of the editing and kept wondering about the hours of film left on the cutting room floor. The second was I was concerned about the ethics of using children's vulnerability as the basis of so much of it.
>
> Q5: What did you like least about the film?
>
> Some of the 'rawness' made me feel a bit voyeuristic.
>
> (Anon. (3), French, white, female, senior lecturer, age 44)
>
> The way in one conversation between the teacher and a pupil, I felt the conversation moved along because of the presence of the camera. He seemed somewhat uncomfortable, but the camera kept rolling.
>
> (David, British, white, male, teacher, age 36)
>
> I found some of the scenes slightly intrusive … the teacher's 1-2-1 scene with the girl who cannot communicate.
>
> (Victoria, British, white, female, teacher, age 29)

These responses are significant as viewer perspectives on what Nichols has called the ethical and ideological costs of documentary's epistephiliac drive.[40]

Conclusion

In this chapter I have shown what can be learned from an investigation of audience perspectives on topics such as documentary's truth claims and conventional epistephilia – issues that have hitherto been addressed largely via text- and production-centred analyses. The study has considered audiences' generic expectations of the documentary mode, and their deployment of notions of 'honesty' and 'sincerity' to characterise Etre et avoir. The focus on this film in particular has also enabled an examination of less-debated subjects such as middle-class taste and Francophilia, which proved crucial to its appeal for the sample under discussion. In Chapter 3, I use another study of a largely middle-class audience, attending the same arthouse cinema, to pursue issues of film form and audience response to a very different kind of documentary, Kevin Macdonald's adaptation of the climbing memoir *Touching the Void.*

Notes

1 David Lockwood, 'Marking out the middle class(es)', in Tim Butler and Mike Savage (eds), *Social Change and the Middle Classes* (London, UCL Press, 1995), p. 1. See also Mike Savage, James Barlow, Peter Dickens and Tony Fielding, *Property, Bureaucracy and Culture: Middle-Class Formation in Contemporary Britain* (London, Routledge, 1992).

2 Ann Gray, *Research Practice for Cultural Studies* (London, Sage, 2003), p. 51

3 The American sociologists Peterson and Kern have argued persuasively that, for middle-aged and younger generations of the American upper and middle classes, barriers between 'high' and 'low' cultural tastes have been eroded, resulting in a shift they characterise as 'from snob to omnivore'. Richard A. Peterson and Roger M. Kern, 'Changing highbrow taste: from snob to omnivore', *American Sociological Review* 61:3 (1996), pp. 900–7. Although she doesn't use the same terms, Charlotte Brunsdon points to 'a class mobility in television tastes' among a particular generation of middle-class feminists engaged in becoming academics. For these women, talking and writing about soap opera may have 'legitimated pleasure … not only for "other women" but also for feminists'. Charlotte Brunsdon, *The Feminist, the Housewife, and the Soap Opera* (Oxford, Oxford University Press, 2000), p. 194. Whether there is any such mobility of cultural taste moving 'upwards' from the so-called 'bottom end' of the social spectrum is still debatable. On this topic, and the suggestion that television may work to increase the 'cultural mobility of viewers', see Maire Messenger Davies and Roberta Pearson, 'Stardom and distinction: Patrick Stewart as an agent of cultural mobility: a study of theatre and film audiences in New York City', in Thomas Austin and Martin Barker (eds), *Contemporary Hollywood Stardom* (London, Arnold, 2003), especially pp. 168–9 and 181. For a summary of responses to the 'cultural omnivore' model, see Skeggs, *Class, Self, Culture*, pp. 143–5.

4 Lopez quoted in Viv Griskop, 'Do the maths', *Telegraph Magazine*, 28 May 2005, p. 41. Thanks to James Montgomery for pointing me to this reference.

5 *Ibid.*, p. 41. *Positif* magazine gave the number of single-class schools in France as 400. Francoise Aude, '*Etre et avoir*: un cas d'ecole', *Positif*, 499 (2002), pp. 40–1. Thanks to Guy Austin for pointing me to this reference and translating it for me.

6 Guy Gauthier, *Un Siecle de Documentaire Francais* (Paris, Armand Colin,

2004), p. 193. The presence of Pacific immigrant children in the class might be taken as one sign of 'contemporary society', however. Thanks to Guy Austin for pointing me to this reference and translating it for me.

7   Aude, '*Etre et avoir*'. The article noted: 'George Lopez is the first to refuse [the school's] validity as a model. How could his method, his authority, and even the "foundations" he gives his pupils, work in an urban environment, within the turbulence of a multicultural society?' The feature also criticised a perceived gender bias in the film: 'If "school" is a feminine word, in *Etre et avoir*, Nicolas Philibert inscribes it mainly as masculine. That's old hat.'

8   Amy Barrett, 'The truth hurts', *Screen International* (21 November 2003), p. 18.

9   Cinema Advertising Association figures to 4 November 2003. Telephone call to CAA research department, 24 November 2003.

10   Additionally, I gave out 120 questionnaires to cinemagoers at the local Odeon cinema, hoping to discover some reasons why many people had not been to see *Etre et avoir*. Only 11 questionnaires were returned – easily the worst rate of return I have experienced in audience research. Of these 11 respondents, nine did not know that the film was showing; one did not get round to seeing it; and one wrote 'the subject matter did not appeal to me'. The larger point here is how hard it is to track down (non-)audiences who care little about any particular film, or, as in this case, know little or nothing about it. This difficulty may be one reason why so many audience studies have focused on fans: as especially committed and often vocal audiences they may be relatively easy to research.

11   In addition to the 36, two female respondents (age 63 and 65) did not give permission to be quoted. Twelve of the 36 were teachers, with another 9 working in similar professions as tutors, lecturers, instructors, counsellors, etc. The full breakdown of the sample is listed in the methodological appendix.

12   See more on this kind of analytical move in terms of class later in this chapter. On the issue of a researcher writing into existence a generic category which may not exist on the same terms for the audiences being researched, see my comments on writing about horror in Austin, *Hollywood, Hype and Audiences*, Chapter 4, especially pp. 116–18.

13   On this topic see various critiques of David Bordwell's overly rational, and consequently rather impoverished, model of spectatorship in fiction film.

14   Nichols, *Representing Reality*, p. 31.

15   Corner, Richardson and Fenton, *Nuclear Reactions*, p. 50.

16   Nichols, *Representing Reality*, p. 142.

17   See for example, Bruzzi, *New Documentary*; Corner, *The Art of Record*;

Carl Plantinga, 'Moving pictures and the rhetoric of non-fiction: two approaches', in David Bordwell and Noell Carroll (eds), *Post-Theory: Reconstructing Film Studies* (Madison, WI, University of Wisconsin Press, 1996); Philip Rosen, *Change Mummified: Cinema, Historicity, Theory* (Minneapolis, University of Minnesota Press, 2001), especially Chapter 6; Brian Winston, *Claiming the Real*.

18 In each case, the 'simplicity' of *Etre et avoir* – in terms of both content matter and its relatively slow pace and 'gentle', unflashy formal treatment – is crucial.

19 Jim Collins, 'Genericity in the nineties: eclectic irony and the new sincerity', in Jim Collins, Hilary Radner and Ava Preacher Collins (eds), *Film Theory Goes to the Movies*, (New York and London, AFI/Routledge, 1993), p. 257.

20 Hill, *'Big Brother'*.

21 For a more detailed critique of such models, see Plantinga, 'Moving pictures and the rhetoric of non-fiction'.

22 Not many members of the sample actually identified themselves as regular viewers of reality tv, so most rejections of the form may be based on limited viewing experience. Three respondents (all younger than the average age of 44) wrote enthusiastically about reality tv. These regular viewers of reality tv refused to characterise it as a debased travesty of documentary traditions.

23 Hill, *'Big Brother'*.

24 This is also evident in statements about attitudes to reality television and radio made in the similarly middle-class sample documented by the current Mass Observation Archive at the University of Sussex. (Directive number 63, summer 2001).

25 In considering class as a possible factor here, I am not suggesting that reality television as a genre only addresses a working-class audience. Its appeal is much wider than this in class terms. See Hill, *Reality TV*.

26 Winston, *Claiming the Real*, pp. 40–7, 230–1, 258.

27 See for example Benny Crick, 'Documentary schooled in the art of feelgood', *Screen International* (4 October 2002), p. 24; Aude, *'Etre et avoir'*. Phil Powrie calls *Etre et avoir* a 'utopian film' which emphasises 'circularity and stability'. Powrie, 'Unfamiliar places: "heterospection" and recent French films on children', *Screen*, 46:3 (2005), pp. 343, 345.

28 Richard Falcon, 'Back to basics', *Sight and Sound*, (NS) 13:7 (2003), p. 29.

29 Another respondent also noted the justification and authority which the film gained through its documentary status: '*Q6: How important to your enjoyment was the fact that the film is a documentary?* Any feelings that it was a bit fey or twee would have been harder to dismiss if the film was not a documentary.' (Haydn, British white, male, Access

student, age 29)

30   Skeggs, *Class, Self, Culture*, p. 152. For Skeggs, a particular variant of
     this middle-class disposition is presented by the practices and self-
     image of the 'cosmopolitan'. *Ibid.*, pp. 155–9.

31   Nichols, *Representing Reality*, p. 271n.

32   It is possible to argue that *Etre et avoir* has precipitated some major
     changes in the way of life which it records. Its consequences and
     impacts include the elevation of Lopez from village schoolteacher to a
     kind of national hero, and more recently his recasting as a national
     villain, following news of his legal action; and the transformation of
     the village, its school and children into a tourist attraction. Reportedly,
     around the film's release, police had to be called to the school to
     restrain members of the media, and one of the pupils, JoJo could not
     go to his judo classes for a while, because of the crush of sightseers.

33   See Amelia Gentleman, 'Defeat for teacher who sued over film prof-
     its', *Guardian*, 29 September 2004, p. 15.

34   Barrett, 'The truth hurts', p. 18.

35   Quoted in Griskop, 'Do the maths', p. 43.

36   For a more detailed discussion of performance and performativity in
     documentary, see Bruzzi, *New Documentary*, pp. 125–80.

37   Nichols, *Representing Reality*, p. 120.

38   Philibert's earlier film, *Le Pays des Sourds* (France, 1993) also features
     a charismatic teacher and an engaging and vulnerable male child, al-
     though each is less central to the film than their counterparts in *Etre et
     avoir*.

39   See Gentleman, 'Defeat for teacher'; Griskop, 'Do the maths'.

40   Nichols, *Representing Reality*, p. 76. A scene that I found uncomfortable
     when I watched the film at the Duke of York was of one of the pupils
     struggling with his maths homework. As the scene unfolded, he be-
     came gradually surrounded by more and more members of his
     working-class family, all trying to help and getting themselves and
     him more confused in the process. Whether intended as comic relief
     or not, this scene was greeted with widespread laughter in the cinema
     – more than any other moment in the film. One of the reasons why I
     found it so uncomfortable was that I read this laughter as middle-
     class mockery of the stupidity of the working classes – a process of
     laughing at, rather than with, those on screen. I mention this not so
     much to display the credentials of a guilty middle-class liberal, but to
     point to one of the difficulties in writing about class in this context.
     Only two members of the sample mentioned this scene. One in a
     statement that was very brief and said that it was funny, but not *how* it
     was funny. The other one suggested finding humour in recognition –
     a process very different from the other response that I suspected but
     was unable to support: '*Q11: Who did you identify and why?* 'The young

boy whose family were attempting to help him with his maths home-work, and getting confused about it. Why? My father wasn't too hot at Maths either!' (Haydn, British white, male, Access student, age 29).

Thus I have no information from the sample to support my own suspicions, or my tendency to privilege class as an *a priori* analytical category in this research – both of which I must admit would have shaped this passage further had I found such material. (Compare Liz Stanley, 'Women have servants and men never eat: issues in reading gender, using the case study of Mass-Observation's 1937 day diaries', *Women's History Review*, 4:1 (1995), on the assumption, made by herself and other feminist researchers, that gender is an *a priori* analytical category, and her suggestion that it is privileged in practices such as archiving, gathering and interpreting qualitative data.) The response of Haydn also served as a reminder that class needs to be understood as a dynamic process, as well as a set of structures and practices. As an Access student, the respondent could be an example of someone on the social journey from working class to middle class – although this is not necessarily the case.

3

'Suspense, fright, emotion, happy ending': documentary form and audience response to *Touching the Void*

Film scholarship needs to take audiences seriously as a means of deepening, and offering some new angles on, debates over the form, ethics and impacts of screen documentary. This chapter uses a case study of the commercially and critically successful mountaineering documentary *Touching the Void* (UK, 2003) as a point of entry into further consideration of these and associated issues. Drawing on original qualitative research among cinemagoers, it follows two key lines of inquiry in particular. Firstly, it pursues how viewers responded to aesthetic aspects such as *Touching the Void*'s use of dramatic reconstructions alongside 'talking heads'-style interviews with the climbers involved in the original event. How did audiences react to such modality shifts, and what implications did these formal mechanisms have for viewers' investments in character and story? Secondly, and relatedly, the chapter traces a mode of engagement which treated *Touching the Void* as an 'inspirational' story of (male) suffering and survival which might carry lessons for everyday life. It compares such responses to others that refused to take up this orientation to the film.

For the research project, conducted in January 2004, 111 questionnaires were given out to cinemagoers attending *Touching the Void* at the Duke of York's Picturehouse, Brighton. A total of 32 completed questionnaires were returned. Six further questionnaires were emailed to me following a request to members of an outdoor enthusiasts' group, Brighton Explorers. Some additional messageboard material and two more questionnaires were gathered via the 'Joe Public' forum on the official Joe Simpson website, www.noordinaryjoe.co.uk. Judging by stated occupations, the vast majority of respondents were middle-class, and most were aged between 30 and 60 – notably older than fiction film audiences that

I have researched. When asked if they had any climbing experience, half of the sample mentioned 'low-level' climbing or hill walking. One third had no experience at all of climbing, and the remainder (just under a fifth) described themselves as reasonably experienced or serious climbers. There was no clear gendered pattern to these responses. Overall, female respondents outnumbered males by a factor of three to two.[1]

Touching the Void is an adaptation of Simpson's account of a climb in the Peruvian Andes in 1985. Simpson, then aged 25, and his expedition partner Simon Yates, aged 21, scaled the hitherto unclimbed west face of Siula Grande, a 21,000ft peak. Descending in a blizzard, Simpson fell and broke his leg. Yates spent several hours lowering Simpson down the side of the mountain, but when Simpson got stuck over the edge of a precipice, Yates had no choice but to cut the rope. Left for dead, Simpson took three days to crawl back down, and made it to base camp a matter of hours before Yates was due to leave. First published in 1988, Simpson's book sold more than 500,000 copies worldwide.[2]

While the rights to make a fictional feature film adaptation became tied up in various ultimately unproductive business deals in Hollywood (including, reportedly, a script designed as a Tom Cruise vehicle),[3] the British television production company Darlow Smithson bought the documentary rights. The film was originally intended for a television premiere on the UK's Channel 4, but was earmarked for a theatrical release after PBS in the US and Film Four and the Film Council in the UK became involved and boosted the production budget to £1.7 million.[4] It was directed by Kevin Macdonald, whose previous film, *One Day in September* (US, 1999) won an Oscar for best documentary. *Touching the Void* was positively received in the British press, grossed £1.5 million in two months in the UK and $4.5 million in four months in the US,[5] and went on to win the British Academy Film and Television Award for outstanding British film of the year.

Marketing

Carl Plantinga has written:

> we typically view a film while knowing that it has been *indexed*, either as fiction or nonfiction. The particular indexing of a film

> mobilizes expectations and activities on the part of the viewer …
> [It] is a process initially begun by the filmmaker, but to function
> normally, it must be 'taken up' by the discursive community.[6]

Indexing thus works very much like the contractual processes of
genre labelling, by mediating between filmmakers and potential
audiences.[7] In the case of *Touching the Void*, the indexing of the
film was deliberately ambiguous. It was marketed as an adaptation of a bestseller, and thus as implicitly fiction (of the action-
adventure genre), at least for those unfamiliar with the original
book.[8]

Press adverts promoted the bestseller angle, as did the trailer
for the film, which began with the following graphics, inserted
between brief close-ups of mountaineering kit and wider
mountainscapes:

> A film by Academy Award winner Kevin Macdonald
> From the international bestseller
> A true story
> Beyond anything you could dare to invent

The phrase 'true story' employed here has a different effect from
labelling the film a documentary. The wording is, again, essentially ambiguous in terms of the status of the film, as many fiction
titles have been promoted as based on real-life events.

The second half of the *Touching the Void* trailer looks and sounds
even more like a fiction film trailer, with faster-paced editing and
dramatic, rapid music. The following words are flashed on the
screen, one at a time until the last line:

> Friendship
> Strength
> Trust
> Courage
> Loyalty
> Fear
> What would you do to survive?

The single-word prompts condense and characterise the film in
terms of its story content, and are followed by an invitation to
view and respond in a particular way. The second-person address
of 'What would you do to survive?' echoes the scenarios of endangerment popularised in reality television over the last two decades,
and also puts into play notions of suffering, endurance and initiative

associated with the 'male melodrama' of war films, thrillers and the action genre.[9] As will become clear, the proposed mode of response based on imagining oneself in Simpson's perilous situation was ultimately taken up by several respondents (of both genders) in the sample.

Film form

Issues of form are crucial to this inquiry, and, I would argue, should be so for any audience research that explores viewers' uses of and responses to a specific text.[10] In the case of *Touching the Void*, the film is an intriguing combination of interviews with Simpson, Yates and non-climber Richard Hawking (who waited for them at base camp during the whole episode), shot frontally using an Interratron,[11] intercut with reconstructed scenes depicting the climb. The two very different formats are mutually supporting. The interviews provide the two climbers in particular with emotional and psychological depth (along with some moments of humour) and give viewers a sense of their interiority, so elaborating on the character subjectivity developed in the reconstructions. The climbing footage, on the other hand, offers the familiar hooks of narrative action and engagement with character, along with spectacular mountain scenery. It also serves to animate and illustrate the climbers' testimony, which in turn underwrites the veracity of the re-enactments. Climbs were filmed in both Peru and the Alps, and included some storyboarded stunt sequences.[12] Simpson and Yates wore 1980s clothing and gear to play themselves on the hardest climbs, while two actors played the pair in close-ups and less technically demanding sequences.

Touching the Void was not Macdonald's first excursion into reconstruction. His previous film, *One Day in September*, told the story of the 1972 Munich Olympics hostage drama through a combination of archive news and promotional footage, supplemented with newly-shot interview material. But it also made limited use of familiar techniques of dramatic reconstruction such as computer animation and 'first-person' point of view shots (the latter used to illustrate a hostage's escape from his captors). However, *One Day in September* stopped well short of the full scale re-enactments employed in *Touching the Void*. Macdonald has expressed some concern about using this technique in the latter film:

[Having filmed interviews with Simpson and Yates] the heart and the skeleton of the film was already there. But what about the flesh? The only option was a technique that sent shivers down my spine: dramatic reconstruction. In film, I believe things should either be documentary or drama. If there is a tendency in modern television I hate, it is the unstoppable march of the dramatic reconstruction to tell the stories of anything from an ancient Egyptian battle to the early life of Paul Gascoigne …

That was the challenge: how to make one of TV's hoariest conventions work on the big screen, how to combine documentary and drama in a way that audiences would accept. The answer we came up with was simple: no half measures. Keep the documentary element (the interviews) straightforward and make the dramatic elements feel as real as possible, filming in naturalistic style with good actors and no apologies.[13]

So how did the audience sample react to the repeated shifts between, in Macdonald's terms, 'documentary' and 'drama'? Perhaps the most commonly cited response to *Touching the Void* emphasised its remarkable narrative, which many viewers had encountered prior to watching the film in its various circulations via word of mouth, reviews and media coverage, or Simpson's book.[14] For instance:

Q1: What were your responses to Touching the Void?

Felt that it was an extraordinary story in many ways in terms of the endurance and capacity to manage what must have been terrifying experiences.

(Anon. (7) British, white, female, therapist, age 36, limited climbing experience)

Amazement at the story; interest in the characters involved.

(Anon. (3), British, white, male, accountant, age 40, no climbing experience)

Amazement about the content and gripping nature of this documentary. Surprisingly a feel-good factor at work.

Q2: Why did you go to see the film?

Because I had heard it was an outstanding film and I had got interested in the issue of how the crucial decision (cutting the rope) had come about.

(Anon. (12), Austrian, white, female, therapist, age 37, no climbing experience)

Knew the story. Love the mountains – have fallen off one myself
(and had to walk for several hours on a broken leg). It had some
excellent reviews.
(Peter, British, white, male, Ph.D. student/painter and decorator, age 37, hill walker)

This common interest in narrative was often bound up with
accompanying investments in both spectacle and character. For
instance, the following respondent, who had read Simpson's book,
enjoyed supplementing his knowledge of the story via audio-visual
access to both the setting of the climb and the participants involved in it:

Q2: Why did you go to see the film?
Because I wanted to hear and see Joe Simpson and Simon Yates,
and I wanted to see the mountain.

Q4: What did you like best about the film?
I liked the way it was laid out, each section seemed to be in a
'satisfying' order; Also the photography gave a good 2D image of
the environment and scale of things.

*Q7: If you have read Joe Simpson's book, how would you compare the
book and the film?*
I think they are incomparable ... you can see or read one and live
without the other, but if you see both you get a more 'complete'
report of the events, emotions, etc.
(Martin, British, white, male, cabinet maker, age 27, some
climbing experience)

Another viewer commented on the different qualities (and implicitly, pleasures) offered by the two different formats:

*Q15: The film combines interviews with re-enactments of the climb. Do
you think these two elements combined successfully or not? Did you pre-
fer one of these elements over the other?*
Yes. No.
It allowed the film to be both poetical and down to earth.
(Anon. (4), no details given.)

Audience members' interest in both characters and the terrain in which they are located is matched in some ways by
Macdonald's repeated use of zooms and reverse zooms to delineate
the relationship between these two elements. Documentary editor and writer Dai Vaughan's comments on the use of the zoom in

one of his own films are relevant here:

> [T]here remain things for which the zoom shot is almost indis-
> pensable ... If you frame for the people, you get no idea of the size
> of the mountain; if you frame for the mountain, I can no longer
> see the people. A slow pull back links the two. In an instance such
> as this, the zoom takes on the grammatical function of a preposi-
> tion.[15]

In *Touching the Void*, zoom shots reiterate Simpson and Yates's
location in the surrounding landscape – often by 'moving back' to
show the vastness of the mountain, which dwarfs the two men
trying to 'conquer' it.

While respondents in the sample were clearly aware of the
reconstructed nature of much of the film, the fact that it was based
on, and authenticated by, interviews with the participants certainly added to its appeal and impact. For example, note the importance of documentary status and evidentiality in the following
response:

> *Q1: What were your responses to* Touching the Void?
> I felt privileged to be able to 'share the experience' with the climb-
> ers. Deepest gratitude for all involved in making the film.
>
> *Q9: How important to your enjoyment was the fact that the film is a
> documentary?*
> It made all the difference. It's only in a true story that we can
> immerse ourselves fully in events shown on screen. A true story
> makes identifying with the heroes easier.
> (Anon. (6), no details given, some climbing experience)

The presence of engaging human characters in the unfolding
story was crucial in inviting viewer involvement. Respondents
'shared the experience' most notably via vicarious emotional up-
heavals, pain and ultimate survival. For instance:

> *Q1: What were your responses to* Touching the Void?
> When Joe breaks his leg you almost felt it, there was an audible
> gasp in my audience – I thought the acting was superb in the
> whole film – every stumble was agonising and I felt physically
> chilled the conditions they filmed in were so horrendous.
> (Carole, British, white, female, senior investment administrator,
> age 38, hill walker, contacted via Joe Public forum)

Admiration for their courage and determination.
Wonder at their skills and endurance.
Fear for their danger.
Sadness for their fate.
Spiritual awareness of Joe's situation and that he came through
in spite of the odds.
Compassion for Simon afterwards and during.
Irritation at their macho attitude towards life.
(Kim, British, white, female, painter and decorator, age 46,
some climbing experience 'as a learner')

Note also the ambivalence in this last account – a combination of admiration and annoyance. (I will discuss examples of viewers resisting the invitation to identify with the climbers in more detail later in this chapter.)

Much as in fiction film, crucial narrative events in the reconstructed scenes are defined by the involvement of, and impact on, human agents. These events appear to occur in the familiar, conventional 'present tense' of fiction film (with appropriate 'classical' style of filming and continuity editing) even though, as a consequence of cutting back to the interviews, the audience is constantly reminded that these events have taken place in the past. Thus viewers are invited to respond to the climb as simultaneously (i) something that happened several years ago, and which is being recalled by the much older protagonists in the 'now'; (ii) a profilmic event shot more recently, involving both professional actors and the real climbers; and (iii) a story which, like fiction, unfolds in the continuous present of classical cinema style.

Footage of 'real people' shot in a mix of retrospective interviews and re-enactments of dramatic episodes that they have been asked to recall and in which they 'play themselves' is a common enough staple of reality television. As Ib Bondebjerg has suggested, this technique 'creates both a dramatic tense' which shifts between 'now' and 'then', and 'security' derived from the knowledge that everything worked out all right in the end.[16] Equally, Simpson's survival is crucial in providing *Touching the Void* with an ultimately happy outcome, and this is signalled to viewers by his appearance in interview footage from the first minute of the film.

A number of respondents noted the significance of the reassuring ending in facilitating their enjoyment of the film. For example:

Q1: What were your responses to Touching the Void?
I really did like that film, I thought it was intelligent, optimistic and enjoyable.

Q9: How important to your enjoyment was the fact that the film is a documentary?
It is a story that could happen to all of us. It is a true story and it is pleasurable to find out that Joe forgave Simon to cut the cord.

Q11: Were there any other factors important to your enjoyment of the film?
Suspense, fright, emotion, happy ending.
(Anon. (21), French, white, female, costumier, age 32, no adult climbing experience)

In a discussion of the influential US television programme *Rescue 911*, Bondebjerg comments:

> The melodramatic effect of placing people at the near edge of disaster, followed by a last minute rescue is very strong here. Everyday life is given a much stronger dimension and meaning, often expressed in the final statement of the people involved: they have come closer to each other, they have learned to value life and to take care of what they have.[17]

Elements of this dynamic exist in *Touching the Void*, and its story of disaster and survival against the odds carried huge emotional clout for some commentators and audiences. But the film is also significantly different from the format of *Rescue 911* and its imitators. Firstly, Simpson and Yates do not constitute the family unit preferred by such shows. (Despite Simpson devoting his memoir to Yates for saving his life, their friendship has in fact waned in the years since the climb, as noted in numerous press articles about the film.) Secondly, Simpson's story is largely one of self-rescue, of endurance and survival without any external intervention. Moreover, he and Yates, while perhaps reckless in some aspects, were talented climbers, deliberately embarked on a risky project. To this extent, *Touching the Void* doesn't quite fit into the melodramatic frame of reality television's 'innocent victim[s] … caught by random forces'.[18] Nevertheless, as will become clear in the following section, respondents often attested to a strong identification with Simpson as they followed his ordeal, and this was for some a large part of the film's appeal and its 'surprising feel-good factor'. Even if Simpson's adventure was pretty far removed from non-climbing viewers' experience at least, it seemed to provide a powerful fantasy scenario for imaginings of heroic perseverance and triumph, both large and small.

Suffering, survival, inspiration

Touching the Void clearly contains elements of melodrama, insofar as Simpson endures and overcomes suffering, even if this is more brutally physical than the largely emotional hurt at the core of so-called 'female-oriented' tear-jerkers.[19] (There was no simple gendered binary in the sample's responses to the film however: it proved either inspirational or problematic to both male and female respondents.) Simpson's trajectory – from successful ascent to disaster, injury, endurance and ultimate survival – can also be seen to accord with a template of (usually male) heroism familiar from many cultural representations. Scenarios of endangerment or accident and survival have been relayed in various formats, from documentaries like Werner Herzog's *Wings of Hope* (2000) and *Little Dieter Needs to Fly* (1997), to published accounts like Aron Ralston's *Between a Rock and a Hard Place* (2004), which was serialised under the newspaper headline 'The day I had to chop off my own arm'.[20]

A similar pattern is evident in many fiction films. In a discussion of male masochism in the films of Clint Eastwood, Paul Smith builds on the work of Paul Willemen to propose a three-stage model of viewer response and pleasure which moves through 'admiration at the hero's body and presence' to seeing him 'injured and brought to breaking point' before 'emerg[ing] triumphant'.[21] This dynamic is offered not just in several of Eastwood's films, but also in the work of other Hollywood action stars, perhaps most obviously Sylvester Stallone in the *Rocky* and *Rambo* franchises. Some viewers' pleasurable vicarious involvement in Simpson's ordeal may have been facilitated by their previous exposure to such fictional and non-fictional portrayals of the suffering and ultimate survivability of the male body.

While it records the persistence of the body in punishing conditions, *Touching the Void* gives relatively little explicit indication of the emotional and psychological trauma endured by the climbers. (The main exception to this is a short sequence which portrays Simpson's increasing disorientation via hectic visuals accompanied by a Boney M song, which he was unable to get out of his head at the time.) By contrast, satellite texts around the film represented moments of delayed mental collapse experienced by both men, notably Simpson's panic attack during the Peruvian shoot, captured on camera in a DVD extra and recalled in the latest edition of his book, and Yates's reported breakdown around the same time.[22]

Some examples of endangerment by proxy and viewers' pleasurably fearful involvement in the film are quoted below:

> *Q1: What were your responses to* Touching the Void*?*
>
> It was a very emotionally charged film for me to watch. I found the part where Joe Simpson described his knee injury particularly distressing! Awe, fear and love of wild nature, and respect for its awesome beauty and its ability to put us in our place in the cosmos.
>
> > (David, British, white, male, mountain guide, age 39)
>
> Excitement, fear, awe, wonder, admiration
>
> *Q19: How would you define a good documentary film?*
>
> Needs a sense of tension – what's going to happen?
> Needs good pictures and engaging characters that you care about.
>
> > (Jack, British, white, male, teacher, age 31, 'a little' climbing
> > experience)

In the next few accounts, the inspirational value of *Touching the Void* is foregrounded:

> *Q1: What were your responses to* Touching the Void*?*
>
> Awe-inspiring, amazing, wonder at the spirit and determination of man.
>
> > (Anon. (16), British, white, female, conference organiser, age
> > 47, some climbing experience)
>
> I found it inspirational. I was incredibly impressed by Joe's determination and will to live … It's a story I would like to try and remember when I am having difficult times. For the first ten minutes or so I thought 'How can this be interesting?' By the end I was totally absorbed.
>
> *Q4: What did you like best about the film?*
>
> The story. The struggle against impossible odds and the ultimate success.
>
> *Q14: Who did you identify with when watching the film and why?*
>
> Joe – mainly because of his tenacity. I would like to think that I

could find that sort of strength if I needed it.

> (Anon. (13), British, no race given, male, visual effects artist,
> age 49, lists walking as a hobby)

Q1: What were your responses to Touching the Void?

Mesmerised, thrilled, fascinated. Real insight into what humans can do.

> (Janet, British, white, female, retired schoolteacher, age 60,
> some climbing experience)

It was very powerful – it made us feel as though we could more effectively put small things in perspective after seeing this couple struggle so bravely against the elements. It gave us a greater appreciation of what a person can do under duress. I was filled with awe and admiration – particularly for the understated way in which the two climbers presented themselves and their story. It was clearly not easy for them.

> (Claire, British, white, female, education officer, age 27, indoor
> climber) (Brighton Explorers)

Q4: What did you like best about the film?

The lesson that something seemingly impossible can be achieved if you keep on trying.

> (Anon. (3) British, white, male, accountant, age 40, lists
> walking as a hobby)

Q14: Who did you identify with when watching the film, and why?

Joe – because I have just fought my way back to life after a serious illness and now I have to fight again after the loss of my partner.

> (Kim, British, white, female, painter and decorator, age 46,
> some climbing experience 'as a learner'; her late partner was a
> keen climber)

This last comment was part of an ambivalent rather than entirely positive response to the film. But the notion of triumph over adversity is clearly important here. As Bill Nichols has suggested in a discussion of the body in documentary, 'Visible, enduring testimony to the body's persistence becomes all the more important as threats of its permanent erasure become more pervasive.'[23] Note also the metaphorical use of the idea of 'fighting' in the last account, which recalls Valerie Walkerdine's analysis of a working-class family watching the fiction film *Rocky 2*. In that study, the trope of fighting operates as a (masculine) 'bid for mastery' both within the film's diegesis and in the social context of the family's everyday life and the self-perception of the father in particular.[24]

In the instance of *Touching the Void*, gender was still an important factor, both within the film and in terms of some responses to it, but notions of inspiration and fighting to survive were not exclusively male.

Another respondent commented rather self-consciously:

Q1: What were your responses to Touching the Void*?*

Good human interest which moved me in terms of the determination from Joe to keep going – which I feel is how we would all like to imagine ourselves reacting to that situation.
(Peter, British, white, male, clerical worker, age 38, 'low-level' climber)

Responses to the film were never simply monolithic. For example, the next account reveals an intriguing coexistence of different modes of engagement. Here, intense vicarious involvement – both anxiety and wonder – is accompanied by a contrastingly detached, almost judgmental response:

Q1: What were your responses to Touching the Void*?*

Gut churning anxiety!

   Amazement and wonder – the glorious mountains; the extraordinary power of human spirit and survival instinct; incredulity – why does anyone want to do it, why do it inappropriately prepared re gas/food etc.

(Linda, British, white, female, administrator, age 52,
non-climber)

One way of making sense of some of the accounts of inspiration laid out above is via John Mepham's concept of 'usable stories'. He notes:

stories are a form of inquiry to which people can turn in their efforts to answer questions [like] What is possible for me, who can I be, what can my life consist of, how can I bring things about? What is it like to be someone else, to be particular kinds of other people, how does it come about that people can be like that?[25]

Mepham is writing here about fiction on television, but his argument is also relevant to screen documentary. Such uses are not necessarily conscious, but, for some viewers of *Touching the Void*, they would include an explicitly stated and highly portable sense of inspiration drawn from Simpson's ordeal. As detailed above, this could be attached to climbing scenarios, or to overcoming illness and grief, or to the small struggles of everyday life.[26] In this light, the trailer's invitation-to-view, 'what would you do to survive?' appears to have a metaphorical reach and resonance beyond its explicit application to the arena of mountaineering.

Some other respondents clearly rejected Simpson as a possible point for investment or engagement, thus either explicitly or implicitly refusing the film's proposal that viewers align themselves to some extent with him. A number felt closer to other people in the film (Yates or Hawking), or even to non-human elements such as the mountains:[27]

> *Q14: Who did you identify with when watching the film and why?*
>
> I think I identified with Simon most because he seemed so ill at ease and unresolved in his telling of the story – he has stayed in my mind and I felt uncomfortable about his apparent distress.
>
> (Anon. (7), British, white, therapist, female, age 36, 'very limited' climbing experience)
>
> The man waiting with the tents because I couldn't imagine myself ever attempting anything like that.
>
> (Julia, British, white, female, environmental health officer, age 36, climbs 'a very small amount')
>
> Identified more with mountains/nature and climate.
>
> (Jo, British, white, female, doctor, age 40, general mountain walking)

The next respondent attests to the involving power of the film as a vicarious experience, but also asserts her difference from the climbers, distancing herself from their behaviour:

> *Q1: What were your responses to* Touching the Void?
>
> Enjoyed it. Felt physically and emotionally exhausted afterwards, as if I had been through the experience as well.
>
> *Q14: Who did you identify with when watching the film and why?*
>
> No one – I wouldn't put myself in that sort of danger.
>
> (Anon. (9), British, white, female, yoga teacher, age 51, climbed briefly when younger)

In an interrogation of the much-debated issue of identification in (fiction) film spectatorship, Murray Smith has argued that in some instances 'alignment' with a character's emotions and state of mind – often encouraged by mechanisms of film form – does not necessarily result in 'allegiance' or positive sympathy for that character.[28] The case above suggests the presence of a doubled perspective that goes one step further than Smith's proposal. What appears to have occurred here is that the viewer felt a degree of alignment and even allegiance with Simpson when watching his ordeal, but that these processes of engagement did not override an awareness of self which emphasised (perhaps intermittently) the difference between her and the climbers. The coexistence of these different modes of relating to characters is of course revealed at the moment of replying to the questionnaire, with its invitation to reflect on the act of viewing, but it may also have coloured this respondent's experience of engagement and disengagement throughout the film.

It is possible that such an assertion of difference between the viewing self and persons represented on screen may be more likely or stronger when the film being watched is a documentary rather than a fiction film. (In the latter, on-screen characters and actions may be less open to questions such as 'am I that kind of person?' or 'would I have done that?' because of the mode's status *as* fiction.) The obverse of this dynamic is the particular potential of documentary to invite the viewer to imagine themselves into the position of someone else, a mechanism that may also be both like and unlike that experienced when watching a fiction film. In each instance, the relationship between documentary and fiction is characterised by similar proposals and processes but important differences of degree.

The patterning of the above responses is not entirely clear. All those quoted in the last few pages are women, but the significance of gender should not simply be taken for granted in these cases. For some women viewers, gender difference may indeed have presented an obstacle to close identification with Simpson, especially given the particular 'adventurer' type of masculinity exhibited in much of the film. But this behaviour may have caused problems for some male cinemagoers too. Equally, as earlier selections from the sample have shown, women as well as men found the film inspirational. It is very likely that factors less immediately obvious than gender, such as values, experience, profession and lifestyle were also relevant in shaping viewers' replies.

Form, ethics, guilt

Perhaps surprisingly, ethical issues were rarely raised in my audience research. Very few respondents voluntarily mentioned ethics – in terms of either film-making decisions or film form. And when presented with a deliberately open question – 'Do you think the film ran into any ethical or moral dilemmas or problems?' – most took this to be a reference to Yates' difficult decision to cut the rope on his partner. These three responses are fairly typical:

> *Q16: Do you think the film ran into any ethical or moral dilemmas or problems?*
>
> Yes – obviously Simon cutting the rope knowing he was sending Joe to his death. A dilemma but justifiable in the circumstances.
>
> (Jane, British, white, female, NHS manager, age 46, no climbing experience)
>
> Yes. How do you judge when, how if you make a life or death decision. Is it ok to save your own life in certain circumstances?
>
> (Anon. (16), British, white, female, conference organiser, age 47, 'minor' climbing experience.)
>
> Yes – this was my main interest in seeing the film … (if you mean cutting the rope aspect).
>
> (Anon. (17) and (18), mother and son completed questionnaire together, British, white, female, teacher, age 54 and British, white, male, school student, age 16)

These and other respondents tended to look past and through film form, treating it as more or less transparent in their accounts and seeking ethical issues in the content of the film itself. Any possible anxiety about the ethics of the documentary gaze in *Touching the Void* is thus displaced instead on to the ethics of the profilmic event: cutting the rope. Why and how might this be the case?

In his examination of the ethical dimensions of documentary form, Bill Nichols proposes a typology of the relations between camera/subject/viewer which pertain when death is filmed and watched. He codifies such relations as a series of gazes – accidental, helpless, endangered, interventional, humane and clinical-professional.[29] These formal-ethical issues become further complicated in a case like *Touching the Void*, where reconstruction is employed. Clearly, the film does not portray death or a re-enactment of it, but it does depict a number of events which carry the risk of injury and death (the entire expedition, Simpson's fall when he breaks his leg, Yates's decision to cut the rope), in addition to Simpson's painful struggle to regain base camp. In such moments, the dilemma of whether or not to intervene, as filmmaker or as viewer, is qualitatively different from the examples of un-reconstructed death and endangerment analysed by Nichols.

Crucially, the camera, and thus audiences, can gain access to a 'good view' of the climb and its crises without having to confront the moral dilemma of how to respond to the endangerment being 'witnessed'. This is in part because the pro-filmic event (the re-enactment) clearly occurs years after the 'real' originary event; the chronological distance is marked in the film by the uniformly retrospective tone of the interviews. Moreover, with their adherence to the conventions of fiction film, including storyboarded stunts, the reconstructed sequences are obviously staged for the camera, and, by implication, the viewer. Thus the gaze that this footage both relays and invites is diametrically opposed in formal terms to the 'accidental gaze' which Nichols characterises via 'chaotic framing, blurred focus, poor sound quality'. As Nichols suggests, these 'signs of "accidentalness"' tend to 'signify contingency and vulnerability for the documentary generally'.[30] However, the style of shooting in *Touching the Void* makes no attempt to deploy these common markers of evidentiality, relying instead on the iterative authentication provided by the interviews.[31] Footage of the climb is periodically supplemented by voice-overs from the interviews and interrupted by cutaways to the climbers talking, both of which serve to reassert its foundation in fact. It may be the case, then, that audience awareness of the reconstructed nature of the events depicted effectively pre-empts or allays any possible guilt in witnessing the crisis moments and pain endured on the mountain.[32]

One rare exception to the general lack of explicit statements about ethics came from this respondent:

Q14: *Who did you identify with when watching the film and why?*

I think I identified with Simon most because he seemed so ill at ease and unresolved in his telling of the story – he has stayed in my mind and I felt uncomfortable about his apparent distress.

(Anon. (7), British, white, female, therapist, age 36, 'very limited' climbing experience)

Perhaps unsurprisingly, given her profession, the same viewer was also disappointed by the film's lack of engagement with the longer term consequences of the climb for Simpson and Yates:

> *Q16: Do you think the film ran into any ethical or moral dilemmas or problems?*
>
> Yes, as outlined above ... Joe in a way came across as hero and Simon implicitly/explicitly as villain, but my question is about the impact of events like that on people's lives – this was left unspoken largely.

In relation to the process of film-making, the questionnaire sample again provided little explicit comment. However, this topic was discussed in the 'Joe Public' forum on Joe Simpson's official website, in a thread largely fired by behind-the-scenes material accompanying the DVD release of *Touching the Void*. This included footage of Macdonald interviewing Simpson, and particularly Yates, in what some contributors felt to be an overly aggressive and insensitive manner.

Much as in the questionnaire returned by the therapist quoted above, Yates's well-being tended to cause more concern than that of Simpson. Even though the DVD shows Simpson suffering a panic attack on his return to the mountain, his partner's denial of any guilt about cutting the rope or unease about returning to Peru provided the impetus for discussion and speculation about both his state of mind and the behaviour of Macdonald. For instance:

> I have just watched the documentary 'Return to Siula Grande' on the DVD.
>
>   Simons viewpoint seems to be that the accident, cutting the rope, his descent and Joe's struggle for survival was just 'something that happened'. He says it has not affected him. Is this the truth do you think or has Simon just built a very good wall to defend himself.
>
> (dr, posted 7 April 2004)

> But I think you have to remember that it is almost 19 years ago since the accident and as Simon says in the commentary he has travelled extensively since and experienced many different things. I think maybe that has pissed him off more than anything. The fact that TTV has focussed on one small part (however traumatic) of his life. Kevin MacD implied that Simon couldn't possibly have got over it which I think was totally patronising and

insensitive.

(Carole, posted 7 April 2004)

I think Simon would have anticipated being asked questions on the trip to Siula Grande, they'd done the interviews by this stage afterall, but I think he was fully justified in being annoyed by the nature of Kevin MacD's questions – if the ones we saw on screen were representative of the type of questions asked. The director seemed obsessed with the issue of unresolved feelings and guilt. He seemed to have a preconceived idea of the reaction he wanted, a reaction that perhaps fitted a therapy TV culture that continually wants people to revisit and dissect experiences – and attracts viewers. Many people are naturally (and slightly morbidly) curious and 'like' to see victims. Sad but true I think.

Also, Kevin MacD is very divorced from the culture of mountaineering, where accidents are not unusual.

(ClaireW, posted 7 April 2004)

Maybe he [Simon] also regrets doing the climb with Joe and all that that has meant since. That's another angle. I wish I'd asked that question when I went to the lecture at Rheged, but it seemed an insensitive question to ask and one that he probably couldnt answer honestly to a stranger.

(Alibali, posted 8 April 2004)

I agree. Whether he feels regret, guilt, whatever is a private thing for him. I don't see why he should be thought to have been under any obligation to reveal his thoughts to the camera. I wonder whether there is a tendency in our 'reality tv' age to expect people to reveal their innermost thoughts and emotions on screen, but why should they?

(ClaireW, posted 8 April 2004)

Having seen the footage from the DVD, ClaireW's concerns about Macdonald's interviewing style seem to me quite reasonable.[33] But there is also in her postings an interesting construction of reality television as bad object. This could be read as a possible displacement of guilt about watching *Touching the Void* – particularly guilt about the behaviour of Macdonald as director probing Yates for the 'benefit' of the film's audiences – on to a convenient 'low culture' stereotype.

Conclusion

In a discussion of drama-documentary and documentary drama on television, Derek Paget notes widespread 'journalistic unease about the form', which has often been indicted for falling between two stools, ending up as both 'bad documentary' and 'bad drama'.[34] He argues that:

> in actuality there are places where [the camera] cannot go or where it has missed its chance of going. In the dramadoc/ docudrama those things which the camera has missed … can still be shown – but only up to a point and at a price. Audiences who accept the extension of the camera's documentary showing do so increasingly within the context of dramatic suspension of disbelief … [But] following the moment of reception, the form's bid for belief is as often *dis*abled by [dramatic] codes and conventions as it is *en*abled. It is dramadoc/docudrama's cultural role to be believed and then disbelieved, so to speak.[35]

With its particular and clearly signalled combination of two distinct formal modes, *Touching the Void* seems to have largely avoided the problems of critical and audience reception that Paget has outlined. Viewer investments in its re-enacted narrative appear to have been strengthened by the verifying function of the accompanying interview material. This footage provided an authentication that could have been lost if the two elements had been merged into a more uniformly dramatised whole. And, for some viewers at least, the film's credibility was a contributory factor in the portable sense of inspiration that they derived from its presentation of Simpson's ordeal. By tracing these and other interfaces between film form and content on the one hand and audience response on the other – including intricacies of identification, and the far from straightforward relationship between gender and genre – this chapter has attempted to add to an understanding of the range and texture of viewer engagements with screen documentary.

In particular, this research has thrown new light on audience reactions to some of the generic proposals made by this mode of story-telling. A central plank of documentary's appeal is its presentation of opportunities to find out about, and somehow connect with, other people 'out there' in the world.[36] One way in which this connection can occur is via empathetic engagement with another's situation. To recall a question posed by John Mepham, 'what is it like to be someone else?' With its invitation-to-view 'what would you do to survive?' *Touching the Void* was marketed and formally organised in order to deliver just such an experience, via investments in character, story and setting. But only the specificities of empirical audience research can show some of the ways in which socially located individuals responded to this offer, and how the invitation was variously taken up (or not), lived out, and, in the research scenario, written about, by both climbers and non-climbers in the audience.

Notes

1 For a complete list of respondents in this study, see the methodological appendix.
2 A film tie-in edition with a new cover was published by Vintage in December 2003.
3 Richard Falcon, 'White ladder', *Sight and Sound*, 14:1 (2004), pp. 34–5.
4 John Plunkett, 'Peak viewing', *Guardian*, G2, 8 December 2003, np, (accessed via Guardian Unlimited website). The film was ultimately distributed by Pathe after the collapse of Film Four.
5 www.imdb.com, accessed October 2004.
6 Plantinga, 'Moving pictures and the rhetoric of non-fiction film: two approaches', pp. 310–11, italics in original. The concept of indexing was originally introduced in Noel Carroll, 'From real to reel: entangled in the nonfiction film', *Philosophic Exchange*, 14 (1983), pp. 5–45. See also Plantinga, *Rhetoric and Representation in Nonfiction Film* (Cambridge, Cambridge University Press, 1997), Chapter 1.
7 On genre, see especially Rick Altman, *Film/Genre* (London, British Film Institute, 1999) and Steve Neale, *Genre and Hollywood* (London, Routledge, 2000).
8 For those who did know the book, its non-fiction status was presumably an asset, not a disadvantage.
9 This key selling point, along with expertise gained from making *Touching The Void*, was exploited by Darlow Smithson to pitch for and subsequently develop the television series *Alive* (in the US titled *I Shouldn't Be Alive*). An international co-production between Discovery Networks, Channel 4 and Granada International comprising ten hour-long programmes, the series 'uses first person testimony and high-end dramatic reconstruction to tell real-life stories of extreme sportsmen, professional adventurers, and ordinary people faced with agonising dilemmas on which survival depends'. The central hook of the project is 'to leave viewers asking, "What would I have done in the same

situation?"', www.darlowsmithson.com/DSpress.html and http://
emol.org/tv/ishouldntbealive accessed December 2005. On the presence of 'melodramatic' elements in 'male-oriented' genres, see Steve
Neale, 'Melo talk: on the meaning and use of the term "melodrama"
in the American trade press', *Velvet Light Trap*, 32 (1993), pp. 66–89,
reworked in his *Genre and Hollywood*.

10   For more on why analysis of textual mechanisms should not be
jettisoned in favour of an exclusive focus on audiences, see Austin,
Hollywood, Hype and Audiences.

11   Justine Wright, editor of the film, speaking at the London Film Festival, 28 October 2003. The Interratron is a system of screens and
lenses developed by American documentary maker Errol Morris to
allow both interviewer and interviewee to look each other in the eye
during filming. The result avoids the common phenomenon of
interviewees looking slightly away from the camera's gaze to an interviewer positioned nearby.

12   Wright, London Film Festival.

13   Kevin Macdonald, 'Return to Siula Grande', *Guardian*, G2, 21 November 2003, p. 4.

14   This particular sample seemed on the whole more aware of and re-
sponsive to reviews than the (generally younger) audiences for Hollywood films that I have researched previously. Yates's reluctant decision
to cut the rope was also borrowed for the opening sequence of *Vertical
Limit* (US, 2000) a Hollywood feature film starring Chris O'Donnell.

15   Vaughan, *For Documentary*, pp. 144–5.

16   Ib Bondebjerg, 'Public discourse/private fascination: hybridization in
"true-life-story" genres', *Media, Culture and Society*, 18 (1996), p. 39.
Stories of real life 'triumph over tragedy' have also been a common
feature in some women's magazines. Thanks to Janice Winship on
this point.

17   *Ibid.*, p. 39.

18   *Ibid.*, p. 37.

19   For further discussions of gender and melodrama, see Neale, 'Melo
talk', and various essays in Christine Gledhill (ed.), *Home is Where the
Heart Is: Studies in Melodrama and the Woman's Film* (London, British
Film Institute, 1987).

20   *Guardian*, 27 September 2004, G2, pp. 1–3; continued on 28 and 29
September 2004.

21   Paul Smith, *Clint Eastwood: A Cultural Production* (London, UCL Press,
1993), p. 156. Smith is drawing on Paul Willemen, 'Looking at the
male', *Framework*, 15–17 (1981), p. 16.

22   Simpson, *Touching the Void*, 'Epilogue: bad memories'; Wright, London Film Festival; Macdonald, 'Return to Siula Grande'.

23   Nichols, *Representing Reality*, p. 238.

24   Valerie Walkerdine, 'Video replay: families, films and fantasy', in Victor Burgin, James Donald and Cora Kaplan (eds), *Formations of Fantasy* (London, Methuen, 1986), pp. 172, 180–1.

25   John Mepham, 'Television fictions: quality and truth telling', *Radical Philosophy*, 57 (1991), p. 22.

26   A review in *Sight and Sound* commented rather disdainfully, 'Simpson is successful on the corporate lecture circuit where middle managers look to him for inspiration'. Falcon, 'White ladder', p. 35.

27   Hawking is quoted in the film saying that, as he waited in the tent, he decided that if only one of the climbers were to survive, he hoped it would be Yates. In a posting to the Joe Public forum he explains that he had found Yates to be 'wonderfully gregarious' while Simpson had been 'very curt'.

28   Smith, *Engaging Characters: Fiction, Emotion and the Cinema* (Oxford, Clarendon Press, 1995), p. 6.

29   Nichols, *Representing Reality*, pp. 82–9.

30   *Ibid.*, p. 82.

31   The accidental gaze of which Nichols writes contrasts with some conventions of documentary form, in that the presence of the witnessing camera is in many ways foregrounded here. Equally, if, as Nichols argues, 'empirical realism suggests that what we see occurred much as if it would have occurred were we not there to see it' (Nichols, *Representing Reality*, p. 224), this common disavowal of the camera's presence in documentary is doubly necessary for the reconstructed elements of the climb in *Touching the Void*. Here, much as in fiction film, viewers are invited to invest emotionally in narrative occurrences which are staged precisely for the camera. I would argue, however, that this disavowal is not absolute, and can comfortably coexist with an awareness of the (re)constructed nature of the profilmic event, again much as in fiction film.

32   By making this suggestion, I am not overlooking the very real dangers involved in staging the story for the camera (none of which were mentioned by respondents). Both Yates and Simpson reportedly expressed concern over the safety of the film crew on the Peruvian shoot. See Macdonald, 'Return to Siula Grande'.

33   A similar concern with Macdonald's style of interviewing was mentioned in a posting by Richard Hawking, the non-climber who met Simpson and Yates in Peru, and who waited at base camp during the entire climb: '... the "on-screen" questions directed at Simon by MacD are not entirely indicative of the multitude of questions he was asked – most were much more persistent and callous. MacD was constantly looking for skeletons in the closet and deep meanings.' (rrhawks, posted 11 April 2004).

34   Derek Paget, *No Other Way to Tell It: Dramadoc/Docudrama on Television*

(Manchester, Manchester University Press, 1998), pp. 80–2.

35 *Ibid.*, p. 82, emphasis in original.

36 Of course, such a world may be near or far from the viewer, and these connections may result in disgust or denial as well as in a recognition of some commonality.

4

'The most confusing tears': home video, sex crime and indeterminacy in *Capturing the Friedmans*

At Thanksgiving in 1987, Arnold Friedman, a musician and computing teacher, was arrested at his family home in Great Neck, Long Island, New York and charged with multiple counts of child molestation.[1] The convictions of Arnold and his youngest son Jesse, then aged 19, the following year were based on accusations of repeated abuse over a period of four years at computer classes held in the basement of the house. In what appears to be a bungled attempt at plea bargaining in the context of a media feeding frenzy around the case, both men pleaded guilty.[2] Arnold died in jail; Jesse – now out of prison under restrictions, having served 13 years inside – is campaigning to clear his own name.

Sixteen years after their arrests, the film *Capturing the Friedmans* (US, 2003) was released. Co-funded by HBO and Notorious Pictures, and distributed by Magnolia Pictures, it grossed an impressive $3 million at the North American box office[3] and was nominated for an Academy Award for best documentary feature. Most of the film centres on the months between the charges and convictions. It deploys extensive camcorder footage from this period inter-cut with earlier home movies shot by Arnold, along with director Andrew Jarecki's retrospective interviews of family members, police, lawyers and alleged victims.

This chapter makes use of close textual analysis of *Capturing the Friedmans*, along with messages posted over 18 months by viewers on the film's official website forum, to pursue a number of lines of inquiry. These include: the film's structural complexity and, for some viewers at least, its ultimate indeterminacy; the implications and consequences of its re-presentation of home movie and video material shot by members of the Friedman family; and an interrogation of documentary form and ethics, engaging with critical concepts of the public and the private, the personal and the political.

A never-ending story?

My discussion of *Capturing the Friedmans* draws upon comments left on the message board at www.capturingthefriedmans.com.[4] Clearly these postings constitute a self-selected sample, with a general bias largely in favour of the film (a relatively small number of hostile comments appear on the site). There is also of course an element of public performance in all postings to the message board. But an awareness of how this context shapes the self-expression of the participants should not lead to a sceptical assumption that such messages are only ever dishonest.[5] Any analysis of such material does need to be wary of ascribing too much significance to 'outliers' who may have extreme reactions, however. Certainly, viewers had to be sufficiently motivated to register their response to the film, whether positive or negative. Hence I would not pretend that the message board offers a statistically representative or comprehensive audience sample.[6] But, in terms of both scale (32,000 words posted) and the range of topics raised, it is suggestive of several viewing strategies and modes of response to the film.[7]

A key avenue of entry to *Capturing the Friedmans* was based on the film's relative ambiguity, condensed in the tagline 'who will you believe?' with its clear proposal to audiences to make up their own minds about what really happened. This invitation was supplemented by the provision of extra-filmic material on the website and later on the DVD.[8] These extensions of the text offered axes of (potential and realised) viewer investment in the film and the story it tells.

One thing the website message board does quite clearly is to invite, and to provide a facility for, ongoing talk about the film after the first moment of watching, so extending the experience of connecting to the family's case, as presented by Jarecki and his collaborators. Furthermore, in the sleeve notes to the UK release of the DVD, Leslie Felperin suggests that this story is incomplete because it's happening in the real world, which exceeds the borders of any film:

> *Capturing the Friedmans*, like all documentaries, can only capture a
> slice of a larger story which can never be wholly contained by a
> feature-length film. The extras on this disc point to the super-
> abundance of this narrative, one that will continue, no doubt, to
> play out over years to come.[9]

The ongoingness of the Friedmans' narrative is crucial here:
its continuation beyond the edges of the frame, beyond even the
extra material on the website and the DVD. Extensibility is often
sought by Hollywood producers and filmmakers, who try to engineer 'immersive' fantasy universes like those of *Star Wars* or *Lord
of the Rings*. The key difference with *Capturing the Friedmans* of course,
is that this is a story of real people 'out there' in the world, people
who are still living with the consequences of a concatenation of
events dating back well beyond the 1980s, and continuing into a
future that will be shaped in part by the release and success of this
film.[10]

Home video

One of the most remarkable features of *Capturing The Friedmans*,
much commented upon in reviews and viewer responses on the
film's website, is the large amount of home movie and home video
footage used in the film. As Jarecki notes in an interview on the
UK DVD, he gained access to 50 hours of such material. This was
split more or less evenly between Arnold Friedman's 8mm home
movies from the 1960s, 1970s and early 1980s, and camcorder
footage shot largely by his eldest son David, including, crucially,
the months between the arrests and convictions of Arnold and
Jesse.[11] So what exactly are the connotations, impacts and consequences of the extensive use of such material in the film?

From the very beginning, *Capturing the Friedmans* deploys
amateur-shot footage, so mobilising implicit claims to immediacy,
veracity and integrity. But this raw material is also carefully edited to follow a narrative arc and so maximise its dramatic effect.
Something of this is apparent in the first sequence of the film,
which in some ways can be viewed as a microcosm of the form of
the larger whole.

Capturing The Friedmans begins with the credit 'An Andrew
Jarecki film' in white on a black screen. The lettering is initially
blurred and takes time to come into focus, much like a common

expectation of home movie footage. The screen remains dark while a slightly hesitant voice-over begins: 'Hi, hi it's me, it's – Oh, we're not ready yet.' An image emerges out of the black during this sentence. It is of a smiling, slightly awkward male teenager in a navy greatcoat, framed from the chest up, somewhere between a medium shot and a medium close-up. He is looking and talking direct to camera, standing in front of a blurred background of foliage and branches. The teenager continues, 'Hi, it's me, Jesse, are we there? yeah, ok good, we're there ...' A clear but relatively unobtrusive intervention from beyond the profilmic world is made when the graphic 'Jesse Friedman' is added to the bottom of the screen. Jesse announces to camera that he is going to conduct an interview with 'Arnold Friedman, my father'. He moves to his right and pulls into the frame a balding, bespectacled and smiling man, who shouts 'tada' and waves theatrically as he moves from off-screen space.

This 47-second sequence is loaded with details that have become codified as signs of amateurishness in home movies and videos. Jesse's enthusiastic performance as presenter/interviewer is hardly that of a seasoned professional. As he talks, his upper body and head are bobbing around, as if he is shifting from foot to foot, making it hard for the person filming to always keep him centred in the frame. The image itself is slightly blurred, and is clearly shot using available light. Strong sunshine throws sharp contrasts on to Jesse's face, obscuring his left eye in shadow. When Jesse moves towards his father, he is too fast for the camera, which lurches in the same direction, capturing just a blur of foliage before settling again on its subjects.

At this moment, another editorial intervention is notable, as the sound of the interview is gradually faded down, carrying on beneath a much louder retrospective voice-over from Jesse, run over the continuing images of father and son: 'I still feel like I knew my father. I don't think that just because there were things in his life that were private and secret and shameful that that means that the father I knew and the things I knew about him were in any way not real.' These words immediately establish a narrative enigma and a degree of suspense. What are the 'shameful' secrets that Arnold Friedman concealed from his son, and presumably, from the world? How exactly were they revealed, and what were the consequences of the revelation?

This pre-credit segment makes a strong implicit claim to evidentiality and intimacy. But, additionally and inevitably, such footage has been selected, arranged and reworked. This has resulted in an economical and gripping first scene, posing questions that, it is implied, the narrative will later resolve. (Ultimately, however, *Capturing the Friedmans* remains relatively open-ended, a point that I shall return to below.) Perhaps surprisingly, this opening can be seen to accord with the conventional demands of fictional screenplay construction delineated in manuals such as Christian Vogler's *The Writer's Journey: Mythic Structure for Storytellers and Screenwriters*, which notes: 'The opening of any story ... has some special burdens to bear. It must hook the reader or viewer, set the tone of story, suggest where it's going, and get across a mass of information without slowing the pace.'[12] Indeed, throughout the film, narration is very carefully controlled with key information withheld from, then delivered to, the audience in a manner designed to engage viewers much as a fictional thriller would.[13]

From this beginning onwards, *Capturing the Friedmans* foregrounds two axes against which documentaries have often been measured. The first proposes a tension between evidentiality and aestheticisation, accommodated in a much-debated balance in John Grierson's famous phrase 'the creative treatment of actuality'.[14] The second concerns the nature of the events portrayed, and can be thought of as a continuum running from issues of private significance to those of public import. While much screen documentary occupies the wide territory between the poles of public and private, and between artifice and 'truth', *Capturing the Friedmans* depends on a particular combination of these four elements.

In a discussion of Abraham Zapruder's famous film of the assassination of President Kennedy, Stella Bruzzi contrasts this accidental and amateur footage of a dramatic public event with the assumed banality of the home movie. She writes:

> The home movie is, virtually by definition, the documentation of the personal and the inconsequential, events of interest only to the family group involved. What makes Zapruder's home movie exceptional is that it happens to capture an event that is not private and trivial but public and of huge importance.[15]

Bruzzi goes on to quote Siegfried Kracauer's argument that 'it is precisely the snapshot quality of [most newsreel and documentary] pictures that makes them appear as authentic documents', with the effect that aesthetic 'beauty' and evidential 'truth' stand in mutual opposition.[16]

Of course, Zapruder's film is not the only exemplar of the proposed dichotomy between films of beauty and truth,[17] nor is it the only exception to the polarisation of public/private significance. For instance, the camcorder revolution of the early 1990s offered some ways to move beyond the second of these binaries. Not only did it spawn a subgenre of low-budget television shows relaying amusing accidents involving pets and children, it also led to more thoughtful attempts to put amateurs' footage on the small screen. One example, the *Video Diaries* strand, which ran on BBC2 during this period, was both an updating of earlier access-to-television initiatives facilitated by new technology,[18] and a way of putting into practice challenges to the rigid polarity of public and private spheres made by feminist thinkers, among others. In the best output from *Video Diaries* and its *Video Nation* offshoot, the slogan 'the personal is political' was enacted on national television.[19]

In a concurrent discussion of home video's incursion into broadcast television in Britain, Peter Keighron identified a new aesthetic of integrity:

> In much the same way as the shaky black-and-white images of *cinema verité* claimed to be somehow closer to reality than Hollywood technicolour, so the video aesthetic can promise the closest shave yet. The wobble of the image, the lurch of the autofocus, the bleeding reds all add up to a new authenticity … The whole 'what you are about to see is the work of an amateur' aspect of the series is no longer merely a negative apology for poor technical quality, but a positive advertisement for the integrity of the amateur.[20]

As Keighron predicted back in 1993, this camcorder aesthetic was rapidly appropriated by other screen formats, from advertising campaigns to 'shakycam' techniques in mainstream film and television drama, to the reality television boom. *Capturing the Friedmans* avoids the glib and reductive nature of many of these borrowings, but it still relies on Keighron's notion of the 'integrity of the amateur'[21] for much of its impact.

The events relayed via home movie and video are doubly mediated, however: once by Arnold's and David's shooting decisions using 8mm camera and camcorder, and again by their

presentation in the finished film. The latter encompasses not only
the selection and placement of this material in the narrative structure of *Capturing the Friedmans*, but also the marketing and promotion of the film as a documentary mystery or thriller, centred on
the tagline 'who will you believe?'[22] (This double mediation is
self-consciously acknowledged in the opening credit sequence,
where the Friedman family members – parents and three sons –
are introduced via a montage of home movie footage, much as if
they were central characters in a television drama.)[23] Additional
use of archive television footage and newly shot interview material, along with editing decisions involving processes of delay and
revelation, render the case into a filmic and suspenseful story.

Viewers' mostly approving comments posted on the film's official website applaud both a sense of accessing the 'real' which is
absent from other less credible media representations, including
reality television,[23] and the narrative structure of the film, which
produced suspense and shocks. Both documentary 'truth' and aesthetic 'beauty' (artifice producing effects and impacts) contribute
to the film's appeal here. On the former, see for instance:

> Jim, posted 28 February 2004:
> Saw the movie and it will remain with me for the rest of my life.
> Very rarely am I so affected by a film. Forget Survivor, Big Brother,
> Fear Factor or the Real World. Capturing the Friedmans is the
> REAL world.

> JV, posted 20 February 2004:
> Great disturbing, thought-provoking, sad funny, pathetic, pessi-
> mistic, hopeful ... REAL! This is reality. May it kill all future TV
> reality shous. Well done.[24]

> Eron, posted 11 July 2003:
> This film puts 'reality television' to shame. Amazing how David
> was filming video diaries before anyone knew what that was.

The terms used by other viewers to discuss the film emphasise
the generic shape and impacts of the narrative. In some accounts,
such factors were prioritised over and above the video format or
intimate subject matter. For example:

> Nansi, posted 18 May 2004:
> I think this is one of the best documentary films I have watched.
> The director edited it brilliantly and effectively because he kept
> the tension going. Jsut when you thought all the card were on

table, boom! He drops another piece of information that turns the issue around. It kept playing with my head as to which side I was leaning towards.

Gary Guthrie, posted 21 July 2003:
Simply captivating. The director's ability to develop a 'plot' through their editing of all the footage, audio, photos, etc. – one akin to a great drama or thriller – is pure genius.

Matthew, posted 5 September 2004:
The great thing about the film was that the issue was not guilt or innocence, but unanswered questions about what happens to a family embroiled in such a controversy. A journey that ends in a Roman suicide by the hero who is also the villain, in a last attempt to redeem himself for the pain that he caused his son and his family. Very satisfying.

Jean-Marc, France, posted 22 April 2004:
An amazing film – the first documentary equivalent of Rashomon, the Kurosawa film where everyone recalls a different version of a same murder.

In the last posting at least, there is also an element of a public performance of knowledge, a display of cultural capital. The film's *Rashomon* effect was, however, problematic for some commentators, of which more below.

Public and private

The opening sequence of *Capturing the Friedmans* implies a blurring of public and private spheres, not only as a consequence of its re-presentation of home video material, but also via its particular focus on family members exposed to public scrutiny. This scrutiny of the Friedmans occurs not only in the mid-1980s, channelled via accusations of abuse and local media attention, but also more recently through the acts of spectatorship and judgement invited by the documentary intervention itself.

The filmmakers have repeatedly stressed their intention to make a film centred on the family members engulfed by a confluence of legal process, media attention and community hysteria. For example, Jarecki commented on the use of home movie extracts in the credits:

We knew that the home movies that the Friedmans had taken over the years were such an important part of the film that we

wanted them to be the centrepiece of the opening titles, but we
wanted to use these titles as a chance to establish the family members firmly at the centre of the story you know, rather than making it a story about a legal case or something less personal.[26]

Certainly the presence and availability of hours of home movies
and videos facilitated the decision to concentrate on family dynamics. Such a decision raises a number of issues, however, including questions of editorial control and ethical concerns (in terms
of both making and watching the film) and debates over whether
or not a 'personal' angle was the best way to approach the legal
case.

For a film dealing with allegations of paedophilia, *Capturing
the Friedmans* may appear surprisingly reticent in its visual representation of such abuse. The molested bodies of the alleged victims are notable by their absence.[27] Instead, the film relies on a
series of indirect mediations of sexual activity. Quite early on,
magazine cover shots and a list of titles taken from the child pornography magazines that Arnold kept in his study are displayed
for the camera. The most vivid – but heavily mediated – representation of sexual activity appears in a sequence where former assistant district attorney Joseph Onorato and retired detective Frances
Galasso, then head of the local Sex Crimes Unit, talk about accusations of abuse made in police interviews with some of Arnold's
computing pupils. A simple black and pink computer-rendered
image of a penis gripped by a fist appears in closeup on the screen.
In a simulation of masturbation, the penis flashes blue and then
red. This brief sequence lasts six seconds, before the camera's gaze
shifts screen right for four more seconds to register a joke scoreboard
or 'petermeter' on the margin of the computer screen.[28] But the
moments of alleged sex crime remain inaccessible to any camera,
and are therefore not audio-visually available in the film. (Nor
were they presented as evidence in the case. Both Arnold and
Jesse pleaded guilty and all the evidence gathered by police was
from alleged victims' testimony, with no physical evidence submitted.)

Of course, the lack of any images of abuse, and the deliberate
avoidance of any attempt at reconstruction, enables the film to
sidestep some ethical pitfalls. But another intimate site of access to
the private *is* arrayed on screen – that of the family in crisis, in the
aftermath of the arrests of Arnold and Jesse. Thus talk about the

alleged sex crimes and their consequences (both contemporane-
ous in 1987, much of it recorded on David's camcorder, and via
retrospective interviews), becomes the focus of the film, rather
than the crimes themselves. In the process family members themselves become key objects of scrutiny.[29] And, as Foucault famously
suggested, sexuality is once again constructed as a prime site of
truth.

Several commentators have noted an increased appetite for
'human interest' stories in television news, current affairs and
documentary, as well as in the reality television boom of the 1990s.
Liesbet van Zoonen calls this process 'intimization'.[30] On a related
development, Anita Biressi writes:

> Entertainment television's enthusiastic adoption of therapeutic
> discourses of revelation, truth-telling and self-exposure, and of
> popular notions of 'trauma' as the kernel of these revelations,
> has seeped into even the most privileged and 'reputable' of forms,
> including news, current affairs and documentary.[31]

Even within this context, however, *Capturing the Friedmans*
stands out as remarkable, in terms of the content, intimacy and
sheer volume of its camcorder footage, as well as the details of the
story it traces.[32] For example, viewers witness repeated family rows,
David's private video diary, and Jesse's last night of freedom. Despite the creeping ubiquity of (largely domestic) real-life trauma
that Biressi locates on American and British television, such material can still retain the power to shock and move audiences. For
some commentators and viewers, the fact that so much 'private'
footage was shot by the Friedmans became symptomatic of the
family's pathology.[33] In terms of both form and content, *Capturing
the Friedmans'* home movies with a difference can be experienced
as raw and shocking, while the family on screen disintegrates:
Elaine doubts her husband Arnold, son David berates Elaine, and
Arnold retreats into an impenetrable silence.

This extreme intimacy taken to the point of intrusion was often greeted by expressions of emotional response in web postings.
For instance:

Nat Saunders, posted 9 April 2004:
The Shaftesbury Avenue Odeon Cinema, London, this afternoon:
not a dry eye in the house by the end of the movie. Whatever the
truth may be, the wreckage left behind was heart-breaking ...

JGR, Toronto, posted 13 August 2003:
This is a very disturbing movie. I cannot stop thinking about it. I
sat at the end of the movie, immobilized in my chair (in tears) at
witnessing the destruction of a family.

Lisa G, Toronto, posted 28 July 2003:
What an incredible film. I was left devastated and then exhila-
rated and then saddened, but mostly deeply, deeply moved. I had
the most confusing tears at the end. Impossible to nail just why I
cried. Thank you for this film.

The intimate revelations, emotional pain, and family dysfunc-
tion presented in *Capturing the Friedmans* may also have functioned
for some audiences as guarantors of veracity. The warrant provided by such onscreen hurt may have validated the evidentiality
of the camcorder material, which might otherwise have been dismissed by sceptical viewers as relatively unconvincing or staged.
Thus, through a combination of both form and content, the home
video footage can become freighted with connotations of authenticity. If Arnold's home movies conform to what Patricia Zimmermann has called the 'hugs, kisses, hamming, and idealized
memories of a contrived family harmony' that have become conventional to the format, [34] then David's camcorder gives the lie to
this ideal. However, while the viewers quoted above largely welcomed the film's affective charge, others raised doubts and anxieties in terms of both its ethics and credibility. For example:

Angek, posted 12 April 2004:
This film was chilling and disturbing. It was beyond belief, to me,
that David was videoing as the family was disintegrating. I thought
that this was either because the truth was unbearable, or because
he was actively trying to divert the viewer from the truth.

Mark, posted 13 August 2003:
While I was moved by what appeared to be the sheer nakedness
of their story, I was equally struck by how much can be hidden
when so much is put out in plain view. Can anyone avoid a little
'acting' when highly distraught and being recorded, especially the
sons who seemed to have dramatic personalities? IMO the personal cameras obscured as much as they revealed.

Grip, posted 27 July 2003:
Wondering aloud to myself if negative comments are allowed
here. I thought the movie felt contrived, controlled, and dare I
say: fake? I found myself staring at the granular footage looking

for signs of digital post-production techniques that might be signs of fraud. Decent documentary, if true. Somehow I'm not completely sold.

Perhaps surprisingly, anxieties about the voyeurism of the film and its proposals to viewers were expressed relatively rarely on the website. Here are some exceptions:

> BM, posted 16 September 2003:
> Saw the film yesterday. Totally wild and voyeristic ... My eyes were glued to the screen the entire time.

> Jennifer Halbach, posted 3 June 2004:
> I enjoyed it a lot and though I knew disater was going to occur and build up, like a car wreck I couldn't help but to watch.

> Peter Bloch-Hansen, posted 26 July 2003:
> ... some of the most fascinating footage I've ever seen in a theatre. It left me wondering, is this entertainment?

The lure of voyeurism, the way viewers felt its appeal despite their concerns, is clearly evident in these ambivalent accounts.

The issue of voyeurism was also raised indirectly by Jarecki in an interview featured on the UK DVD. The relevant passage is worth quoting at length:

> that [home video] material turned out to be so intensely personal that it really gave a different cast to the whole, to the whole film. I think what's so unique about that material is not just that, you know, it's the most personal record of the breakdown of the family that you can imagine, I mean, from inside the house. It's sort of like you know, you read a news story in the paper and you wonder, 'what was it really like in that house, I wonder what that husband said to that wife on the morning before the murder happened', or something like that. Well, here you can go into the house, you know, the family brings you into their own house, with their own camera, and so that's important, I think, but the function of that material in this documentary is that you know in a normal documentary you have two characters who are telling you conflicting things and you have to decide who you believe, but you never met either one of them before, you don't necessarily have enough information to go on, and you don't have any primary source material, you weren't there, but here, because the Friedmans are giving you their home video material, suddenly you're there, you're inside the house, and you have enough material to be able to start to make some judgements about whether

you think this family is just you know, a group of incredibly vi-
cious criminals, or … maybe a seemingly or largely pretty average
family that could have been in the wrong place at the wrong time
… well you know that's something you can suddenly start to
judge for yourself because you have that primary experience with
them.

In the first part of this statement, discussing the hypothetical
murder, Jarecki constructs a revealing voyeuristic fantasy of gaining access to the scene of a crime and the people involved in it.[35]
Not only does this celebration of getting 'inside the house' elide
the multiple interventions of Jarecki and his crew, it also pro-
motes an epistephiliac dream of a particular kind: a disembodied
audio-visual mobility that documentary has often claimed to provide – achieved in this instance via home video, itself coded (not
unproblematically) as a new plateau of intimacy and evidentiality.

Jarecki moves on from this initial expression of voyeuristic
pleasure to justify it in terms of giving viewers the chance to judge
for themselves. From such a perspective, *Capturing the Friedmans*
can be seen as an instance of a common device in American popular
culture that Carol Clover has termed the 'jury challenge'. Clover
argues that the fictional trial movie or courtroom drama 'positions
us not as passive spectators, but as active viewers with a job to
do'.[36] Despite the rather unhelpful binary between passive and
active spectatorship suggested here, Clover's general point can be
usefully applied to *Capturing the Friedmans'* presentation of a real-
life criminal case. The jury challenge is made very clear in the
invitation-to-view of the film's tagline: 'who will you believe?'[37]
Jarecki's comments above endorse this viewing strategy, trading
on the familiar myth that to see is to know, as if the images in the
Friedmans' home videos hold a truth, perhaps not self-evident,
but available for the attentive viewer to decipher.

Contradiction and indeterminacy

Some reviewers have celebrated *Capturing the Friedmans* as a self-
reflexive examination of the limits of film as a medium of record,
whether intentional or not.[37] In interviews, Jarecki himself presents the film as an interrogation of processes of memory and a
demonstration of the elusiveness of truth, at least in people's recollections. The invitation to 'judge for yourself' works partly in

tension with these two readings of the film, especially the first one. By contrast, the jury challenge is grounded at some level on the veracity of (parts of) what the viewer sees and hears, insofar as the film, with its parade of competing discourses, characters and voices, is proposed as worth watching in order to come to some kind of conclusion, even if it is that there is no easy answer.

Capturing the Friedmans is structured not only as a dramatic and carefully paced narrative of a family wrecked by a criminal investigation and subsequent convictions. The film is also assembled and experienced as an interchange of accusations, allegations and counter arguments, a composite of edited segments from interviews with police, prosecutors, former computer students and family members, as well as from the Friedmans' home movies and videos. The resulting mix of conflicting perspectives was praised by commentators and by some viewers, but also proved controversial.

As David Bordwell has suggested, ambiguity in fictional storytelling is very much a convention of (European) art cinema, in terms of both textual mechanisms and viewing strategies: 'Put crudely, the slogan of the art cinema might be, "When in doubt, read for maximum ambiguity."'[39] Ambiguity is not always tolerated by audiences, however, in either fiction or non-fiction. Judging by website postings, *Capturing the Friedmans'* deliberate avoidance of moralising certainty and closure was perplexing for some viewers. But it proved productive for others in stimulating a range of speculations, interpretations and judgements by people making up their own minds about the rights and wrongs of the case. (For some, as will soon become clear, the film was clearly legible and left little room for doubt, despite its promoted ambiguity.)

The first contradiction of the police case against Arnold and Jesse comes 17 minutes into the film, in an interview with Judd Maltin, Jesse's best friend from high school. As editor and co-producer Richard Hankin notes in a DVD commentary, Maltin here functions as a 'character witness' for Jesse. (More detailed allegations of abuse and refutations of those allegations, along with concerns about police interview tactics and the use of hypnosis to retrieve children's memories, follow a few minutes later.) Hankin stresses the difficulty and significance of deciding when to first introduce material contradicting the police and prosecution case, and this choice is indeed fundamental to the structure and impact of the film. According to Jarecki in the same commentary, the first cut initially showed the case entirely from the police perspective, and ran for 45 minutes before any opposing argument was offered, with radically different results: 'what we found was that if you then added in another layer of complexity and another set of people to believe after that, there was no going back ... it was just kind of an afterthought to say there was any doubt.' Ultimately, in the final version, counter arguments against the police case are not left so late.

An example of the finished film's interlacing structure comes a few minutes after Maltin's interview. Verbally graphic accusations about sodomy, rape and a bizarre sexualised game of 'leap-frog' recounted by investigating detectives and a former computer student are inter-cut with an interview with another student, who describes the classes as 'as ordinary and as boring as you could possibly imagine' and rejects accusations of abuse as a 'grotesque fantasy'. The editing strategy in this three-minute segment rapidly establishes the coexistence of differing perspectives and discourses on the case, achieving a multivocality that persists throughout the film.

The following accounts respond positively to the film's ambiguity and multivocality, expressing this in terms of the jury challenge ('searching' for the truth 'like an investigator'), and/or the enjoyment of an unusual degree of freedom to form opinions, leading to discussions after the moment of viewing:

> monica, posted 14 April 2004:
> as a film student, I really loved this film ... I appreciated the neutrality, and even more with the DVD the extra materials, so that you really do feel like an investigator searching for what the real and definitive truth here really is ... I can't say I'm sure of anything after watching this film, not of Arnie or Jessie's innocence or guilt ...

> Josh, posted 18 April 2004:
> This is a uniquely honest film, Thank you for allowing the viewer room to form our own opinions. Very compelling.

> Elizabeth, posted 28 January 2004:
> I love how no judgement was made by the filmmakers and that you are open to assume what you think happened.

Tracey Hoyt, Toronto, Canada, posted 27 July 2003:
My friends and I had a very intense discussion about it during dinner afterwards. This is the true sign of an excellent documentary: we left asking more questions and debated over who was really telling the truth.

Philippe, posted 15 April 2004:
I have been violently shaken by this moive. What is truth? What is a human being? How real can a relationship be? How the American society can do such things? And who can I trust? And who am I? Bravo ...

Others posting messages appeared more certain of Arnold and Jesse's innocence or guilt:

Julian Glasgow, Scotland, posted 6 September 2004:
No physical evidence, just a bunch of brainwashed kids telling fairytales so that their parents could be compensated and have something to do. The U.S. legal system is f— and even more f— is the fact that no one did something about this. May your dad rest in peace and Good luck Jesse. Get out of the U.S. and come to the U.K.

Mike Watson, posted 9 February 2004:
Arnold and Jessie are obviously guilty and this is just another example of Hollywood liberals trying to make people feel sorry for scumbags.

CJ, posted 15 March 2004:
What sick perverted father/son team would rape and molest boys TOGETHER? I mean ... REALLY! IT sounds like a bad perverted horror movie. And yet, this was reality for Jesse and Arnold.

Note in this last posting how the genre of the horror film offers a ready-made cultural trope through which to figure child abuse, a taboo topic that otherwise stands at the limits of representability as almost 'unimaginable'.[39]

For some commentators, in contrast to those viewers quoted above, the film's balancing act constituted a missed opportunity. A review of the DVD release on the American website *Slate* criticised the filmmakers for prioritising dramatic imperatives over honesty and accuracy. Responding to extra material available on the DVD but excluded from the feature film, Harvey A. Silvergate and Carl Takei accused *Capturing the Friedmans* of backing away from an unambiguous declaration of a miscarriage of justice in favour of a spurious – if dramatically effective – even-handedness:

> Containing hours of previously unreleased footage and archival
> material, the DVD makes it clear that Jarecki decided to maintain
> a studied ambiguity. He had compelling evidence that the
> Friedmans had been railroaded by a criminal-justice system in
> the grips of hysteria. This evidence presumably was omitted for
> dramatic effect ... Jarecki argues that he had to maintain balance
> so that the film would be taken seriously by viewers ... [He]
> continues to maintain that if the film had been less evenhanded
> the audience would not have thought deeply about where the
> truth lay. We think, however, that Jarecki underestimates his au-
> dience.[41]

It is clear that the mystery and jury challenge elements of the
film were indeed crucial to its commercial and critical success.
However, viewer comments posted on the *Capturing the Friedmans*
website (all self-selected of course) suggest that many people ap-
preciated a film that withheld judgement precisely because it required audience involvement and thought. While some viewers
using the message board found the film confusing or frustrating,
others found it either clear enough proof of a miscarriage of justice, or a serious rather than futile offer to make up their own
minds on the 'evidence' presented. It is not my purpose at this
point to make a judgement on these criticisms and defences of the
film, but to show how dramatic form, marketing imperatives, audience viewing strategies, and journalistic notions of accuracy to
the facts do not always converge neatly in documentary.

A decade before the release of *Capturing the Friedmans*, Bill
Nichols argued that a 'shift of epistemological proportions' had
occurred in the field of documentary:

> Traditionally, the word *documentary* has suggested fullness and
> completion, knowledge and fact, explanations of the social world
> and its motivating mechanisms. More recently, though, docu-
> mentary has come to suggest incompleteness and uncertainty,
> recollection and impression, images of personal worlds and their
> subjective construction ... What counts as knowledge is not what
> it used to be.[42]

Capturing the Friedmans shows how an emerging politics of location in documentary – offering explorations rather than conclu-
sions, emphasising specificity and multiple subjectivities rather than
generalising 'objective' certainties – can be commercially expedi-
ent when it borrows from fiction film genres (the thriller, the

melodrama) that provide a framework which may, at least partially, motivate and manage such ambiguity and doubt.

The personal and the political

In contrast to some reviewers' criticisms about the prioritisation of a marketable mystery above valid concerns about police procedure, or about a proliferation of images proving nothing, for some viewers posting on the website, *Capturing the Friedmans* told the complicated story of a miscarriage of justice about which, ultimately, there could be little doubt.

For example:

> Diane F, posted 31 August 2004:
> I was surprised that I was able to see and feel the humanity in Arnold as I clearly feel he is a pedophile and there were probably victims other than the two he admitted to. I do believe the computer group was left untouched and Jesse was sacrificed by both parents. The justice system and media are a disgrace. Peace to the family.[43]

> Louise, posted 17 August 2004:
> This is such a heartbreaking story. While we know that Arnold was not altogether innocent, there is no doubt in my mind that both he and Jesse were in no way guilty of the crimes they were accused of here. It is such a gross abuse of power and miscarriage of justice by the authorities and police.

> Jay Silver, posted 1 August 2004:
> The most egregious form of police misconduct ever filmed first hand. Through all of this, does it not occur to anyone, that there is not one shred of physical evidence ... Anyone who took part of the media should be ashamed of themselves ... NEVER HAD A CHANCE!

In a discussion of television documentary, Myra Macdonald has suggested that in some cases, 'the personal can become political, moving the audience beyond a fleeting fix of voyeurism to fresh perceptions about the workings of the contemporary or historical world.'[44] How might this be true for *Capturing the Friedmans*? I would argue that (for some but not all of its audiences) the film can be seen as effectively humanising, and so rendering watchable, engaging, and 'real', issues of police procedure, legal process, media panic, community hysteria, and 'deviant' sexuality. These topics of undoubted significance in the public sphere gain a degree of salience via the domestic focus and individual pain relayed in the filmic treatment of the case.

In his DVD commentary, Jarecki says:

> One of our goals in the way that we wanted to portray the film, it was really ... in a very human way, you know when we have a case like this, there's a tendency in the media for the family to become very dehumanised. I also think that the Friedmans felt that if they shared all their private material with us including all this home video material, it's true that some people would say 'oh, those guys are crazy for videotaping everything', but you really couldn't get through this material [as a viewer] and not think of this family as a group of human beings, you know, flawed human beings but very real.
>
> There's a tendency in a case like this to characterise the people you've been reading about in the newspaper as monsters and I think once we call someone a monster we don't really learn anything about them any more, it's sort of, you know they're obviously a whole different species from us, and so it was important for us that we really show the humanity of this family and the fragility of the family.

Jarecki's argument does not easily excuse the intrusion and voyeurism mobilised by the film and via the act(s) of watching it. I certainly don't want to take this and others of his proposed justifications for granted. But some viewers posting on the website, however representative or not they might be, do indeed attest to the film's success, whether intended by its makers or not, in rendering the personal political and the political personal.

In these cases at least, *Capturing the Friedmans* becomes a vivid example of the third level of meaning proposed by John Corner in his triple-decker model:

> A level at which viewers and readers attach a generalized significance to what they have seen and heard, evaluating it (perhaps in relation to its perceived presuppositions and entailments if it has propositional force) and locating it within a negotiated place in their knowledge or memory, where it may continue to do modifying work on other constituents of their consciousness (and, indeed, of their unconscious).[45]

Here are some examples of the consequences of watching – and thinking about – *Capturing the Friedmans* in terms of the personal and political dimensions of its story:

> Tess, Indiana, posted 4 September 2004:
> I saw the film about six months ago, but parts of it still haunt me
> … I felt I could begin to understand facts of the Friedman's lives
> that never would have been available without such a great movie.
> my heart hurts for the entire family …
>
> Maria Cristina, posted 6 July 2003:
> You have turned my night inside out. My mind is twisting. I am so
> upset by what this family suffered, the unanswered questions,
> the lives ruined. And more than anything, the fact that we will
> never truly know what happened. I wish you could have tied the
> movie up with a nice pink bow, captured the bad guys and re-
> deem us all. And I am left waiting with my naievete. Realizing that
> life doesn't work that way; only bad movies.
>
> Emily, posted 29 June 2003:
> I saw this film last night, and I couldn't fall asleep until 5 am
> because my brain wouldn't turn off … I feel like my life has
> changed because I'll never look at news and media the same way
> … However I'll gladly trade my peaceful night's sleep for being rid
> of a certain amount of ignorance that I formerly possessed.

In some of these examples, and others quoted earlier, viewers have become engaged in feeling and thinking about not just this family or this case, but beyond the particular instance to its implications for and about institutional processes and popular attitudes to sex crime in the United States.

No discussion of *Capturing The Friedmans* should ignore the film's undoubted voyeurism, or its clear acts of mediation and attendant lack of (impossible) transparency. But to watch stories about 'the world' presented by documentaries such as this is not necessarily to feel nothing beyond the lures of voyeurism, nor to fall automatically into the trap of naive positivism (despite some such implications in Jarecki's comments about home video taking audiences 'inside the house' to offer a 'primary experience'). Ultimately, what I want to acknowledge, and in some ways defend here is a critically unfashionable mode of viewing documentaries in order to find out, and be moved by, things that are not always available via first-hand experience. Even if this inevitably entails reliance upon the decisions and mediations of filmmakers, it should not be ridiculed as unthinking or gullible, easily dismissed as 'credulous' from the standpoint of 'sophisticated' academic scepticism. In the end, all this does not reduce the responsibility confronting any filmmakers attempting to make a documentary, but rather increases it. As the writer and documentary editor Dai Vaughan has suggested:

> Documentary will be consequent upon what it appears to show, rather than upon what it necessarily does show; and the relationship between the two is a matter for the filmmakers' ethics, inaccessible to the viewer. Yet the assumptions which the viewer makes about this relationship, on the basis of signals intended or unintended, will inform his [sic] perception of the film. To make a documentary is therefore to persuade the viewer that what appears to be is.[46]

This investigation of *Capturing the Friedmans* has explored some of the multiple and tangled ways in which such ethical issues interact with questions of film form, marketing logics, and viewing strategies, both proposed and realised.

Notes

1   Investigators' first lead was the interception of child pornography sent to him in the mail.
2   The two trials were the first to be televised in Nassau County.
3   The film grossed a further $1 million overseas. Source: www.box officemojo.com
4   Visitors to the site are invited: 'Tell us your thoughts about *Capturing the Friedmans*', and are asked to submit 'name' and 'comment'.
5   For more on questions of mediation and self expression in audience research, see Thomas Austin, *Hollywood, Hype and Audiences: Selling and Watching Popular Film in the 1990s* (Manchester, Manchester University Press), pp. 25–6.
6   Some ethical issues also arise here, in that I am making use of web postings which, while clearly made to a public forum, were not done so in the knowledge that I would comment upon them in published research. While I have inevitably made selections from a large amount of material I have tried to treat statements with respect, and not to misrepresent them. I have also followed generally established research procedures, which hold that 'it is not necessary to explicitly seek permission for recording and analyzing publicly posted messages'. Katherine M. Clegg Smith, '"Electronic eavesdropping": the ethical issues involved in conducting a virtual ethnography', in Mark D. Johns, Shing-Ling Sarina Chen and G. Jon Hall (eds), *Online Social Research: Methods, Issues and Ethics* (New York, Peter Lang, 2004), p. 230. Thanks

to Gerarda Cashman for pointing me to this reference.

7   Postings were made mainly by viewers in the US, but there were also some from Canada, Europe, Latin America, and Israel. A few mention personal connections to the subject matter, as victims of abuse, or relations of victims, as psychologists or lawyers, and some are students told to watch the film for a class. But the vast majority do not present themselves in any of these terms.

8   Material on the DVD includes more family home movies and footage of the prosecution's 'star witness', information about another suspect never charged, Jesse's life out of prison, arguments among people featured in the film at its New York premiere, director's commentary and interview, and Jarecki's original short film about David's work as a professional birthday party clown.

9   This issue is particularly acute in the case of screen documentary. Stanely Cavell also points to what lies outside the frame in his more general comparison between painting and photography and, by extension, film: 'You can always ask, of an area photographed, what lies adjacent to that area, beyond the frame. ... We might say: a painting is a world; a photograph is of the world. ... The implied presence of the rest of the world, and its explicit rejection, are as essential to the experience of a photograph as what it explicitly presents.' Stanley Cavell, *The World Viewed: Reflections on the Ontology of Film*, enlarged edition, (Cambridge, MA, Harvard University Press, 1979), pp. 165–6, 23–4, cited in Joe Moran, 'Childhood, class and memory in the *Seven Up* films', *Screen*, 43:4 (2002), p. 400.

10 For a persuasive critique of the myth of informed consent in documentary, which draws in part on the unforeseeable and ongoing consequences of agreeing to be filmed, see Brian Winston, *Claiming the Real: the Documentary Film Revisited* (London, British Film Institute, 1995), pp. 219–29.

11 Following David's lead, Jesse made covert audio recordings of his parents, one of which is used in the film. Having recorded the camcorder material, David stored it away without ever having watched it, according to Jarecki's commentary on the DVD. As Jarecki also notes in both DVD interview and commentary, gaining access to the family members, and to this footage, took time and involved some negotiations. For instance, he was put in touch with Elaine Friedman, David's mother and Arnold's wife, after offering David a tape of his childhood appearance on the *Candid Camera* television show.

12 Christian Vogler, *The Writer's Journey: Mythic Structure for Storytellers and Screenwriters* (2nd edition, London, Pan Books, 1999), p. 81.

13 Information withheld for quite some time includes the (separate) guilty pleas of father and son, the sentences they received, and Arnold's suicide in prison by an overdose of antidepressants, from which Jesse

received $250,000 life insurance.

14   Paul Rotha, *The Documentary Film* (2nd edition, London, Faber, 1952), p. 70. For further discussion of this slippery phrase, see Winston, *Claiming the Real*, especially pp. 11–14 and 24–9.

15   Stella Bruzzi, *New Documentary: A Critical Introduction* (London, Routledge, 2000), p. 14. As Bruzzi rightly notes, not only are (degrees of) editorial intervention and aestheticisation inevitable, they are not necessarily detrimental to documentary's conventional truth claims.

16   Kracauer cited in Paul Arthur, 'On the virtues and limitations of collage', *Documentary Box* 11, (1997), p. 3.

17   A similar binarism has been labelled by some film makers the 'Zapruder quotient'. 'If you had a very high quotient of total amateurism in terms of technique, but the content was superb, what you were filming was absolutely riveting, that was 100% on the Zapruder curve.' Mike Wadleigh in *Late Show Special*, BBC2, 22 November 1993, cited in Michael Chanan, 'On documentary: the Zapruder quotient' *Filmwaves*, 4 (nd), accessed online at: mchanan.dial.pipex.com/ zapruder.htm. A contrasting attitude, which refuses the opposition of notions of 'beauty' and 'truth', is evident in some of the films and writings of Werner Herzog. See Thomas Austin, '"… to leave the confinements of his humanness": authorial voice and constructions of nature in Werner Herzog's *Grizzly Man*', forthcoming 2008.

18   Peter Keighron, 'What's up doc?', *Sight and Sound* (NS), 3:10 (1993), pp. 24–5.

19   I will return to this concept below.

20   *Ibid.*, 24.

21   *Ibid.*, 24.

22   In a discussion of the 'academically neglected tradition of documentary journalism', John Corner writes: 'television documentary journalism attempted where possible to place the viewer as 'witness' to the 'evidence' of its own inquiry. This was very different from the kind of audience position encouraged in classic documentary cinema, where it was largely *manifest* if under-appreciated realities … which were portrayed.' John Corner, 'Visibility as truth and spectacle in TV documentary realism', in Ib Bondebjerg (ed.), *Moving Images, Culture and the Mind* (Luton, University of Luton Press, 2000), p. 145, italics in original. *Capturing the Friedmans* also deploys an investigative dynamic, but it draws from screen fiction as well as journalism, stresses contradictions and refuses conventional closure. In terms of its engagement with competing recollections, as well as its successful marketing as a non-fiction thriller, it is reminiscent of Errol Morris' celebrated *The Thin Blue Line* (US, 1988).

23   This style of introduction to the family is mimicked on the film's website via sections devoted to each member.

24 For more on distinctions made by some audiences between documentary as a site of the authentic and reality television as essentially inauthentic, see chapter two.

25 All quotations taken from web postings are verbatim, including some errors in spelling and grammar.

26 Andrew Jarecki, director's commentary on DVD.

27 A partial exception to this is an interview with one alleged victim who slumps across a sofa while being filmed. His pose, along with the lighting used to conceal his face, tends to focus attention on his body. On how the filmmakers ended up shooting the interview this way, see Jarecki's commentary on the DVD.

28 In director's commentary on the DVD, Jarecki explains that the footage is a reconstruction of one of the Commodore 64 computer games found in the Friedmans' house.

29 The Friedmans' Jewishness will not be pursued here. It is not an explicit point of comment, either in the film or on the mesage board: among 32,000 words posted about the film, the word 'Jewish' came up just three times.

30 Liesbet van Zoonen, 'A tyranny of intimacy? Women, femininity and television news', in Peter Dahlgren and Colin Sparks (eds), *Communication and Citizenship* (London, Routledge, 1991), p. 217, cited in Myra Macdonald, 'Politicizing the personal: women's voices in British television documentaries', in Cynthia Carter, Gill Branston and Stuart Allan (eds), *News, Gender and Power* (London, Routledge, 1998), p. 105.

31 Anita Biressi, 'Inside/out: private trauma and public knowledge in true crime documentary', *Screen*, 45:4 (2004), p. 401.

32 Jonathan Caouette's autobiographical *Tarnation* (US, 2004) is another recent cinematic example of this trend.

33 As Jarecki says in his DVD commentary: 'it's true that some people would say ' "oh, those guys are crazy for videotaping everything".'

34 Patricia R. Zimmermann, *Reel Families: A Social History of Amateur Film* (Bloomington, Indiana University Press, 1995), p. 150. Zimmermann notes how home video often conforms to this template. But she also offers a contrasting description of how it is used in fiction films like *Down and Out in Beverley Hills* (US, 1986) in a way that could be applied to *Capturing the Friedmans*: 'the male child of an emotionally dysfunctional couple wields the camera like a scalpel, surgically opening up and exposing family secrets'. *Ibid.*, 145. Thanks to Paul Ward for pointing me to this book.

35 In the case of the Friedmans, Seth, the middle brother, is a notable absence for much of the film. He refused to be interviewed by Jarecki, and appears less often than his brothers in featured home movie and video footage.

36   Carol Clover, 'Judging audiences: the case of the trial movie', in Christine Gledhill and Linda Williams (eds), *Reinventing Film Studies* (London, Arnold, 2000), p. 246.

37   The second person address here has some similarities with the tagline 'what would you do to survive?', used to promote the mountaineering documentary *Touching the Void* (UK 2003). I have argued in chapter two that this proposal invites empathy and vicarious participation with the climbers in the film, whereas in the case of *Capturing the Friedmans*, the invitation is to weigh up the evidence and come to some kind of conclusion about competing points of view voiced on screen.

38   See for instance the following comments in *Scope*: '*Capturing The Friedmans* is best understood as a film about the limits of film. This is not what Jarecki thinks, but it is nonetheless what the film does best. … What finally makes the film important is its ability to raise questions about our faith in the visual – not whom we believe, but what, in the end, do we see?' Deborah Shaller, '*Capturing the Friedmans*', *Scope*, (NS) 1 (2005), accessed online at: www.nottingham.ac.uk/film/journal/.

39   David Bordwell, 'The art cinema as mode of film practice', *Film Criticism*, 4:1 (1979), p. 60.

40   For a discussion of how the common fictional figure of the serial killer can be used to as a device through which to consider real-life abuse, see Biressi, 'Inside/out'.

41   Harvey A. Silvergate and Carl Takei, 'Mistrial: The *Capturing the Friedmans* DVD sheds new light on the case', *Slate*, posted 27 February 2004, accessed at: http://slate.msn.com/id/2096296/. See also criticisms of the film's ambiguity made by investigate journalist Debbie Nathan (who features briefly in the flm), cited by Shaller in '*Capturing the Friedmans*'.

42   Bill Nichols, *Blurred Boundaries: Questions of Meaning in Contemporary Culture* (Bloomington, Indiana University Press, 1994), p.1.

43   Acccording to 'My Story', a document Arnold Friedman wrote while in jail, he had sexual activity with two boys at a summer resort when he was in his 40s.

44   Macdonald, 'Politicizing the Personal', pp. 105–6.

45   John Corner, 'Meaning, genre and context: the problematics of "public knowledge" in the new audience studies', in James Curran and Michael Gurevitch (eds), *Mass Media and Society* (London, Edward Arnold 1991), p. 272.

46   Dai Vaughan, *For Documentary: Twelve Essays* (Berkeley, University of California Press, 1999), p. 59, italics in original.

5

Approaching the invisible centre: middle-class identity and documentary film

So far in this book I have considered various engagements with screen documentary made by viewers other than myself. In this chapter I turn attention to some of my own responses to documentary films, and explore how my identity, particularly its middle-class aspect, has shaped these reactions. The purpose behind this move is not to wallow in narcissism, nor to 'restore' a middle-class, white and male subjectivity to the centre stage of film and media studies – if it has ever been truly displaced – although both these accusations might be levelled at me.[1] Instead, I aim to acknowledge, foreground and so begin to interrogate my own, particular privileged subjectivity as researcher, rather than to pass it off as invisible, unremarkable, or irrelevant.

Some similar steps have already been taken within the field of audience studies. Often borrowing from feminist thought, qualitative audience research has embraced self-reflexivity more willingly than some other sectors of media, film and cultural studies.[2] My argument here is undoubtedly influenced by work within both feminist and audience studies traditions that has focused on 'speaking positions' in order to avoid the universalising assumptions of supposedly 'objective' research. But my particular concern with middle-class identity addresses a topic that remains underexamined in much work on the media. Hopefully, this chapter will both clarify the position from which I have conducted the research in this book, and act as a spur towards more critical thinking about class, in all its manifestations and complexities, within film and media studies.

If the cultural and social power of whiteness as a normative dimension of identity lies in its ability to obfuscate its own specificity, to render itself 'normal', taken for granted, invisible, the same is true of middle classness.[3] However, while constructions of white-ness have been subjected to increasing academic scrutiny in the last decade or so, middle classness remains somewhat under-ex-amined, certainly as regards the vast majority of work on film and the media.[4] This is generally true in terms of studies of production and consumption as well as analyses of textual representation.[5] In the following pages I attempt to open up this core identity to fur-ther investigation by grappling with my own middle-classness, and with two documentary films which, inadvertently or other-wise, have led me to confront this element of my identity. Al-though this chapter lacks the scope or detail to be called a fully-fledged piece of autoethnography, it borrows from that criti-cal tradition an interest in self-examination in order to query some of the assumptions and practices of academic discourse. [6]

Becoming conspicuous on the grounds of class identity is some-thing that is not usually welcomed by members of the nebulous, fragmented, but nevertheless highly significant social group known in Britain as 'the middle class'. This is especially true, in my expe-rience, within the university sector. Such reluctance is encour-aged by the fact that, despite some genuine attempts to widen participation, the student population in British higher education remains predominantly middle-class. And, although a decline in wage levels compared to other professions, shifts towards casualisation, and the rationale of the market have eroded in-comes and job security for many, academic employees in British higher education are still best thought of as middle-class.[7] (I am following the influential work of Pierre Bourdieu,[8] and more re-cently, Mike Savage *et al.*, in classifying intellectual workers as positioned beyond the working class largely because of their greater holdings of institutionally sanctioned cultural capital, which can be translated into *some* social and economic advantages.)[9]

Middle-class characters and concerns are repeatedly repre-sented in popular film – both fiction and documentary. But the critical tools with which to approach the *classed nature* of such por-trayals need to be refined and developed. The same is true of class-sensitive perspectives on the media industries and media audiences. On the latter, Jostein Gripsrud suggests that many academic cel-ebrations of consumers of popular culture are tacitly motivated in part by the desire of upwardly mobile entrants into academia for a 'symbolic homecoming' to their social origins in the working classes or non-academic middle classes.[10] Similarly, Rita Felski notes that, 'only too conscious of the charges of aridity and abstraction often levelled at intellectual work', cultural critics such as John Fiske 'eagerly ally themselves with the image of a vital, sensual, popular body'.[11] By contrast, she argues, intellectuals from the lower middle class often feel ashamed of, and alienated from, their origins.

In fact, most of the academics in the field who are actually explicit about their own writing positions appear far more comfortable thinking about themselves as gendered, raced and sexual subjects than as classed ones. Commenting on the ways in which class became more or less 'unspeakable' in American humanities discourses (particularly film studies) during the 1980s and 1990s, David E. James suggests that this was due to three factors. First, not enough working-class people were admitted into higher education. Second, where affirmative action did lead to the enrolment of working-class women or people of colour, they were admitted and their identities theoretically validated 'under the designation of their sexual or ethnic identities ... while their class background was ignored'. Finally, 'although all other identities have been eminently assimilable to the bourgeois academy, allowing female, black, and queer people to live privileged lives as female, black and queer academics ... the best a person from the working class can hope for is precisely that, to be *from* the working class, and in this displacement to be deprived of the possibility of speaking either as or for the working class'.[12] The exceptions to academics' general silence about their own class have tended to be accounts written by precisely those who entered the academy from working-class backgrounds, and who have had to negotiate this mobility.[13] But middle-classness has remained largely unmarked, naturalised in countless ways, an invisible centre at the heart of most academics' social identities.[14]

Discussing the need for a full and systematic elaboration of class as a tool of cultural analysis, Chuck Kleinhans writes:

> It would have to include an explanation of production and diffusion as well as texts themselves. It would have to account for class differences in audience reception. It would have to develop across, between, and within diverse media. And it would have to consider the interrelation of class with gender, race, ethnicity, age/ generation, region, and so on.[15]

As Kleinhans himself notes, this is a hugely ambitious task. Like his work, my own is an inevitably partial and limited investigation of class, but it moves in a rather different direction. Kleinhans' symptomatic reading of class tensions in Hollywood action films absents his own class identity (as does Douglas Kellner's analysis of class in the *Poltergeist* films, published in the same collection).[16] By contrast, I focus here on two films that have prompted me to think about my membership of the middle class.

I should point out here that I think of myself as belonging to what might be loosely called the *Guardian*-reading English middle class. (*The Guardian* is the British daily newspaper traditionally read by the left/liberal middle classes, particularly public sector employees.) My mother grew up in a lower middle-class family, and my father in a rural working-class one. Both my parents worked in the public sector: she as a school secretary and then a social worker, he as a teacher.[17]

The catalyst for my recent thinking about class was provided by two documentaries from the United States: the award-winning HBO film *Paradise Lost: The Child Murders at Robin Hood Hills* (US, 1996), directed by Bruce Sinofsky and Joe Berlinger, and its sequel, *Paradise Lost 2: Revelations* (US, 2000). The two films foregrounded issues of class for me by staging some interactions or collisions between (white) members of the working and middle classes. In this analysis, I trace the differing conditions under which these mediated meetings took place, and my responses to them. As numerous writers have noted, class identity is formed and experienced not just in terms of social, cultural and economic practices and structures, but also through emotional ties and psychological investments. Accordingly, I have tried to pay attention to these dimensions of my viewing behaviour.

Like the questionnaire entries and web postings analysed in previous chapters, statements made here about my personal response to the films must be considered as performative acts made about feelings and engagements, rather than as transparent reproductions of these. As a consequence, my account of the viewing process should be seen as in part a form of self-presentation, offering (whether deliberately or accidentally) particular constructions of self-identity. An awareness of this presentational dimension should not invalidate what I am arguing here, but should pre-empt any simplistic claims to objective truth.

Paradise Lost

Bill Nichols has suggested that one of film documentary's dominant modes of construction has been to frame its subjects as 'other'. In class terms, this results in a middle-class argument that positions its working-class subjects, most notably via the voyeuristic paternalism of what Brian Winston has termed 'victim-documentary'.[18] As Nichols puts it: 'The voice of authority resides with the text itself rather than those recruited to it'.[19] Historically, as Beverley Skeggs summarises, '"the working class" as a category came into effect through middle-class conceptualizations. These conceptualizations were produced from anxiety about social order and through attempts by the middle class to consolidate *their* identity and power by distancing them from definable "others".'[20] This 'classing gaze' (in Lynette Finch's phrase) typically elevated moral issues over those of economics, to focus on 'social problems' like 'bad' language, drinking, and children's behaviour.[21]

At first glance, the *Paradise Lost* films appear to fit these templates pretty closely. They follow a criminal investigation into three child murders committed in West Memphis, Arkansas. The mutilated bodies of the 8-year-old boys were found in a small wood at the back of a truck wash on the edge of the interstate highway. Police arrested three local teenagers and charged them with murder, alleged to be the result of ritualistic occult practices. In the process of tracking the initial court hearings, convictions, and subsequent appeals of the three, the films present West Memphis as a bleak 'white trash' settlement of trailer parks and bungalows, a breeding ground for Christian fundamentalism and religious hysteria, with (in the second film) undercurrents of child abuse and drug use. Issues of morality and social class are overlaid here with the connotations of the films' semi-rural setting in Arkansas, one of the poorest states in the USA. Rural America, in particular the rural South, has become associated with the white working class in many popular discourses and representations.[22] The Americaness of the location carries a particular charge of otherness for this English viewer, even while it recalls other, often fictional, portrayals of white trash.

I found both *Paradise Lost* films hugely affecting and compelling. Like many other viewers, I was moved and outraged by what seemed to be a clear miscarriage of justice uncovered by the filmmakers. But, alongside these highly significant achievements, the films were also troubling – because of the means through which they had elicited these responses, and because of their treatment of class.

By combining court footage and interviews with police, lawyers, accused and the victims' families, the implicit invitation made to the viewer, particularly in the first film, is to act as a member of the jury and so come to her/his own verdict on the case. (As discussed in Chapter 4, a similar strategy was employed by the makers of *Capturing the Friedmans*.) Co-director Joe Berlinger has said of *Paradise Lost*:

> We wanted to treat the audience like jurors so we reduced it to the elements we felt motivated the jury. But it does still trouble me: talking to people after the film came out, maybe 20 per cent felt the three were guilty based on what they had seen in the film. That sobering realisation changed our approach for the second, which is more of an advocacy film.[23]

While responding to the 'jury challenge' proposition, I felt uncomfortable about the films' construction of the inhabitants of West Memphis and in particular of the 'antihero' John Mark Byers, stepfather of one of the dead boys. The films essentially have two 'stars', and each is charismatic in his own way. The first is Damien Echols, alleged 'ringleader' of the teenagers. Sentenced to death at the age of 19, he is initially presented as rather self-absorbed but is increasingly articulate in interviews conducted on death row. The other is the fascinating and apparently unstable Byers, a part-time preacher. Perhaps because of restricted access to Echols (and due to the fact that no other members of the victims' families were prepared to take part in the second film), the filmmakers return repeatedly to Byers over the course of the two documentaries, shooting him in a number of bizarre performances to camera.

Such posturings may not have been explicitly invited by Berlinger and Sinofsky, but they do seem to have been at least indirectly encouraged by the presence of the filmmakers, and of several other television crews and journalists in West Memphis. Questioned on this point, Berlinger has commented:

> Some people definitely did [perform for the camera] but there's a documentary legitimacy to that because they're unwittingly

revealing something about themselves ... We never purposely stage a situation, but the camera can encourage people to do things they might not otherwise do.[24]

Byers' performances include, in the first film: making threats to the (absent) accused direct to camera on a visit to the crime scene; repeatedly shooting with his vintage pistol three pumpkins that he has named after the accused; taking Polaroids and praying at his stepson's grave. Due, it seems, to his eloquence and enthusiasm for such rituals, in addition to allegations about his involvement in the crime, Byers proves vital to the structure and content of the film (over and above his wife, and any of the other victims' families). His performances provide frequent punctuation to the edited court footage. In the second film, he is filmed in close-up crying and talking to his wife's grave; returning to the crime scene and symbolically 'burying' the accused trio before setting fire to their 'graves'; and brandishing a bible and warning the accused, direct to camera, 'Hell awaits you'. Finally – inter-cut with closing credits announcing the failure of Damien Echols's appeal, and Byers' conviction after filming for selling prescription drugs to an undercover police officer – he is shown in his lounge lip-synching to his own tape-recording of a hymn, cut at a local recording studio.

A relentless process of 'othering' runs through both films, particularly in the depiction of Byers as a white trash grotesque. But a new dynamic is introduced in the sequel. The change occurs with the introduction of members of the Free the West Memphis Three Support Group. These apparently middle-class out-of-towners of both genders – drawn from both coasts as well as some Midwestern states – operate very much as surrogates for the audience (many members of the campaign were alerted to the case by watching the first film) and, perhaps for the filmmakers themselves.[25] This is due not only to their questioning the official verdict of Satanist murder committed by the three teenagers (for which the central evidence was a highly contentious confession made by one of the accused) but also due to their geographical and class locations. Thus Arkansans, both middle-class and working-class, are placed alongside, and explicitly judged by, members of the East and West Coast middle classes.

The campaigners are readable as middle-class via an accretion of details such as clothing (they often wear casual clothes, but

appear in suits outside the courtroom), and their relations to technology (they are shown using a large personal computer and
speaker phone in order to publish a conversation with Echols on
the group's website).[26] Their middle-classness is also coded via
their voices. The distinctive southern accent of Arkansans tends to
be readable as a sign of working-class 'backwardness' in the two
films.[27] To this extent, the lack of equally distinctive accents among
the campaigners (at least for an English viewer) renders them
'unmarked' in class terms. It is only their presence in the milieu of
West Memphis that makes them conspicuous, standing out as
middle-class.

In watching and listening to the support group as they con-
versed with the convicted men's families and their lawyers, and
argued with Byers outside the courthouse, I began to confront my
own judgmental and voyeuristic attitude towards the Arkansans,
an attitude encouraged by the organisation of the films themselves.
Well-meaning, avowedly liberal, and committed to notions of justice, I recognised the campaigners as admirably more active and
less inert versions of my own self-image.[28] But I also saw them
enjoying class privileges and confidence similar to my own, and
deploying a similar gaze, both pitying and condemning, towards
the 'white trash' people of West Memphis. The consequent effect
for me as a viewer (whether intended by the filmmakers or not)
was to question my own position as a hitherto 'invisible' judge of
not just the criminal case but the community as well.

This juxtaposition of classes became even more acute with
footage of the mothers of two of the accused, Damien Echols and
Jason Baldwin, in Los Angeles for the (never aired) recording of a
television talk show. After watching a total of more than three
hours of footage shot in Arkansas, seeing the two women riding in
a huge black limousine to the television studio was slightly shocking – as if they had travelled not just to another state, but to the
territory of another class. Why did the presence of these two working-class Arkansan mothers in middle-class Californian environments feel so odd, so 'unnatural'? Perhaps because of the relative
lack of mobility of (some) working-class people, constrained as
they may be by limited economic and social resources.[29]

Equally, why did the arrival of the support group in West Memphis, while causing some tension and dissonance, not feel so
strange? Because middle-class mobility across and between

different social and physical landscapes is taken for granted. *Paradise Lost 2* shows this familiar binary of middle-class freedom to move, into West Memphis and out again, and working-class immobility, wherein leaving West Memphis for Los Angeles seems much more of an upheaval. In doing so, the film spurred me to think about my own comfortable, unquestioned mobility as, partially at least, a classed privilege.[30]

During the LA visit, Pam Echols joked with campaigners about how many people there wore black, while 'you'd get into trouble for that in some places'. She told them how Damien wore black partly because someone had told him he looked sexy in it. Later, invited to admire a 'dapper' photograph of her son on the support group website, she reacted with a strained smile. These moments were to some extent about a set of disconnections around regional and class differences. But they were also about attempts to connect across the gaps, and to deal with various human emotions – pain, grief, embarrassment, sympathy.

Thus, for me, the class dynamics of *Paradise Lost 2* were complicated by attempts made by its participants (and perhaps, I inferred, by its off-screen makers) to connect across regional and class divides. But these efforts coexisted with the 'righteous mission' of socially-oriented documentary,[31] and its mobilisation of a gaze both sympathetic and condescendingly judgemental. The classed dimension of this mission – and my own more or less willing participation in it – became ultimately foregrounded in an unsettling manner while watching the second film.

Conclusion

In this brief chapter I have approached the invisible centre of middle-classness by tracing representations in two documentary film texts, and by considering the classed gaze on offer to the audience of such films. I have also tried to critically explore my own responses as a middle-class viewer. In the process I have demonstrated some ways in which screen representations of middle-class characters can be examined precisely *as* classed, rather than as simply neutral or taken for granted. The classed nature of such portrayals, the exact characteristics ascribed to the middle class, and the invitations made to a middle-class viewer are perhaps most readily available for analysis in films that stage meetings between members of the middle and working classes, such as the two discussed here.

If notions of class are to return to a position of significance in cultural analysis, much more extensive work needs to be done, including investigations of the affiliations, perspectives, assumptions and privileges enjoyed by academics occupying their own classed positions. This approach is needed for a full and self-reflexive understanding of the prism of middle classness through which the majority of academics in the field view their objects of study. But any such move should not deflect attention away from other dimensions in which class is an even more pressing but equally neglected issue. These include not only textual representations of class – in both documentary and fiction – but also conditions of production and labour relations within the film and television industries, and empirical studies of the place of class in reception. In addition, all such work also needs to attend to intersections between class and gender, ethnicity and sexuality, as I have only intermittently attempted to do here.

Notes

1   For a powerful critique of the tacit restoration of gendered and classed privileges via some discourses of self-reflexivity and confession, see Skeggs, *Class, Self, Culture*, pp. 131–4. She writes: 'We have to ask … who is representing themself as reflexive, as having a self worth knowing, a voice worth hearing … [A]ccess to [social and cultural] resources is what makes reflexivity, although this is rarely acknowledged in claims for the reflexive self.' *Ibid.*, p. 133–4.

2   See Gray, *Research Practice for Cultural Studies*, especially pp. 33–5, for a summary of some such work within audience studies. See also Sandra Harding (ed.), *Feminism and Methodology* (Milton Keynes, Open University Press, 1987); Brunsdon, *The Feminist, the Housewife, and the Soap Opera*.

3   On constructions of whiteness, see Richard Dyer, *White* (London, Routledge, 1997); John Gabriel, *Whitewash: Racialized Politics and the Media* (London, Routledge, 1998).

4   This is not the case in sociology or social history. On conceptualising links between class and culture, see Skeggs, *Class, Self, Culture*. For work on the British middle classes see Mike Savage, James Barlow, Peter Dickens and Tony Fielding, *Property, Bureaucracy and Culture: Middle-Class Formation in Contemporary Britain* (London, Routledge, 1992); and Tim Butler and Mike Savage (eds), *Social Change and the Middle Classes* (London, UCL Press, 1995). On the American

professional middle class from the 1960s to the 1980s see Barbara Ehrenreich, *Fear of Falling: The Inner Life of the Middle Class* (New York, Harper Perennial, 1990). For an account of changing cultural tastes among American 'highbrows' from the 1980s to the 1990s, see Peterson and Kern, 'Changing highbrow taste', pp. 900–7.

5 On the place of class in the emergence and institutionalisation of cultural studies in Britain, see Nannette Aldred and Martin Ryle (eds), *Teaching Culture: The Long Revolution in Cultural Studies* (Leicester, NIACE, 1999). See also Graham Murdock's call for a return to class analysis in cultural and media studies in 'Reconstructing the ruined tower: contemporary communications and questions of class', in James Curran and Michael Gurevitch (eds), *Mass Media and Society*, 3rd edn., (London, Arnold, 2000), pp. 7–26. For examples of audience studies that do address class, see Andrea Press, *Women Watching Television: Gender, Class and Generation in the American Television Experience* (Philadelphia, University of Pennsylvania Press, 1991); Andrea Press and Elizabeth Cole, 'Women like us: working-class women respond to television representations of abortion', in Jon Cruz and Justin Lewis (eds), *Viewing Reading, Listening: Audiences and Cultural Reception* (Boulder, CO, Westview Press, 1994), pp. 55–80; Ellen Seiter, *Television and New Media Audiences* (Oxford, Oxford University Press, 1999).

6 See Matt Hills, *Fan Cultures* (London, Routledge, 2002), pp. 71–89 for an excellent consideration of the uses and limitations of autoethnography, including the problem of narcissism, which I have doubtless succumbed to here.

7 See also Murdock, 'Reconstructing the ruined tower', pp. 19–20. This is not to suggest that all academics are identical in class terms. They will of course have differing pasts and family backgrounds.

8 Pierre Bourdieu, *Distinction: A Social Critique of the Judgement of Taste* (London, Routledge, 1986). For critiques of Bourdieu's model that still retain a sense of its usefulness, see Lyn Thomas, *Fans, Feminisms and 'Quality' Media* (London, Routledge, 2002), Chapter 1; Skeggs, *Class, Self, Culture*, pp. 141–7.

9 Academics come under the third of Savage *et al.*'s subdivisions of the British middle classes: entrepreneurial, managerial and professional. As noted in Chapter 2, these groupings are 'differentiated mainly by their respective command of property, organizational and cultural assets'. Lockwood, 'Marking out the middle class(es)', p. 1. Within the professional middle class, those employed by the state in education, health and welfare are characterised as having 'cultural assets but not much money' relative to other middle-class subgroups, and are compared to Bourdieu's category of 'intellectuals'. Savage *et al.* point to this group's interest in so-called 'high culture', but also to its above average participation in outdoor activities and yoga (but not

team sports), and below average consumption of alcohol. 'This ascetic lifestyle can be associated with the 'habitus' of this particular group, one reflecting their often expert knowledge of the body and their separation from the world of business. Thus, their habitus can be seen as simultaneously a product of deliberate choice (one rejecting competitive individualism and marketplace values) while at the same time being a rationalisation of their comparatively low incomes.' Savage *et al.*, *Property, Bureaucracy and Culture*, pp. 109–10.

10   Jostein Gripsrud, '"High culture" revisited', *Cultural Studies*, 3:2 (1989), pp. 194–207.

11   Rita Felski, 'Nothing to declare: identity, shame, and the lower middle class', *PMLA*, 115:1 (2000), p. 35.

12   David E. James, 'Introduction: Is there class in this text?', in David E. James and Rick Berg (eds), *The Hidden Foundation: Cinema and the Question of Class* (Minneapolis, University of Minnesota Press, 1996), pp. 2–3, italics in original. Charlotte Brunsdon takes a slightly different perspective when she writes of middle-class feminists' neglect of class in the 1970s: 'Put simply, non-working-class white women would be available to have a primarily gendered identification precisely because they were not *already* identified as, for example, black and/or working class ... those least encumbered by other identities subject to structural discrimination are most available to explore what they experience as a primary self-definition and site for discrimination, their gender.' Brunsdon, *The Feminist, the Housewife, and the Soap Opera*, pp. 206–7, italics in original.

13   For excellent examples of this kind of writing, see Carolyn Steedman, *Landscape for a Good Woman: A Story of Two Lives* (London, Virago, 1986); Annette Kuhn, *Family Secrets: Acts of Memory and Imagination* (London, Verso, 1995); Beverley Skeggs, *Formations of Class and Gender: Becoming Respectable* (London, Sage, 1997); Joanne Lacey , 'Discursive mothers and academic fandom: class, generation and the production of theory', in Sally R. Munt (ed.), *Cultural Studies and the Working Class: Subject to Change* (London, Cassell, 2000), pp. 36–50.

14   For a rare, if rather underdeveloped, exception, see Ellen Seiter, 'Making distinctions in tv audience research: case study of a troubling interview', *Cultural Studies*, 4:1 (1990), pp. 61–84. See also Seiter, *Television and New Media Audiences*, Chapter 3.

15   Chuck Kleinhans, 'Class in action', in James and Berg (eds), *The Hidden Foundation*, p. 240.

16   Douglas Kellner, 'Poltergeists, gender and class in the age of Reagan and Bush', in James and Berg (eds), *The Hidden Foundation*, pp. 217–39.

17   By concentrating on my middle-classness, I am inevitably prioritising this above other facets of my 'dominant' identity, namely my maleness, whiteness, heterosexuality and able-bodiedness. For a

consideration of male heterosexuality in terms of film audiences see Austin, *Hollywood, Hype and Audiences*, pp. 77–97.

18 Winston, *Claiming the Real*, pp. 40–7, 230–1, 258.
19 Nichols, *Representing Reality*, p.37.
20 Skeggs, *Formations of Class and Gender*, p. 4, italics in original.
21 Lynette Finch, *The Classing Gaze* (London, Allen and Unwin, 1993), p. 10, cited in Skeggs. Both disapproving and (more recently) celebratory equations of the working class with notions of the unruly body overlook what Felski calls 'an important tradition of respectability in working-class life'. Felski, 'Nothing to declare', p. 35.
22 See, for example, Matt Wray and Annalee Newitz (eds), *White Trash: Race and Class in America* (New York and London, Routledge, 1997).
23 Joe Berlinger interviewed in James Bell, 'Memphis Blues', *Sight and Sound* (NS), 15:6 (2005), p. 87.
24 *Ibid.*
25 What the viewer and filmmakers share is invisibility and freedom from on-screen scrutiny.
26 The campaign website is: www.wm3.org.
27 Some of those speaking with an accent are middle-class professionals such as lawyers and journalists, but in these cases the accent, while often less overt, still marks them out.
28 In making this point I am not suggesting that there are no significant differences between being middle-class in the USA and being middle-class in Britain.
29 I am thinking here of habitual mobility, rather than working-class migrations seeking better opportunities. For more on (im)mobility and class, see Diane Reay, 'Children's urban landscapes: configurations of class and space', in Munt (ed.), *Cultural Studies and the Working Class*, pp. 151–64.
30 Of course, mobility in social and physical space also has important dimensions in terms of gender, race and (dis)ability.
31 Trinh T. Minh-ha, 'The totalizing quest of meaning', in Michael Renov (ed.), *Theorizing Documentary* (New York, Routledge, 1993), pp. 90–107.

6
'Our planet reveals its secrets': wildlife documentaries on television

In recent years wildlife documentaries have enjoyed an enhanced profile and growing presence in theatrical and DVD markets, thanks to hits like *La Marche de l'Empereur/March of the Penguins* and *Le Peuple Migratuer/Winged Migration*, along with IMAX films such as *Galapagos* (US, 1999) and *Africa's Elephant Kingdom* (US, 1998).[1] But it is on television – both mainstream broadcasters and, increasingly, specialist channels – that wildlife documentaries have been a more enduring fixture, even while the genre has been subject to almost constant change. This chapter examines recent commercial and formal developments in wildlife documentaries on television. It also draws on original qualitative audience studies to look at the responses of viewers to a range of wildlife programming, from high budget 'blue-chip' series to hybrids borrowing celebrity presenters and formats from 'reality television' and other popular genres. What are some of the expectations and engagements, pleasures or irritations, understandings or confusions, derived from this material? Before attempting to answer these questions, it is necessary to consider some of the commercial contexts in which wildlife television is embedded.

Production contexts

From an industrial perspective, as Simon Cottle has noted, 'Wildlife programmes are especially commercially useful because they have a long "shelf life", their subject matter and universal appeal can seemingly cross different cultures, and they can easily be repackaged and dubbed.'[2] But a series of external shocks and new demands has changed the economic climate in television: 'New technologies of production and delivery, heightened competitiveness, industrial centralization, fragmenting audiences and internationalizing markets have all dramatically impacted on the "production ecology" of natural history programmes.'[3]

In the late 1990s, the UK industry was confronted with a downturn in demand for so-called 'blue-chip' or 'upmarket' programming. As Cottle notes, this shakeout was due in part to 'a previous over-supply of these "heavy investment" programmes by a proliferation of small-scale independents, and the shift in commissioning to low-cost programmes'.[4] Significant commercial pressures remain, particularly in relation to commissioning strategies, budget constraints and scheduling. For instance, when interviewed in 2005, Harry Marshall, of independent production company Icon Films was cautiously optimistic, but stressed the highly competitive multi-channel arena in which natural history television now exists:

> Generally wildlife filmmaking is in quite a good state. Some think it's going downhill but the truth is, it is now having to stand up to all comers. Natural history used to have its Sunday evening family slot, but now it's out there in the deep pelagic waters of weekdays at eight, having to do battle with soaps and reality TV and much more competitive scheduling. It is catering for exactly the same audiences and with exactly the same levels of boredom and has to capture their attention.[5]

This industrial context has driven formal innovations and the development of new generic hybrids. Among these is the 'action man' format, led by imports such as the late Steve Irwin's *Crocodile Hunter* series, which became the most watched programme on the Animal Planet channel in the late 1990s.[6] British broadcasters have responded with a number of attempts to reposition wildlife on television, including more personality-fronted shows and borrowings from popular formats such as soaps, 'reality television' and drama. The following comments from executives in British production companies testify to this:

> [W]e believe that attention to storyline, character and innovative approaches are much more important than simply filming the natural behaviour and habitats of animals – the traditional focus of many natural history shows.
>
> Viewers are no longer looking for big budget films which

concentrate on animal behaviour in isolation. They want identifi-
able stories and strong people-based narratives. We are introducing more science, history, animation and fantasy in our films.[7]

Similar shifts, including the drive to recruit celebrities to lead
audiences into documentary topics, are apparent across the wider
terrain of popular factual programming on British television. Richard Klein, the newly appointed documentary commissioner at
the BBC, responsible for 275 hours of television per year, commented in 2005: 'Documentaries can be seen as a rather painful
dose of medicine, and I believe we are there to entertain people
... We can use that pool of BBC1 talent the audience enjoy, Paul
Merton, Jack Dee, Lisa Tarbuck, Victoria Wood.'[8]

The casting of celebrity presenters does not have to work in
opposition to 'difficult' content, although such combinations are
relatively rare. A recent instance of the convergence of commercial imperatives, celebrity appearances and serious subject matter
is *Last Chance to Save*, launched on Sky One in 2005. The series was
one of the first commissioned by a new wildlife unit formed through
the collaboration of Sky One and Tiger Aspect Productions, and
should be located within the context of a concerted re-branding of
Sky One as more 'upmarket' around this period. Documentaries
were envisaged as one of the totems of this reorientation.[9] *Last
Chance to Save*'s presenters included Joanna Lumley, Griff Rhys Jones
and Vic Reeves. The Sky One website described the series thus:
'Following a team of experts assisted by a well known personality,
each documentary will highlight the plight of some of the world's
most endangered animals, including the Orang-utans of Borneo,
Kenya's Black Rhino, Rwanda's Mountain Gorillas and the Giant
Leatherback Turtles of French Guiana.' The channel's 'sponsorship
opportunities' information clarified the commercial logic behind
this initiative. The proposed benefits to potential sponsors of the
show included: 'opportunity to communicate with a younger group
of viewers, averaging higher disposable income than their terrestrial counterparts' and 'salient brand association – quality, contemporary and exclusive'.[10] Such motivations do not undermine
the campaigning ethos of the series, but they do illustrate something of the economic climate in which decisions about the commissioning and scheduling of documentaries are made, and the
market-driven criteria by which such decisions may have to be
justified.

Some practitioners and commentators have lamented increased commercialisation, 'dumbing down', and perceived Americanisation in the field. Walter Koehler, from Austrian production company ORF said of wildlife programming in the UK:

> This British obsession with genres is unbelievable. One minute commissioning editors want programmes without history but with scientists, next it is without scientists. Then if you include one, they reject it 'because the audience won't understand it'. The biggest problem in the UK is losing your culture because of American markets. The BBC was influenced by Discovery and it has changed the way you tell stories and make programmes. Programmes like *Pride* are fun but they aren't natural history.[11]

Other programme makers are more optimistic about what they see as diversification rather than dumbing down. Brian Leith was executive producer of *Deep Jungle*, which deployed computer-generated imagery (CGI), intercut between multiple storylines, and was promoted by ITV1 in May 2005 as 'Indiana Jones meets the Planet of the Apes'. He commented:

> Just as the natural world has changed, so have natural history programmes. And they needed to. They'd got into a rut. Film-makers would go to remote places, film everything that moved, return and cut it in the editing room thinking that was film. They'd lost all sense of narrative, making little effort to bring it alive to new audiences … The time is right to draw on all these new techniques to engage new audiences. It is not dumbing down. It is a noble cause to get people interested and entertain them at the same time.[12]

Alastair Fothergill, formerly head of the BBC's Natural History Unit, and producer of 'blue-chip' series *The Blue Planet* (2001) and *Planet Earth* (2006), has worked at different points on the spectrum of wildlife television. He notes the commercial pressure to find new audiences and to split costs through international co-production, not just on prestige projects.[13] But he also claims that *The Blue Planet* 'came at a time when lots of people were saying [blue-chip] natural history is dead and it completely disproved that'.[14] Fothergill also seems more comfortable than some with borrowing narrative techniques from television drama and soap opera:

> Like any other genre, there are good and bad times. What has happened now is that the BBC has broadened its approach and is

trying new techniques … With *Big Cat Diary* we knew we'd got natural stories but we weren't making cliffhangers. So the producer went to *EastEnders* [a long-running BBC soap] for advice on how to make it more gripping. We've had to improve storytelling. We can't just rely on beautiful photos, that just won't work any more … *Big Cat* was very successful and we moved it across [from BBC2] to BBC1 as *Big Cat Week* and got 6 million viewers across a week, putting it firmly in the top ten … We have had to look more aggressively at the schedule and work with the slots.[15]

Keith Scholey, Fothergill's successor as head of the Natural History Unit, also stresses the need for diversity in the BBC's wildlife programming in order to reach multiple audiences:

We're trying to create new formats and using new technology to move us on. I would [also] say the modern way of doing the traditional format has proved to be as successful as ever. So that is our strategy now. It's not to put all your eggs in one basket, it's to spread it around, to have lots of diversity.[16]

New hybrids

I will now turn to two recent examples of inter-genre hybridisation selected from the range of wildlife programming broadcast by the BBC in 2005. Both these series are reminiscent of what Todd Gitlin, writing about American television in the 1970s and 1980s, has called the 'recombinant form'. This strategy 'assumes that selected features of recent hits can be spliced together to make a eugenic success'.[17]

Springwatch With Bill Oddie was broadcast live on weekdays on BBC2 between 8 and 9p.m. for three weeks in May and June 2005. A repackaged and updated version of *Britain Goes Wild With Bill Oddie* from 2004, it focused on changes in the flora and fauna of the UK in spring and encouraged viewers to take an interest in indigenous rather than 'exotic' wildlife and environments. In the first programme in the series, co-presenter Kate Humble introduced a montage of images with this line: 'our cameras have been up and down the country since Spring really sprung, picking up these iconic images just for you'. Overlaid with acoustic guitar music, the sequence comprised quickly edited close-ups of a red squirrel, a hedgehog, a robin, tree blossom, ladybirds, fox cubs, a bee, a mouse, a snake, seabirds, a frog and a butterfly.[18]

In important ways *Springwatch* resembles the established formats of both the news bulletin and the 'magazine' show (pioneered in the UK by *Nationwide* and *That's Life* in the 1970s). Despite their differences, such programmes typically share a conventional formal organisation whereby presenter figures provide continuity, embodying a familiar visual and vocal framework into which a series of more or less discrete sequences, both live and pre-recorded, can be inserted. This is a canonical example of what John Ellis has termed television's 'segmental' form, one that he also locates to differing degrees in advertising spots and popular drama.[19]

Springwatch has three presenters led by Bill Oddie, formerly a star of the 1970s comedy show *The Goodies*, more recently returned to television as a bird-watcher and host of wildlife programmes. Oddie is joined on screen by Humble, while live and pre-recorded segments shot 'on location' from London to the Isle of Mull are fronted by Simon King. The pairing of Oddie and Humble as hosts is highly conventional in popular television: the older male and the younger female. Oddie is privileged over Humble in that he usually speaks first, often interrupts her, and is portrayed as possessing greater expertise on the subject of the natural world. The couple are typically arranged for the camera standing by a farm gate, or (in an almost parodic gesture to daytime magazine shows like *This Morning* or *Richard and Judy*) sitting on a sofa inside a barn, with a coffee table in front of them and bank of television monitors to one side.

The series is characterised by regular inter-cutting between footage from fifty live cameras on the Devon farm where Oddie and Humble are located, and material presented by King. Much as in a news bulletin or magazine show, the rate of cutting is kept quite high, with a rhetoric of liveness carried by an editing pattern which alternates between recorded items, live footage including 'updates', and shots of the presenters, who deliver a mix of scripted and spontaneous responses to each other and to what is being shown on the cameras. For instance, in a typical programme, the first 12 minutes comprised nine relatively discrete segments, including live footage of blue tits and swallows, and a pre-recorded sequence of a jackdaw fledgling with live commentary from Oddie and Humble, along with a report from Simon King at the London

Wetlands Centre, which also mixed live and recorded material.[20] *Springwatch* is clearly designed to mobilise already familiar codes and conventions of popular television, drawing on a presenter-fronted 'live' segmental format into which any content, from real-life crime to sports coverage to natural history, can be inserted.

My second example, also from the BBC, draws on fictional and 'reality television' depictions of crime, and deploys CGI, an authoritative narrator, expert interviews and repackaged archive footage to create a tightly budgeted but distinctive series. *Animal Crime Scene*, broadcast weekly for an hour at 8p.m. on BBC1 in August and September 2005, is a BBC/Animal Planet co-production.[21] An opening voice-over, accompanying images of a 'crime scene' being cordoned off by investigators, explains:

> Imagine a murder investigation where all the characters are animals. An innocent victim and of course all the usual suspects. Join me at the crime scene to play detective and track down the killer. Aided by the latest forensic science, we'll uncover the evidence. So, as our murder mystery unfolds, can you figure out who did it?[22]

This introduction is in part a pastiche of real crime shows like *Crimewatch UK*, where viewers are solicited to provide evidence in unsolved cases. Equally, with its stress on investigative procedure and forensic research, the series borrows from a popular sub-genre of screen crime fiction, and recent American television hits such as *CSI: Crime Scene Investigation* (CBS, launched in 2000) in particular.

Each programme in the series takes the 'murder' of one animal (a caribou, a gazelle, a green turtle) and works through a number of hypotheses about possible killers. The process is illustrated with a combination of library footage of predators, some brief interviews with experts on the relevant animals, and staged sequences of actors in white coats studying computer screens and samples of hair and blood in the mocked-up 'crime lab'. CGI is used to track possible movements of animals in and out of the 'crime scene'.

Animal Crime Scene's voice-over is provided by Sir David Attenborough, one of the most experienced and respected presenters in British wildlife television, famous for his work on groundbreaking series like *Life on Earth* (1979), *The Life of Birds* (1998) and *The Blue Planet*. Although Attenborough never appears on camera, his gravitas is essential in supporting the programme's bids for authority and credibility. However, Attenborough's 'blue-chip' persona and upper middle-class voice make for an uncomfortable fit with a commentary in which he has to deliver scripted puns about 'Arctic assassins' and the hunt for a 'cold blooded killer'.[23] His participation in the series provides an interesting point of contrast to his reported dismay at Time-Life Video's sensationalist promotion of his series *The Trials of Life* in the US in 1991. According to Gregg Mitman, Time-Life Video advertised the twelve-hour series 'by condensing all the attack scenes ... into a brief promotional spot. A voice-over barked, "See up close how the law of the jungle is kill or be killed ... Find out why they call them animals." Sir David Attenborough was so disturbed by this exploitative sensationalism that he considered taking legal action.'[24] It may be seen as a measure of changing expectations and commissioning pressures in the arena of natural history television that Attenborough has since chosen to participate in a populist 'recombination' like *Animal Crime Scene*, which embeds its informational content within a highly dramatic genre framework.

So far I have considered some recent tendencies in the industrial organisation and textual characteristics of wildlife documentaries on television. In the remainder of the chapter I examine audiences' perspectives on this output. I assess contexts of viewing, the perspectives of non-viewers, and a range of responses from those who watch these programmes regularly.

Audience research

The audience research project encompassed three separate stages. Firstly, in a pilot study I distributed questionnaires among final year students at the University of Sussex during the summer of 2005. Following this study the questionnaire was refined and handed out to 27 sixth-formers from an inner London college who were visiting the campus on a short residential course. This was a group that was socially mixed, in terms of (self-identified) class and ethnicity, and thus stood in contrast to the pilot sample and the subsequent Mass Observation Archive sample, both of which were largely white and predominantly middle class.[25]

The final phase of audience research made use of the Mass Observation Archive, a national 'life writing' resource based at the University of Sussex. In addition to housing material gathered during the 1930s and 1940s, the archive administers a self-selected sample of 500 current 'correspondents', who are invited to write in response to a regular series of 'directives' on their everyday lives and opinions, covering topics as diverse as gardening, the royal family and UFOs, as well as, occasionally, media use. In summer 2005 I arranged for a directive to be sent out, asking for correspondents to write about their viewing experiences and opinions of wildlife documentaries.[26] I read and analysed 170 responses between October and December 2005.

The current Mass Observation sample is largely white and the majority of correspondents are middle-aged and older, with far more from the middle classes than the working classes.[27] This, and the fact that it is a self-selected sample, means it has no claims to being representative of the population as a whole. Nevertheless, the sample's size, the range of identities, locations and experiences that correspondents draw on, and the depth and richness of many of their accounts, make it a significant and valuable research resource.

The format of correspondents' written replies threw up some particular issues. Each directive includes the following request: 'As usual, please start all three parts of your reply on a new sheet of paper with your M-O number, (NOT name), sex, age, marital status, the town or village where you live and your occupation or former occupation.'[28] Accordingly, correspondents usually preceded their remarks with these biographical details, although further, more idiosyncratic, information was sometimes added. However, details of ethnicity and sexual orientation were rarely if ever declared outright. I assumed that the majority of correspondents were white and heterosexual, and that these two normative dimensions of identity were often simply taken for granted as 'obvious', unremarkable and not worth stating. This assumption was largely confirmed by staff at the archive. (Nevertheless, it is clear from a subsequent directive on sexual activity that the sample does include some gay, bisexual and lesbian correspondents.) The fact that neither sexual orientation nor ethnicity is usually prioritised, in the way that other facets of identity such as gender are, significantly reduces their visibility – and thus the ability of any researcher to argue for or against their relevance – outside particular directives which explicitly raise such topics.

The additional information provided varied widely, from details of hobbies, to family members, to exact location when writing the account. The material generated from the directive was thus highly self-presentational, not just in terms of correspondents' statements of behaviour and opinion, but in their assertions of identity to start with. This should not be considered a problem, an obstacle to some more 'transparent' access to response, but as a potentially useful means of exploring senses of self, claims to status and distinction, and revelations of 'common sense' assumptions.

Contexts of viewing

Television viewing, like other forms of media use, is always shaped and informed by a number of contexts – commercial, social, personal.[29] There is never an impermeable boundary between viewer experience of a text and the multiple contexts in which text and viewer are situated. The following instances highlight some of the micro-social settings in which the event of watching television takes place. They draw attention in particular to the interpersonal relations within which acts of viewing are embedded:

Q 5: Do you usually watch wildlife docs on your own or with anyone else? Please give details.

I'll usually be at the table with my grandparents on Sunday evenings, if antiques roadshow isn't being shown, wildlife programmes are on the TV in the background, often without the volume loud enough to hear them though. If big cat diary is on before dinner is served we'll sit round and watch while catching up with weekly goings on in our family.

(Becky, age 21, white, British, female, university student, middle-class) (pilot study)

The last documentary I watched was last night. It was about Killer sharks, I watched it because sharks are really scary and my children were interested … I really enjoyed finding out about them but was depressed by the over fishing and the decline in the population of sharks. My youngest son has Shark Top Trumps and so I have become more interested in them.

(I am a 40 year old married woman with two children/I have changed career from Occupational therapy to administration and have been doing volunteer work and courses to improve my skills. I am working part time temporarily in a HE College. I live in N Wales but I am not Welsh.) (J2891)

[The last documentary watched was] on Discovery channel. It was filmed at Steve Irwin's zoo in Australia. My 25 yr old son called me in to watch it as he'd visited it last year ... It wasn't so much the Discovery Channel programme I enjoyed – it was spending time relaxing with my son and listening to him recounting his travels.

(Female, 52 years, married + 2 children, p/t recruitment advisor, Plymouth) (B1215)

In the last two instances, television viewing functions in part at least as an element of the mother's emotional and social work as caretaker in the family, in each case bonding with the son by watching a programme with him. The next extracts propose the family as either a source of comfort and enjoyment, nostalgically recalled, or as a locus of obligations. (For others, the family may be an ambiguous mix of such duties and pleasures.)

[recalling growing up in 1950s and 1960s] Television in those days was black and white and there won't have been the technology in the photography that there is today, but then we lapped it up as it was all on the magic lantern and it was very cosy watching it with sister, mummy and daddy.

(Female caseworker, separated, 56, Disley) (T1843)

Q8: Do you usually watch wildlife docs on your own or with anyone else? (please give details).

If I do, I watch it because my gran is and I can't switch the TV.

(Anon. (5), age 16, black, British, female, college student, working-class)

I watched [*Springwatch*] because I was on holiday in Dorset with my parents and they wanted to watch it. I wouldn't have chosen to watch it myself because this type of programme leaves me cold. I only ever watch them if I'm with my parents and it's something they're keen on seeing. So I guess I watch them maybe once or twice a year, and I'm usually doing something else while they're on (reading or, in the case of Springwatch, a Soduko puzzle).

(Female, age 36, single, London education researcher) (J3141)

The following two accounts emphasise the intermittent attention that can, on occasions, be granted to television – specifically the interruptibility of the act of watching, and the possibility of engaging with more than one media form at the same time:[30]

The series Coast has been well worth watching, and is one such programme to show mini-documentaries. I'll usually sit through the ones on Coast – the marine biologist seems well read and has an obvious enthusiasm which comes over well. Her slots were only a couple of minutes each and sometimes they'll catch my attention. Other times I'll sit through them apathetically, or do something else (draw the curtains/go to the kitchen for a biscuit etc ...)

(Male, age 23, single, living in [?], Shropshire, working full-time in a factory making tiles) (E2977)

They are very restful to watch and not very demanding. Most of the information is not new to me so I am inclined to read a book at the same time.

(Female, 61, married, Odiham) (C2078)

The complex particularities of viewing contexts will, of course, have impacted on all those respondents quoted in this and other chapters, but their impacts are not always traceable and will not always be so clearly stated as here.[31]

Non-viewers: apologies and assertions

As I noted in Chapter 2, it is not very easy for an audience researcher to locate refusing viewers – those who deliberately avoided a film or programme – or others who failed to find the item to start with, and who may be even harder to identify and track down. One benefit of using the Mass Observation Archive for this chapter was that several correspondents who did not actually watch wildlife documentaries still responded to my directive, perhaps out of a sense of loyalty to, or investment in, the larger project. Some of these non-viewers usually deliberately avoided the genre, while others did not prioritise it in their viewing choices, and a handful had little or no opportunity to watch documentaries, as they did not have access to a television.[32] In either case, respondents' expressed reasoning for not watching or enjoying wildlife documentaries revealed significant ways of thinking about both the genre, their own senses of self, and, indirectly, the research process itself.

The research scenario is best thought of as an event that presents both an opportunity and a threat to those being researched. The opportunity is the chance to express one's opinions or experiences, and, by implication at least, to be listened to and taken seriously. In the process, one may also have the chance to project (consciously or not) a particular self-identity, or to rework a sense of self – which is always potentially open to further revisions, and so is never ultimately finished or completed. (Researchers can be seen to take part in somewhat similar acts of self-presentation.) The risk is to have one's identity exposed, misread or painfully (re)constituted, in front of, and by, others – peers, other research subjects, or the researcher/s themselves.

The specific nature of any research procedure undertaken, whether based on focus groups, one-to-one interviews, question-naires, or any other method, will of course shape these issues in important ways. Whatever the particular instance, the process of producing identities in audience research should be acknowledged and interrogated rather than be quietly ignored. This should not lead to a self-critical paralysis on the part of the researcher, how-ever. Only the false goal of attaining some transparent, unmedi-ated access to respondents' states of mind or emotion would insist that respondents' statements can and should escape such contex-tual factors.[33]

In the present study, one possible risk for some respondents was that of appearing uninformed, ignorant or uninteresting by confessing to not watching documentaries. Some apologetic ad-missions revealed an internalisation of judgements presumed to be made by the researcher/s, as invisible addressee/s of these ac-counts.[34] For instance:

> I cannot remember watching a wildlife documentary … I am sure it's a gap in my experience but for myself I am interested in people and how they tick … Perhaps people like me should be better educated. It's a bit late now!
>
> (F, 77 years, married, Bristol, formerly tutor in adult education) (M2629)

> Why do I immediately feel guilt at admitting that I hardly ever watch wildlife programmes? I know I should (why?), but I just don't.
>
> (F, 61 years, married, village near Exeter, primary school teacher) (R1227)

> This directive has made me feel slightly guilty for not taking ad-vantage of the provision of wildlife programmes that I know to be interesting and informative. Will try to do better!
>
> (Female, 68 years, widow, Brighton, retired nurse/civil servant) (L1991)

These comments are shaped by a number of overlapping factors.

Firstly, they attest to the prevalence of discourses which elevate documentary as culturally or morally superior to (often unspecified) 'lower' cultural forms. Thus Bill Nichols's notion of documentary as a 'discourse of sobriety' appears to have some purchase among some (non)viewers of the mode.[34] The statements also reveal assumptions that public perception of the status of the individual viewer may be shaped by their admitted viewing habits. In these cases, a degree of self-reproach or self-incrimination is presented. Finally, they may be seen as in part anticipating the demands and expectations of the researcher/s, and signalling an awareness of failure to provide 'the right answers'.

For others, the status of the genre was realised in terms of family pressures to watch, which were experienced either as childhood obedience to parental regulations, or as parental encouragement of offspring:

> As a child Sunday afternoons, once lunch was out of the way, meant a couple of fidgety hours spent watching nature documentaries on television, such programmes were, I gather, thought in our household to be improving in some way, rather like going to church or joining the scouts.
> (Male, single, age 34, Stoke-on-Trent, Warehouse operative)
> (C3167)
> ... the only person in our house who watches wildlife programmes is my son. I suppose we encourage him to watch them because we hope they will foster an appreciation of the natural world in him.
> (Female, married, Dwygyfylchi, Housewife/mother) (P3213)

Some respondents were more assertive in their rejections of the genre. It is notable that in the (admittedly limited) examples quoted here, the split between apologetic and assertive non-viewers appears to be a gendered one, with females falling into the former category and males into the latter. The terminology in the next accounts works to construct certain distinctions of self as non-viewer from viewing others, who are characterised by contrast as pretentious, snobbish and/or dishonest in their perceived bids for kudos and cultural capital. For instance:

> It seems that there is a 'snob appeal' to wildlife documentaries. I have heard people who like to delude themselves that they watch very little television say 'I only have it on for the news, and the wildlife programmes.'

> (Gender: male. Age: 38. Marital status: single. Home: Birming-
> ham. Occupation: University Administrator) (B 3227)

> Yawn, on the whole ... They've become one of the great WOR-
> THY things that you can admit to watching without being dis-
> missed as brain dead couch potato. When I was at school it was
> the news ... Now you get the brownie points ... for claiming to
> watch a long succession of small furry animals knobbing each
> other to a David Attenborough commentary. It turns you from a
> couch potato into an environmentalist.

> (Male, 54, single, Wisbech, distance learning tutor) (M2854)

To summarise, any research scenario is crossed by relations of
power, between researcher, researched and constructed 'others'.
It offers a forum for self-presentation and the production of identity, which may be construed as either a risk or an opportunity.
Consequently, the particularities of the research event may elicit
either apologies or assertions of superiority and bids for distinction, as well as shaping modes of response in other, perhaps less
evident, ways.

Moving pictures: spectacle, travelogue, argument

My analysis of more positive audience responses to wildlife documentaries begins with a statement that synthesises several reasons for watching, and pleasures derived from, these programmes.

> I find myself entranced by them. The places in the world that I
> may only ever visit through them ... It is like having a concen-
> trated education and dose of beauty all in one. They are informa-
> tive and gorgeous. When would I be at the bottom of the sea with
> the knowledge to know what I was looking at?

> I just bought a colour TV to watch wildlife programmes. Black
> and white was sufficient for everything else but the wildlife
> programmes really demand to be seen in all their colourful beauty.

> (Female, 53, single, London, reception/information worker)
> (H2418)

This account offers a glimpse of the rarely remarked upon (because now so common) visual attractions of colour television,[36]
and raises the more widely discussed promise of virtual travel experienced through viewing. It also foregrounds two other important and interlinked dimensions of watching natural history

documentaries: spectacle and informational content. In this chapter I will interrogate each of the three components – spectacle, travelogue, argument – in turn, and investigate some of the imbrications between them.

Crucially, screen documentary's displays of 'colourful beauty' are not often static, but are typically shown in motion. Variations in the speed of moving images may further develop both spectacularisation and argument. For example, slow-motion may be used to enhance the visibility of insects' wing movements in flight, or time-lapse photography used to render changes in weather and time of day, or seasonal rhythms.

Viewers' enjoyment of unashamedly spectacular – and mobile – displays of planet earth's wonders, its landscapes, its oceans, and its creatures, recall Tom Gunning's influential notion of the 'cinema of attractions'. For Gunning, the American cinema until 1906 or 1907 was a largely 'exhibitionist cinema' centred on 'inciting visual curiosity and supplying pleasure through an exciting spectacle – a unique event, whether fictional or documentary, that is of interest in itself.'[37] Gunning locates in early cinema 'a particular aesthetics of display, of showmanship, defined by the goal of assaulting viewers with sensational, supernatural, scientific, sentimental, or otherwise stimulating sights, as opposed to enveloping them into the illusion of a fictional narrative.'[38] He also writes of: 'The Lumière tradition of "placing the world within one's reach" through travel films and topicals'.[39] Some such attractions – of accessing the world in spectacular forms – are evident in some viewers' accounts of their responses to wildlife documentaries on television.[40] For example:

> I saw a very good documentary about wild life under the seas round Australia and New Zealand. The animals were absolutely amazing in their shape and colours and I admire greatly the photographers and everyone concerned with showing these wonders that we would never see otherwise.
> (F, married, Staines, Middx, ex-civil servant, age 73, 3 children, 4 grandchildren) (B2065)

> Documentaries show us things which we would not normally notice or have the opportunity to see, to give us a better idea of the world's riches.
> (Female, aged 38, single, living in the Isle of Man, civil servant specialising in Government pension schemes) (B3019)

A significant element of the appeal of animals – including mediations of them via television and film – is their motility, the fascinating ability to move independently, beyond any arrangement or performance produced by humans organising them. This is what Lorraine Daston and Gregg Mitman call 'the active reality of animals'.[41] They write:

> As Aristotle remarked, the distinctive mark of the animal is self-locomotion; they move themselves, with all of the roaming autonomy movement implies ... animals are not our marionettes, our automata ... They are symbols with a life of their own. We use them to perform our thoughts, feelings, and fantasies, because, alone of all our myriad symbols, they can perform ... We may orchestrate their performance, but complete mastery is an illusion.[42]

Again, this way of thinking about wildlife documentary recalls some writing on early cinema. Dai Vaughan has commented that the 'essential triumph' of the Lumière brothers in films such as *Le Déjeuner de Bébé* (France, 1895) or *A Boat Leaving Harbour* was 'the harnessing of spontaneity', in capturing the (non-human) movements of leaves and waves.[43] He writes: 'The movements of photographed people were accepted without demur because they were perceived as performance, as simply a new mode of self-projection, but that the inanimate should participate in self-projection was astonishing.'[44] Of course in most wildlife television, it is not so much the movements of inanimate objects but the non-human agency of animals which fascinates. The shapes and colours mentioned repeatedly in viewer accounts are manifested through the motions of creatures on screen.

The aesthetics of televised wildlife documentary have recently been considered by Helen Wheatley. In a useful formal analysis of BBC1's hit series *The Blue Planet*, Wheatley locates moments 'where the *beauty* of what was being shown was emphasized above all else', and suggests that these were 'marked out as moments of "quality" within the discourse surrounding the programme'.[45] However, her argument also inadvertently reveals the pitfalls of reductive viewer categorisations, which I hope to avoid here.

Having noted *The Blue Planet*'s relatively slow pace, 'cinematic' visual aspirations and orchestral score, Wheatley argues that 'the audiovisual pleasures of [the series] are best enjoyed by those with the capital (both cultural and actual) to appreciate them'.[46] In contrast, I would disagree with any suggestion that such moments are only ever present in 'prestige' programming like *The Blue Planet*, or that their audience appeal is so restricted. Access to a colour television would probably be considered essential by viewers watching this kind of material, but beyond this point Wheatley's proposals become problematic, relying as they do on under-supported assumptions about the determining forces of cultural taste and disposable income. Clearly, such factors may be relevant, but they should not be assumed to always be so in a straightforward or monolithic fashion.

There is a circularity to Wheatley's argument. First, she characterises *The Blue Planet* as adhering to 'upper-middle-class taste codes'.[47] Then she draws on an audience survey, which, as she herself admits, probably excludes viewers from outside this taste bracket: 'These particular viewers ... had admittedly, already singled themselves out as '"discerning viewers"' by attending a live screening of series highlights accompanied by the BBC Orchestra and the choir of Magdalen College, Oxford'.[48] The stocks of cultural and economic capital required to attend such an event exceed those needed to enjoy *The Blue Planet* on television, but Wheatley's analysis lacks the scope to move beyond this narrow sample. As a result she attributes to the series an audience address that is inappropriately narrow. For *The Blue Planet*'s viewing figures to have peaked at more than 12 million,[48] it must have attracted viewers beyond 'upper-middle class' taste groups, however Wheatley might define them. Moreover, although I make no claims for statistical accuracy, my own audience research suggests that viewers from a range of economic, social and cultural backgrounds enjoy this kind of programming.[50]

The popularity among audiences of spectacular visual displays should not be simply assumed, of course. Certainly, its significance varied across the samples under discussion. Thus, while some wrote enthusiastically about previously unseen sights and wonders, others appeared ambivalent about such material. For example:

> I generally find them too slow – like a series of beautiful snapshots that I might dip in and out of but not want to sit down and watch from end to end ... It's the fact that it's a world normally hidden that appeals.
> (female, 53, married, 2 children, part-time basic skills tutor and classroom assistant supporting adults with learning difficulties (ex-librarian), Brighton) (no number given)

In addition, the persistence of a presentational aesthetic in wildlife documentaries cannot be taken for granted. Its presence, extent and significance is not uniform but varies from case to case.[51] Some wildlife programmes work very deliberately to harness their spectacular attractions, anchoring them within narrative frameworks.

At times, as already noted, programmes may borrow from established fictional formats like soap operas or crime series. They may also operate to construct either animals (often named and anthropomorphised) or humans, or both, as significant agents in the story. For instance, in an analysis of the use of anthropomorphic tropes in her documentary about the rehabilitation of formerly captive orang-utans *The Disenchanted Forest* (2002), which was broadcast to over 250 countries worldwide, director Sarita Siegel commented: 'Strong human and animal characters establish an emotional identification with the audience.'[52] (One consequence of anthropomorphism may be the effective naturalisation of human gender norms via depictions of animal behaviours, particularly male rivalry, sex, reproduction and the 'survival of the fittest'. In a critique of such tendencies, Barbara Crowther comments: 'a handful of core structures are found to recur constantly. These story-types themselves tend to reflect androcentrism and patriarchal relationships.')[53]

Several respondents in the audience samples attested to being engaged and moved by just such devices, sometimes despite their misgivings. For example, here is a relatively rare (for this study) male admission of emotional attachment and response:[54]

> The last programme I watched was Elephant Diaries on TV about a month ago. It followed a group of orphaned elephants at a sanctuary over a year. It made me want to pack up work and go and work with elephants. I was reluctant to watch it because I know I'll get emotionally involved and then I have to watch it every week.
>
> My wife, Gerry, started watching it and I caught a couple of minutes and that was it – I was hooked. The problem with most wildlife programmes is they're very emotionally manipulative but even though I know that I [can't?] help being engaged by them … I hate those programmes which follow a family or community of animals and give them names and personalities. Sure, animals have different personalities but giving them names is humanising them too much … Having said all the above I still get

carried away with being emotionally engaged by the animals and their individual characteristics. It's a dilemma I can't resolve; the emotional involvement is what makes a programme good but also what creates this illusion.

(Male, 42, Cheltenham, journalist) (V3091)

The next respondent writes technical reviews of programmes for the BBC Resources department, and felt engaged by some programmes despite her initial professional distance:

The last new wildlife series that I had to review was Big Cat Diary. I was surprised by how I was drawn into the programme and the events that were developing ... The show neatly played to an audience that is used to being fed a diet of soaps. There were characters that you got to know and you followed their everyday life. The focus would switch between the various groups that were being followed and so the audience got to follow each storyline, never focussing on one group for too long and always leaving the story on a little cliffhanger so that you wanted to keep watching to see what would happen.

(Female, 32, single, London, VT editor/videotape operator (television)) (C3038)

Processes of memory and recall may play a part in weakening narrative architecture to partially detach, isolate or reify spectacular images or sequences from their settings in story or argument.[55] Nevertheless, it is best to think of moments of display and the mechanisms of characterisation and narrative or argumentational structuring as largely co-present in most documentary texts, although viewers may prioritise one over the other in their chosen modes of viewing.[56] To return to the first respondent quoted in this section, a further statement reiterates the appeal of a form that is both 'informative and gorgeous':

The world teems with life and wildlife documentaries give us an opportunity to learn more about our world, its beauty, its vastness, its singularity and plurality, its joy and its pain.

(Female, 53, single, London, reception/information worker) (H2418)

Certainly, in the audience samples, the appeal of a presentational aesthetic through which the wonders of the natural world could be accessed appeared to be significant for many viewers. But such statements did not exclude informational content. See, for instance:

> The octopus who can manoeuvre into a bottle is just 'Oh my God,
> how can it do that?' The list goes on and on. I'm sure that you can
> be totally amazed by most animals of our planet whether it be on
> land, sky or sea. Our planet reveals its secrets slowly and fascinat-
> ingly. I cannot see how you can ever be bored watching documen-
> taries like these ...
>
> (Female, 45, married [living with] husband, daughter (19), son
> (12), father-in-law, Conwy, shopkeeper) (M3147)

> I prefer exotic settings to the urban fox type subject. The latter
> does not impart any new information, which is another key ele-
> ment. Documentaries should always provide some new infor-
> mation to be engaging. I know foxes eat my rubbish, what they
> look like and how clever they are. I don't know much about the
> giant sloth apart from their great fingernails.
>
> (Female, 30, single, London, compliance manager) (M3055)

> I think you need to be curious about everything in order to like
> any kind of documentary. It is not just pretty picture of fish or
> something on screen. The bloke talking is trying to educate us
> about what he is interested in.
>
> (Female, age 50, divorced, carer, Limavady) (C1191)

> All animals, but especially wild animals, are very different from
> us, and when a documentary really grabs my attention it's be-
> cause while I'm watching I feel as though I've been transported
> invisibly into a completely different world, with a whole different
> set of appearances and appropriate behaviours. A couple of ex-
> amples spring to mind: one of the Cousteau films, about the life
> of the octopus, and a scene from, I think, Life on Earth, in which
> a mantis caught and devoured some other insect. These creatures
> were from our own planet but they looked and acted as though
> they were from somewhere completely alien. And when that
> happens I realise how incredibly varied life on our planet really is,
> and how many ways there are of experiencing being alive. A
> good documentary leaves you with a sense of wonder.
>
> (Male, 46, married, civil servant, living in east Boldon)
> (M3190)

Here, and in some of the accounts quoted earlier, the pleasures of
being informed, of becoming knowledgeable, are apparent. So too
are those of virtual travel, of being taken elsewhere via the act of
viewing. As I shall suggest below, not all viewers want to be taken
so far afield, but the lure of the travelogue in wildlife documenta-

ries remains an important (extra)textual promise and commonly mobilised mode of viewing.

I have argued so far that gaining virtual access to the previously hidden 'wonders of the world' – via both spectacle and argument – is one of the key pleasures derived from wildlife documentary programmes by some enjoying viewers. It is a short step from making this suggestion to assuming that such attractions are to be delivered via engagement with the 'exotic'. Certainly, the promise of accessing the 'exotic' is raised in a number of audience responses. But two important points need to be borne in mind here. The first is that the properties of the 'exotic' and the 'familiar' or 'everyday' are not innate, residing within objects, but are always contingent and relational. The second caveat is that not all novelties are far away. It may be possible to render exotic, outlandish and spectacular flora and fauna hitherto considered to be familiar, quotidian, and undeserving of notice.

Notions of the exotic and the familiar are dependent on, and shaped by, prevailing circumstances. Thus, details of present location, and experiences of mobility between or to this and other locations, become significant for each individual respondent deploying such terms. A useful reminder of the contextual nature of these ideas is provided by David Morley. In his book *Home Territories* he notes:

> The question of what (or who) belongs where and, conversely, of what constitutes the exotic for whom, in which circumstances, is perhaps best captured in a (possibly apocryphal) story told about the French surrealist writer Raymond Roussell's trip to Africa in the early part of the twentieth century. Prior to his departure, Roussell's mother urged him to send her the most exotic thing he could find, as a present. Some months passed after Roussell's departure before a parcel arrived. His mother opened it, in great excitement, to discover within an electric fire. It was, as the accompanying note explained, the most exotic thing he had been able to find in Africa at that time.[57]

In the case of animals, many are commonly rendered 'exotic' by being put 'out of place', either in zoos or via media representations which bring them into the domestic sphere. As Gail Davies comments in her analysis of zoos: 'This geographical displacement [of the 'wild' animals on display] is part of what constitutes their attraction, and the process of decontextualisation alone can serve to give exotic value to certain animal species, the majority of which are never seen by people in nature.'[58]

Given the contingent nature of the exotic and the familiar, for some viewers the jungles of Asia may be not so much an exotic location as a reminder of a past workplace:

> At one time in my life I used to log timber in Burma and British Guyana (now Guyana) so tropical rain forest programmes will be watched. I regret now that I was so busy with the job I had that I had little time to watch the wildlife … Wildlife memories do spring to life again in watching programmes and the ones where new techniques enable cameramen to get to the top of trees and see the life up there are fascinating. Logging teak with elephants was one of the joys of my working life: I am so prejudiced in their favour that I can't look at programmes about the African elephant!
>
> (Married male, age 84, cathedral city in the south, retired senior business executive) (B 2240)

A recent instance of the process whereby creatures largely assumed to be familiar or unremarkable are radically defamiliarised and so converted into a spectacle of the previously unseen is *Life in the Undergrowth*, a BBC1 series focusing on invertebrates broadcast in November and December 2005. By employing new technology – including miniaturised cameras and magnifying lenses – the series promises the viewer virtual access to a world that has been overlooked, if never quite invisible.[59] Something of this process of defamiliarisation enabled by changes in scale is evident in the combination of commentary and images in the opening sequence of the first episode. David Attenborough's voice-over, accompanying a startling close-up of a snail's head and its emerging tentacles, begins: 'An eye, from another world … we don't often see a snail that way, and that is because we've only recently had the tiny lenses and electronic cameras that we need to explore this miniature world.'[60]

Life in the Undergrowth visits overseas locations such as Venezuela, Australia, the Amazon and North America, but it also offers a new look at relatively familiar creatures like earthworms, snails and slugs. What makes them appear extraordinary is the way that they are filmed. For example, colour, motion and shifts in scale combine in staggeringly beautiful shots of a pink-orange velvet worm crawling through leaves, a microscopic springtail ('the size of a full stop') catapulting in slow motion, or slugs mating in close-up. In the latter sequence, which runs for more than three minutes, accompanied by gentle violin music and Attenborough's reverently hushed voice-over, two leopard slugs entwine around each other while spiralling gently downwards on 'a rope of mucous'. Their bluish male organs extend and fan out together into 'a translucent flower-like globe' before sperm is exchanged. Attenborough's unhurried voice-over delivers biological information but also calls attention to the visual beauty of the images. These two functions combine in an invitation to be moved through both knowledge and aesthetic experience, to respond with awe at what is being relayed on screen.

The spectacular use of enlargements, tricks of scale and slow-motion recalls the trick photography of early cinema in which the apparatus of image production was also very much part of the show as a technological marvel in its own right.[61] The appeal of *Life in the Undergrowth*'s presentational aesthetic is noted in the following newspaper review: 'State-of-the-art footage of bluebottles and hoverflies, coupled with a profile of the world's largest insect, The Titan Beetle, make for such a cornucopian visual feast so filling in its own right you're almost incapable of absorbing the narrative content.'[62]

So what exactly is the role of argument in such an exhibition-ist subgenre of screen documentary? Certainly, the images of the slugs mating, and many others, in some ways exceed an informational or argumentational function. However, a spectacular or presentational aesthetic is not incompatible with informational content (in the form of either narrative or argument). It is more a question of how any programme combines these two elements, which are often complexly intertwined.

In the case of wildlife documentaries, argumentation may draw on editing patterns, shot selection and graphics as well as music and voice to set images into context, narrating them, elaborating them and working to clarify or anchor their meaning.[63] Commentary may, for example, call attention to issues of species rarity, scale, details of life cycle, mating and feeding, bio-technical function and prowess and the like. It may also explicitly proclaim the rarity or novelty of what is being shown, as in some of Attenborough's assertions in *Life in the Undergrowth*. Or it may foreground the experiences, feelings and thoughts of the presenter/s – a point to which I return below.

In some of these instances, vocal narration (whether via onscreen delivery or disembodied voice-over) follows the already hybridised formats of television documentary journalism. [64] John Corner has noted the significance of anchoring devices deployed to impose coherence on the diverse material that such programmes commonly use:

> The varieties of documentary journalism (magazine formats at the lighter end, series like *World in Action* and *Panorama* at the other) often drew on a very wide range of visual material, having different origins and different kinds of status in relation to their topic. Together with the radical time/space disjunctions over which a programme might work, this frequently required strong presentation and voice-over to provide continuity and narrative development across the diversity of material. [65]

Corner's analysis is certainly relevant to the functions of voice-overs and onscreen presenters in wildlife documentaries, including programmes already discussed in this chapter, like *Life in the Undergrowth*, *Springwatch* and *Animal Crime Scene*. Such more or less overt narrational interventions may attempt to elicit a response from viewers that is not simply cognitive or emotional – if the two can ever be fully separated – but combines both, as in the example of the slugs sequence from *Life in the Undergrowth*. Of course, how actual social audiences respond to such invitations needs to be investigated rather than taken for granted.

Epistephilia and 'inappropriate' or troublesome knowledges

As discussed in Chapter 2, a frequently discussed motive for watching screen documentaries is epistephilia. Bill Nichols writes: 'Documentary convention spawns an epistephilia. It posits an organizing agency that possesses information and knowledge, a text that conveys it, and a subject who will gain it.' [66] Such a will to knowledge is evident in several viewer statements about wildlife documentaries. But some of these also complicate and problematise assumptions about watching documentary as a straightforwardly epistephiliac practice.

The significance of informational content and a desire to gain knowledge through viewing is evident in the following accounts:

A good documentary relies very much on the ability and appeal of the presenter. My favourites are Bill Oddie and Ray Mears. For me, both have just the right touch: fairly low beat and a touch of modesty, with a bit of humour thrown in. I try and watch all their programmes, as I hope to learn something.

(Male, age 76, married, Oxford, retired chartered surveyor) (B1509)

My favourite programmes simply are anything David Attenborough does. He keeps you interested from the word go. Life on earth and The Blue Planet have never been beaten in my eyes. They are educational and interesting, which makes both my children and I want to watch and learn.

(Female, 38 years old, divorced, Kentallen, post office clerk) (B3220)

Some viewers took the opportunity to present a particular self-image, which was contrasted with constructions of 'other' television audiences. In the following case, documentaries and their discerning audiences – which include the respondent – are clearly distinguished as superior to 'lesser' programmes and those who watch them. (This is of course precisely the kind of claim to distinction that is noted and ridiculed by some of the non-viewers quoted above.)

Compared with the general level of drivel that appears on British TV, wildlife programmes stand out like a beacon ... I would think these programmes do require a certain level of attention (rather than any particular intellect or scientific background), and that may be a challenge to much of the general TV audience, more accustomed to slumping in front of utterly undemanding soaps, so-called reality TV shows, and game shows.

(Age 56, Caucasian male. Married with three 'children', all at University in England ... retired in 2004 as a business development director of a 'top three' pharmaceutical company ... B.Sc., Ph.D., D.Sc (Medicine) – all London University. Currently spending 2 weeks in Spain where we have a house) (R3198)

While claiming to have learned things from his viewing, this respondent goes on to make an admission about the limits of this knowledge, in terms of its failure to mobilise any kind of consequent action on his part:

One learns much of the species, of the environment, and of the challenges which each faces. To be honest it does end there – as entertainment. I have not felt moved to any action (e.g. to join an animal or environmental charity). I do see it principally as entertainment.

Thus, strategies of distinction coexist here with a distinctly less pious confession, although it is not entirely clear whether the latter is a comfortable or a guilty admission. Either way, it provides a point of contrast with claims made on behalf of the genre by some practitioners and viewers.

Of course, this tension confronts documentary and nonfiction in general, beyond any particular subgenre. As Bill Nichols asks:

> What position do we occupy when we encounter tales about the historical world? ... Do such tales not blur the boundary between aesthetics and action? Are they not meant to serve a cautionary or galvanizing role? Do they not also become yet another form of commodity consumption at the same time as they urge us, directly or indirectly, to do more than simply consume them?[67]

I return to some of these questions towards the end of this chapter.

Other respondents readily admitted to not learning anything, thus (whether deliberately or inadvertently) countering some familiar bids for status made on behalf of documentary and its audiences:

> For many years I have watched wildlife documentaries, always on television. Two presenters that I can remember are David Attenborough and Bill Oddie. Usually my wife watches them with me. I have usually been impressed and enjoy watching them. I am not aware of having learned anything from them but I do consider them to make good television.
>
> (Age 82, male, married, retired, served 43[?] years in aviation. During the war I held a commission in the RAF. Living in Spelthorne) (B1442)
>
> *Q12: How important are the following? (please give reasons for your answer if you can)*
>
> *Factual information*
>
> Not really that important – to be honest I can't really ever remember much of the factual information projected through these programmes
>
> (Anon. (7), age 21, white British female student, middle-class [also writes that she watches at least two wildlife documentaries a week])

It is important to keep in mind that the exact type and tenor of information sought by viewers of wildlife documentaries may vary. This does not simply apply to questions of choosing the 'exotic' over the 'local' or vice versa. For example, the following respondent expressed disappointment at the lack of emotional and corporeal information relayed by documentary presenters:

> I cannot stand the way that David Attenborough talks on his documentaries and that has spoiled most of them for me. The silly thing is that I love the photography and subjects of his documentaries, it is just his voice that I do not want to listen to. In fact it is generally the way documentaries are made that make I do not want to watch them ... I want wildlife documentary presenters who enthuse the way someone would chat to a friend about their holidays. With thoughts and feelings and sensory information about how the rain feels on their faces and their feet are covered in blisters, not to mention mosquito bites etc. Not someone determined to teach me something ... I never feel that documentaries give me the experience of being there. Too much sensory information is missing.
>
> (Female, 40 years of age, married, Herstmonceux, special needs assistant) (H2911)

This account complicates any assumptions about a straightforward and monolithic espistephilia prevailing among documentary audiences. Instead, it poses the question, what particular kinds of knowledge are prioritised within the genre and the dominant modes of viewing, discussing and writing about it?

Much like many other statements by viewers, journalists, and scholars on the topic, the respondent here asserts the centrality of the knowing presenter in wildlife documentary, but, crucially, this figure is rethought as a corporeal and emotional being. Some respondents and critics have praised the contagious enthusiasm of favoured presenters, from Attenborough to Bill Oddie to Steve Irwin, but this statement goes further. The notion of the presenter as a (usually male) rational, and still relatively unfeeling source of expertise is unequivocally replaced with one of him as an embodied, feeling and sensory person. While not explicitly mentioned here, such a revision of the presenter ideal, from more or less disembodied expert to emotional and physical surrogate for the viewer, also raises the issue of gender norms and binaries, which have traditionally aligned the mind with masculinity and the body with feminity.

Following the influential work of Michel Foucault in particular, many scholars have explored the complex ways in which knowledge and power are enmeshed in cultural and social spheres.[68] This is certainly true of writing on documentary, which can be seen to set a premium on knowledge of various kinds, in terms of both its (extra)textual organisation and commonly proposed viewing strategies. But knowledge is not always empowering. It can also become freighted with the burdens of guilt, anger and impotence, so effectively disempowering the recipient who may be unable to act decisively upon such knowledge. This dilemma is evident in the respondents' accounts which follow.

In the following two instances, so-called 'negative' or 'bad news' issues like hunting, poaching and animal (or human) suffering are to be avoided, possibly because they are felt to constitute calls to intervention which may be considered unrealistic or impossible to answer by the individuals concerned:[69]

> When the pics of what poachers and the remaining great white hunters in South Africa come on, I just switch over or off; I have had enough trouble in life, thanks, and there is nothing I can do.
> (grandmother, p/t teacher, Croydon, 72 years) (A1292)

> I know there's all sorts of suffering in the world, among humans and animals, but if I can't do anything to reduce it, I don't want to be a spectator. It feels shameful to write such a thing, but I'm happier burying my head in the sand.
> (I am female, 42 (born August 1963), married and living in Linlithgow in the county of West Lothian in Scotland. I am a personal finance journalist and am also working on my first novel. I'm writing this on Friday, August 12, 2005.) (M3132)

By contrast with the above accounts, the next one criticises 'positive' rather than 'negative' representations of wildlife. [70] It does this by offering a critique of human impacts on natural environments, one which by implication is lacking (or at least only ever implicit) in the programmes under discussion. What is shared with the earlier comments is a sense of impotence, and a desire not to be reminded (even indirectly) of something already known – in this case, the onward creep of environmental degradation:

> I marked time on this piece for ages trying to remember when I last watched a wildlife documentary. It is so long ago I can't remember. It really made me think why I stopped watching. I have come to the conclusion that there were two reasons.

The first was that I found them irritating, the sanctimonious tones of David Attenborough, the breathless excitement of Bill Oddie ...

The other is more difficult to explain, irritation in a different form. The expert going on about the wonders of the rhinoceros and the elephant, while others see them as millions of pounds worth of powdered rhino horn or ivory. The rain forests of Borneo and the Amazon, the first is a source of exotic hardwood the latter cluttering up good grazing land which could be used to raise cattle and soya to keep McDonalds in business. One thing I have learned in the past seventy years is that anything which has a bottom line with a lot of noughts wins. Especially as the greedy are also generally selfish and not in the least worried about what's going to happen beyond their self indulgent lifetime. Knowing that made watching wildlife programmes by dedicated and well intentioned aficionados only serve to raise my blood pressure.

(Male, 71 years, retired LGV driver, widower, Basildon) (R470)

In his influential essay 'Why look at animals?' John Berger argues that knowledge is produced at a cost, that of distance: '[Animals] are objects of our ever-extending knowledge. What we know about them is an index of our power, and thus an index of what separates us from them. The more we know, the further away they are.'[71] While this process of distancing or separation is undoubtedly significant, Berger neglects a further ramification, illustrated by the above extract. This is the possibility that an individual may enter temporarily into some kind of denial of what they know, exerting agency not to seek knowledge but to avoid or shield oneself from it, because that knowledge comes at too high a price: anger, guilt, and impotence.

In the same essay, Berger suggests that zoos are paradoxical monuments to loss. This is what makes them so disappointing: they are products of the historic destruction of the very animals and habitats that they hope to 'preserve'. Zoos can then be seen as part of what Michael Watts, following Berger, calls a 'gigantic act of enclosure' enforced on animals by the twin motors of modernity and capitalism.[72] Watts writes: 'The zoo is unequivocally about loss and captivity, and the very antithesis of the fecundity and freedom which nature purportedly signifies.'[73]

Natural history programmes often present a similarly abundant, pristine, perfectly functioning (and vividly telegenic) nature. In the process they tend to not only conceal their means of production,[74] but also, as Simon Cottle has noted, to evacuate the realities of environmental damage.[75] It is these environmental threats which the respondent quoted above is all too aware of, presumably via other media sources. And it is the chasm between these two sets of representations, these two different mediated knowledges, which has led to his refusal to continue watching wildlife documentaries.

The profilmic and animal–human interactions

The drive to know – or to avoid knowing – is bound up with documentary's generic concern with the profilmic, with referents 'out there' in the world. As a result of this concern (and as discussed in Chapter 2), screen documentary may have particular consequences for its subjects as well as for its audiences. For example, Bill Nichols suggests that semiotics is an inadequate tool with which to confront the various impacts of documentary on 'those who have their image "taken"'.[76] Nichols is writing about human subjects appearing in documentary, but it can be argued that the mode's representations of non-human subjects including animals, and audiences' engagements with these representations, are also significantly shaped by its claims to portray something of the world. This is the reason why accusations of 'faked' footage have proved controversial whether related to human or animal subjects.[77]

In an analysis of animals on screen, Jonathan Burt has proposed that such images always gesture to the profilmic, and in particular to issues of welfare and treatment – both in general, and in relation to the particular film or television programme being watched.[78] He writes: 'This rupturing effect of the animal image is mainly exemplified by the manner in which our attention is constantly drawn beyond the image and, in that sense, beyond the aesthetic and semiotic framework of the film.'[79] Burt's suggestion relates to animals in screen fictions, but it may also be applicable to animals in documentary. However, this kind of response needs to be investigated further, rather than being simply assumed to be the case.

In my audience studies, several respondents did express concern for the welfare of the animals portrayed, whether or not such issues were raised directly on screen. (On occasions the aesthetic and semiotic frameworks of documentary texts may already point to issues of animal welfare and treatment. But in other instances, such issues remain tacit, bracketed off from the texts' main attractions and propositions, if sometimes allowed marginal or indirect reference via 'making of' interviews, spin-offs or websites.)

In some instances, presenters may operate as emotional surrogates for viewers, relaying their concerns and anxieties. This function can overlap with presenters' channelling of audience desires for knowledge. The two functions are best thought of as sometimes intertwined, rather than necessarily polarised, and any balance between them will vary from case to case. A number of successful television formats, including *Elephant Diary*, *Big Cat Diary*, *Springwatch*, and many celebrity-fronted shows, play on such dynamics by foregrounding human–animal interactions.[80] (This trend contrasts with recent theatrical hits like *Le Peuple Migrateur/ Winged Migration* and *La Marche de l'empereur/March of the Penguins*, and the main sections of the blockbuster television series *Planet Earth*, all of which keep humans off screen, along with earlier traditions in British and American wildlife films. On the latter, Mitman notes: 'As the success of both [Walt] Disney and [Marlon] Perkins made evident, making nature entertaining on film depended in part upon the removal of any signs of human presence.')[81]

The significance of the presenter as an emotional relay point for the viewer is foregrounded in this respondent's comments:

> Another wildlife programme I watched fairly recently was Big Cat Diary, which consisted of families of lions, cheetahs and leopards in their natural terrain persistently stalked by camera crews in off-road vehicles. What I recall most about this is the relief on the faces of the presenters when they spotted their feline friends after a lengthy absence, and the concern if a particular cat appeared weak, malnourished or in danger.
> (Male, 36, single, Stamford, Lincolnshire, Screen printer/ engraver/sign maker) (M3217)

Some viewers were enthusiastic about the roles of presenters (whether 'experts' or celebrities from other realms of popular culture) in fronting wildlife footage and so inviting particular emotional and cognitive responses to it. Others objected to presenters getting in the way of the animals on screen. In 2004 the former punk rock singer John Lydon capitalised on his recent appearance in ITV's successful reality television series *I'm a Celebrity Get me Out of Here* by making wildlife programmes for both Channel Five and Discovery. Here is an angry response to one of those shows, *John Lydon's Shark Attack*:

> *Q13: What do you think of celebrity-led wildlife docs, like John Lydon on sharks, Amanda Burton on lions, etc?*
>
> I hated the John Lydon on sharks one!!!!! First of all he is a prick, second he is so loud and irritating, third he is a prick! I love sharks, they are my favourite animal but he completely destroyed the documentary. This is my point about channel 5 documentaries, we want to see the animals not some crap celebrity chatting shit trying to boost his flagging reputation. I really really hate this type of wildlife documentary, I am not interested in the lives of 'celebrities' if I was I would watch celebrity love island. If there is a programme on sharks that is what I want to see and be educated on.
>
> (Henry, age 21, white, British, male, student, middle-class)
>
> (pilot study)

As this account shows, not all viewers want to watch an emotional or intellectual surrogate responding to animals on their behalf. In this case, the animals (sharks) are seen to inhabit a world 'out there' that is more compelling than the celebrity framework through which their activities are mediated.

Mediated and direct experiences, engagement and escape

While presenters from Attenborough to Lydon may travel the world as part of the filming process, one of the major appeals of wildlife programming attested to by viewers and commentators is the promise of gaining virtual access to elsewhere. Of course, the proliferation of mediations offering experiences grounded in what John B. Thompson has called 'non-local knowledge' is a key characteristic of the contemporary media array. But, as Thompson notes, 'non-local knowledge is always appropriated by individuals in specific locales and the practical significance of this knowledge – what it means to individuals and how it is used by them – is always dependent on the interests of recipients and on the resources they bring to bear on the process of appropriation.'[82]

In the case of wildlife on television, direct, unmediated

experience of screened locations and animals may be impossible for many viewers, due to general inaccessibility or contextual factors such as economic and physical constraints. Alternatively, for some audiences, documentaries may constitute an incitement to travel, to attempt to improve on mediated experiences by seeking more direct ones. In either case, the motivations for both viewer and tourist can be thought of in terms of 'push' and 'pull' factors. These dynamics can be mutually supporting, but are not necessarily so.

The following accounts describe a range of push and pull elements, showing how contextual conditions can shape predispositions, modes of viewing and types of response:

Q4: Do you ever watch any wildlife documentaries on tv?

Please say why you do/don't watch them.

Yes, as we live in the city we don't come across many animals so to see what animals there are in the world is quite fascinating.
(Fatima, age 18, British Asian female, student, working-class)

Q4: Do you ever watch any wildlife documentaries on tv?

Please say why you do/don't watch them.

Yes – only wildlife documentaries that are set somewhere exotic, because I see animals that I have never seen before and some of their behaviour is so human like.
(Anon. (7), age 17, black British Caribbean female, student, working-class)

Q19: Is there anything else you'd like to say about wildlife documentaries?

I think wildlife documentaries are so fascinating and they really need to be about real life. I enjoy them a lot as they offer escapism to other lands and places.
(Jenna, age 21, white, British, female, student, middle-class) (pilot study)

They appeal to me because I have no intention of travelling to Africa, the Brazilian rainforest or the polar icecaps. They are my preferred sightseeing mode. They probably do appeal largely to people who will never go on safari, or take that sort of holiday.
(Female, age 75, divorced, Cobham, Surrey, formerly CAB adviser) (M1395)

Wildlife documentaries take us to places that ordinary Joes don't get to see. I am fortunate enough to have seen the wildlife of Australia in the natural habitat and close to hand, and also an

American Bald Headed eagle in the USA, but there are many more animals I would dearly love to see, and television enables me to do that.

(Female, 38, married, Sheffield, Homemaker) (B3185)

The drive for knowledge (watching for argument and informational content as well as for access to the spectacular and inaccessible) can coexist with the kind of touristic gaze attested to above. This is made explicit in the next two accounts:

Q10: How would you characterise a good/enjoyable wildlife doc?
Have to show you things that you never knew existed to be interesting – like the Blue Planet made you realise everything that goes on under the ocean, and that's what made it interesting.

Q13: How important to you are the following? (please give reasons for your answer if you can)
The kind of animal shown
Ordinary animals can be boring – exotic ones we don't usually see are better.

(Fergus, age 18, white English male, student, working-class)

Q12 How important are the following? (please give reasons for your answer if you can)
Setting and scenery
Sometimes more important [than the wildlife]. As someone who hasn't travelled further than package holiday to Turkey, and craving a gap year – wildlife documentaries are one of the ways in which I can take in some sights I otherwise wouldn't be able to. These are often filmed particularly well without being too exaggerated. I would say I'm more into exotic locations for docs, I like being surprised by what is shown to me.

Factual information
Yeah very important to me, not down to intricate detail, but I want to know things which impress me (knowing the wingspan of an eagle say, or temperatures of locations, hard to describe but I want to be taught)

(Becky, age 21, white, British, female, student, middle-class)
(pilot study)

Most of the respondents quoted so far in this section imply that mediated experiences of wildlife and locations act as substitutes for direct experience (which may or may not be anticipated in the future). For some, the mediation may operate – for the self or imagined others – as an invitation to travel, to seek just such an engagement with the 'real', however unlikely or potentially damaging the realisation of this ambition may be. See for example these two differing responses:

> The last thing I watched was about brown bears in Canada ... It has inspired me to want to go to Canada to see bears for myself if or when I win enough money to go ... Hopefully animal documentaries inspire us to be kind to living things and maybe go on a safari to see them for real.
>
> (Female, age 50, divorced, carer, Limavady) (C1191)

> I don't like documentaries exploring remote places, as I think people should stay out of them.
>
> (Female, 46, single, Shetland, single parent) (C41)

For the next person, an increased reliance on mediations is to be expected among the housebound. Interestingly, this situation is considered a future possibility, rather than being denied, avoided, or used to make a judgement of others:

> It is not that I am not interested in the outdoors; I walk in the countryside regularly and am at my happiest out of doors. For me general wildlife programmes provide a vicarious experience. However if/when the time comes that I am housebound these are programmes that I will watch and enjoy.
>
> (Female, 68 years, widow, Brighton, retired nurse/civil servant)
> (L1991)

Other respondents, perhaps with greater access to the natural world, validated direct experiences over mediated ones, matching the local to the former category, and the faraway or inaccessible to the latter. For instance:

> Recently, sitting in my beautiful sitting-room overlooking trees and fields, at dusk, I've watched a white owl swooping past my enormous window and gliding and dropping on the prey in the grasses, or perching nearby on a pole and slowly extending its enormous wings as it turned its face towards me and I've thought 'this is worth 20 films'!
>
> (Female, widow, retired, 84) (F1560)

> I have a bee hive now, very instructive just to sit and gape at the comings and goings. And I have a wormery and a fish pond. And more pigeons than you can point a flame thrower at. What need I an Oddie?
>
> (Male, 54, single, Wisbech, distance learning tutor) (M2854)

By contrast, in the next account, mediation adds values unattainable through direct experience:

> I suppose one of the most worthwhile and exciting things I've done has been a week in the Kruger game park among wild animals ... But there's no way you could experience the closeup activities of this vast variety of insects, animals and birds that television has to offer.
> (Male, age 86, retired civil servant, Cheam, widower) (G2134)

The following respondents lament the shortage of programming on domestic topics, and/or stress the use value of documentaries which stimulate further, first-hand engagement with (local) nature:

> I would love to see more [programmes] about the common creatures of this country. For example I see earwigs all the time but I know more about a seahorse that lives hundreds of miles away and I have to pay to see in a sealife centre. And how about the sparrow, when will we get a good look into their lives. It would be great to see it on tv and then be able to see that creature in real life having its life on your doorstep.
> (I am a married mum of three. I live in the south east of England. I was born in 1952, married in 1971, my children were born in 1972, 1976 and 1980. I am the manageress of a florist shop and I have 4 grandchildren ... so far.) (D156)

> The last wildlife documentary I watched was a video on red kites at the Red Kite Centre in Wales and before that a DVD at home on red kites. We have red kites frequently flying over our village and took the opportunity whilst on holiday to find out more ... I prefer to sit and watch the birds in the garden than sit and watch a film about lions or elephants.
> (Female, age 55, married, village in Bucks, School secretary) (C1786)

> Some of the items in Springwatch were filmed in the London Wetlands Centre at Barnes in West London and I was keen to go there myself. I did so last week when I joined a group of friends for a visit followed by a barbecue supper. A direct result of watching a wildlife programme – one extends one's horizons and I found myself bird-watching for the first time.
> (Female, age 65, widowed, living London Docklands, working p/t Librarian) (H2673)

Having noted these responses, I want to return to the (often strongly felt) motivations for seeking mediated experience presented at the start of this section. Such viewer investments should not be underestimated. It has proved relatively easy for critics to locate in ideas and constructions of nature, including those of television audiences, evidence of numerous ailments and misdemeanours, ranging from idealistic sentimentality to selfish touristic aspirations to a widespread alienation from the natural world which can only be intensified by reliance on television. For instance, in 1998 the columnist Polly Toynbee reacted to a flurry of 'SOS animal programmes' (about pets as well as 'wild' animals) including *Pet Rescue*, *Animal Hospital Revisited*, *Wildlife SOS*, and *Animal Rescuers*, with this criticism:

> What are we coming to? Blue Peter pets we all loved and grew up with, but we did grow up. Now we have infantile animal sentimentality for adults too. In a world of human atrocity, this sick obsession with animals has turned into serious decadence. Why weep over rodeo horses when there are the orphans of Kosovo also available for our tears? If we want vicarious suffering, let's have more tales of starving Sudanese babies.[83]

Citing Toynbee, Burt comments:

> This tone of austerity and discipline colours a good deal of contemporary critical writing on modern animal imagery ... It is not always clear what this austerity is refusing. However, it is based, structurally at least, on assumptions that most human–animal relations in modernity are in various ways wrongful – either sentimental or hollow or a disconcerting combination of the two.[84]

An earlier example of this way of thinking is found in Berger's essay 'Why look at animals?' He writes:

> 'Nature' ... acquires the meaning of what has grown organically, what was not created by man, in contrast to the artificial structures of human civilisation. At the same time, it can be understood as that aspect of human inwardness which has remained natural, or at least tends or longs to become natural once more. According to this view of nature, the life of a wild animal becomes an ideal, an ideal internalised as a feeling surrounding a repressed desire. The image of a wild animal becomes the starting point of a daydream.[85]

Berger proposes that the animal image, the starting-point of the daydream, is 'a point from which the day-dreamer departs with his back turned'. He illustrates this prevalent state of 'confusion' about wild animals with the following news story:

> London housewife Barbara Carter won a 'grant a wish' charity contest, and said she wanted to kiss and cuddle a lion. Wednesday night she was in a hospital in shock and with throat wounds. Mrs Carter, 46, was taken to the lions' compound of the safari park at Bewdley, Wednesday. As she bent forward to stroke the lioness, Suki, it pounced and dragged her to the ground. Wardens later said, 'We seem to have made a bad error of judgment. We have always regarded the lioness as perfectly safe'.[86]

The impulses, desires and situations behind this kind of 'daydream' – an idealisation of nature that is often impractical and sometimes dangerous, but is widely promoted via some mediations of nature – need to be interrogated further.[87] In their generalising tendencies, diagnoses and indictments like those quoted above run the risk of neglecting the complex and particular ways in which engaging with cultural representations of nature – including wildlife documentaries on television – may be at least in part a response to social conditions and lived experience. Berger's notion of the 'daydream' suggests something of this, but fails to pursue it sufficiently.[88]

The following respondent's statement raises some of these issues:

> I love the serenity of Africa and all wildlife regions that take us from the ugly industrial world into a natural habitat more so because I live in an industrial wasteland of workaday commerce.
>
> My wife loves any animal film and would watch Babe forever, I think cats, dogs, rabbits, forever appealing, even foxes with the horrible 'vermin' tag are God's creatures.
>
> I was reprimanded for feeding birds, with a warning from my local council, which is part of my natural culture, no longer permissible. Now with an overwhelming foreign culture now ruling the roost.
>
> Such is life, people worry about car or roof damage or petty deeds of the new age of materialism, now rife in all its glory, Whatever happened to the love of natural surroundings. Yes – I am very annoyed.
>
> (Married, male, retired builder, East London) (R40)

This is an account of trying to connect with the natural world in two ways, via both mediated and direct engagements with 'nature'.

The former combines a temporary respite or escape from the 'industrial wasteland' of the locality with the consoling pleasures of televised constructions of Africa as Edenic – a well established trope in western cultures.[89] The second attempt is towards a more direct experiential engagement with the locality – feeding the birds – although prohibition threatens to foreclose this activity. Linking both responses is a sense of loss, disappointment and resentment, which appears to verge on xenophobia or even racism at one point (the 'overwhelmingly foreign culture ruling the roost'.)[90]

Nostalgic recollections of a past characterised as less blighted by the forces of urbanisation, technology and commerce, and offering more direct engagements with the natural world, were also evident in other accounts. As one respondent put it:

> If anything the wildlife and nature studies put on TV may bring man and his current behaviour to a halt in an effort to save the treasures that are left and rebuild those tree lined avenues of my childhood, trees that at one time was the home of birds and insects in profusion and now have been removed to allow the cars to clutter up the neighbourhood.
> (Male, 79 yoa, married, Ottery St Mary, retired Administrator)
> (L1504)

Comments like those quoted here should not be dismissed as the predictable complaints of the elderly. They may attest to very real feelings of exclusion and alienation felt by some older people in contemporary society.[91] Moreover, they may have a wider pertinence, in terms of attitudes towards nature and urban or semi-urban living that resonate beyond the category of the 'elderly', a label that can be used unthinkingly to bracket off older age groups from younger ones.

A pessimistic reading of these accounts would posit the viewers as exemplary of the alienation of modern capitalist society from the natural world in general, and 'wild' or 'free' animals in particular. According to this interpretation, the desire to connect becomes a measure of estrangement, and any attempts to close that gap are doomed to failure, shaped as they are by stunted, reductive and ultimately illusory cultural representations of animals. The responses certainly chime with Berger's lament about the growing distance between humans and animals. But the two viewers quoted are not simply reliant on mediations of nature as an alternative to first-hand experience of the natural world. While the former feeds local birds, the latter (who also enjoys watching 'exotic sites we shall never visit') was inspired by a Bill Oddie documentary to build a bee box in his garden.

The sense of loss and nostalgia evident in these viewer statements also requires an analysis that rejects making easy judgements. As Ben Highmore has argued, in a discussion of the routines of everyday life, 'Perhaps one of the sentiments most often associated with everyday life (and disparaged no doubt because of this) is nostalgia.'[92] Highmore cites C. Nadia Seremetakis, noting that, in contrast to general academic suspicion of nostalgia, her work 'shows how nostalgia can join together the individual and the social by grounding everyday life in a loosely historical recognition that how we live now is neither inevitable, nor necessary'.[93] A similar kind of understanding, prompted by the distinct but related processes of watching wildlife on television and being asked to think and write about this activity, can be traced in the two responses above.

Another reading of these and other audience engagements with wildlife documentaries might draw on the emergent body of work on 'biophilia' to point to humans' 'innate tendency to focus on life and lifelike processes', with the result that 'to the degree that we come to understand other organisms, we will place greater value on them, and on ourselves'.[94] The theory of biophilia (and its opposite, biophobia) is potentially compatible with both pessimistic and optimistic approaches to representations of wildlife, in that it stresses humans' need to connect with nature, rather than the success or otherwise of any such attempts. However, the usefulness of writings on biophilia in this instance is hampered by a tendency to prioritise first-hand experience of life forms over mediations of them, and to pay only limited attention to the role of popular culture in producing constructions of nature.

One small exception to this myopia is a study of children's increasing reliance on television over direct experience for their understandings of the natural world, part of a larger project on changing social conditions among Native American people living in the Sonoran Desert on the borderlands of the US and Mexico. Its authors, Gary Paul Nabhan and Sara St. Antoine, conclude that 'replacing direct experience with television-mediated education discourages children from making their own observations and forming their own opinions of the natural world; instead they inherit those of the TV program's writers and editors.'[95] They quote Robert Michael Pyle: 'A [unmediated] banana slug face-to-face means much more than a Komodo dragon seen on television. With rhinos mating in the living room, who will care about the creatures next door?'[96]

This critique raises serious questions about the formation of attitudes to nature among children in particular, which are beyond the scope of this chapter. I will, however, raise three points briefly here. Firstly, there is a danger in enforcing a rigid distinction between the 'educational' on the one hand and the spheres of fantasy and play on the other. Nabhan and St. Antoine's work does not investigate the complex interfaces between knowledge formation, fantasy and experience, both mediated and direct.[97] It also tends to polarise television watching and first-hand experience, neglecting the microsocial contexts of viewing (whether alone or with others) and how modes of engagement and response may draw on understandings gained from other sources (including direct experience) to mediate and interact with programming. Thirdly, in its particular focus on children of Native Americans, the study laments the contamination of a hitherto 'innocent' (non)audience, and (inevitably) has very little to say about adult and/or already urbanised audiences. Equally, the citation of Pyle's argument has a rhetorical force, but his logic is not entirely convincing because it begs too many questions about what viewers of all ages really do with television. The accounts of many of the viewers quoted above suggest that mediated and direct engagements with nature are not necessarily mutually exclusive after all.

Concerns about the allure of televised nature outshining unmediated encounters have also been raised by some documentary practitioners. For example, in 1997, Petra Regent, then series editor for Survival Anglia, said that she was less worried about the (rare) mistreatment of animals during filming than about false expectations of nature being created:

> This is more insidious. Programme makers like to claim their programmes create a love for nature, which leads to an interest in conservation. But I think they may be creating false impression. Especially in Britain, people may go and be disappointed about a less spectacular nature. There's a danger they may not think it is deserving of protection.[98]

The newspaper article that quoted Regent contrasted her point of view with that of Alastair Fothergill, of the BBC's Natural History Unit. Fothergill insisted that the spectacularisation of nature created a love of the natural world that was needed to make people care about conservation. In a more recent interview to promote the BBC/Discovery/NHK blockbuster series *Planet Earth*, Fothergill elaborated on this point: 'How can you care about the polar bear if you don't see why its life is dominated by the amount of ice it has, and therefore by global warming?'[99] However, global warming is never mentioned directly in the sequence featuring polar bears (or anywhere else in the first five episodes of *Planet Earth*). Instead, the programme relies on the viewer to make the connection. As the journalist interviewing Fothergill noted, to do otherwise would be to become 'political' and so threaten the series' commercial prospects: 'the series grinds no political axe (as none hoping to sell to 100 countries can afford to do)'.[100]

At the time of writing, the first episodes of *Planet Earth* are being broadcast on BBC1. So far, human activities and impacts have been evacuated from its depiction of the planet, apart from footage of film crews in a regular 'behind the scenes' supplementary sequence entitled 'Planet Earth Diaries'. Urgent problems such as climate change, habitat destruction, hunting and pollution are notably absent from this spectacularly telegenic vision of earth and its wildlife.[101]

In his book *Animals in Film* Jonathan Burt is, like Fothergill, relatively optimistic, suggesting that, on occasions at least, successful documentaries may reconnect viewers with nature in a positive way. Commenting on BBC television series such as *Life on Earth* (1979) *The Living Planet* (1991) and *State of the Planet* (2000), he writes of 'the way in which film uses the visual to suggest that it is this [act of] seeing that actually integrates us with the natural world.' Burt continues:

> The moral message of these films is implicit in the way in which the images of animals and environment are tied together and in the way that, as witnesses, we too become co-opted within this depiction of nature … The act of linking the images creates the vulnerable networks that will be best served by us looking at them in appreciation rather than acting upon them detrimentally. Despite the significance of film technology in constructing these images, the shared glance with the gorilla [in *Life on Earth*] suggests that we are looking from within nature and not at nature.

> Thus, rather than seeing nature films of this kind as a replacement for reality, they seem more like the point of entry for our engagement with the natural world: an active moral gaze made possible, even structured, by the technology of modernity.[102]

Burt goes on to ask a question that he can't really answer adequately: 'is the audience that is configured by this view of the natural world any more than a consumer of this imagery or can the implicitly moral message of such films create the conditions for a more positive engagement with the natural world?'[103] I would argue that, rather than being necessarily transformative by itself, material of this (or any other) propositional potential has to be relocated in the web of experiences, understandings, orientations and knowledges brought to the media encounter by any and every viewer. Whether greeted with irritation, indifference or pleasure, or even, on occasions, welcomed as something like an epiphany, television programming only ever makes sense and gains (or fails to achieve) significance within the particular social situations of its individual viewers.

This is not to devolve the responsibility for making meaning entirely to audiences. Nor is it to take for granted the familiar self-justifications of the professional discourse relayed by Fothergill and others in the industry. The (often internalised) commercial constraints under which documentary practitioners and television commissioners and schedulers operate are too important for that. Despite the range and variety of subgenres and textual hybrids screened in the multi-channel television era, pressing issues of environmental depletion, global warming, and the largely negative impacts of international tourism (often encouraged via media representations – including but not limited to – wildlife programming)[104] remain beyond the pale, for the most part unspeakable. Fothergill's latest series, *Planet Earth*, provides yet another example of the deliberate evasion of these 'difficult' topics.

Conclusion

There are no easy answers to the complex and interconnected issues of separation and connection, direct and mediated experience, the 'familiar' and the 'exotic', knowledge and diversion, spectacle and argument, raised here. However, it seems to me that these ongoing debates should provide more valid and nuanced tools with which to interrogate the diverse roles, uses and impacts of wildlife programming and viewing than blanket generalisations about modernity and capitalism. The twin traps of oversimplifying a variety of representational strategies, and of speaking of/for a monolithic, passive or deluded audience, haunt some of the most provocative thinking on the interfaces between human culture and nature. The range of programming and viewer responses analysed in this chapter suggests that assumptions about the audience embedded in some critiques of constructions of nature do not come close to telling the full story of wildlife documentaries on television and their audiences.

Ultimately, Burt's question about moral messages and positive audience engagements must be situated within a larger debate about the potential of the media to inform and galvanise publics. Why is this potential only intermittently realised? How might steps be taken to fulfil it more successfully? As John B. Thompson argues, since the media's development has helped to create and fuel a growing awareness of global interconnectedness, media *could* play a crucial role in the renewal of a form of 'moral-practical reflection which would provide some reasoned guidance for the conduct of human affairs' (including human impacts on the non-human world). Whether such an enhanced sense of responsibility could develop, and whether it could be put into practice successfully is, Thompson suggests, 'difficult to say'. But, he concludes, this attempt 'might be the best – the only – option we have'.[104] I return to documentary's role in this debate in the concluding chapter.

Notes

1   *Galapagos* grossed $15 million in the US, and ranks as the sixteenth highest grossing IMAX film in the US; *Africa's Elephant Kingdom* ranks two places lower with a gross of $13.5 million. www.boxoffice mojo.com, accessed October 2005.
2   Simon Cottle, 'Producing nature(s): on the changing production ecology of natural history TV', *Media, Culture and Society*, 26:1 (2004), p. 86.
3   *Ibid.*, p. 82.
4   *Ibid.*, p. 88.
5   Quoted in Ros Coward, 'Back to nature', *Guardian*, 9 May 2005, G2, p. 7.
6   Cottle, 'Producing nature(s)', pp. 91–2. For an analysis of Irwin's self-

promotion and some of his shows, see Mark L Berrettini, "Danger! Danger! Danger!" or When animals might attack: adventure activism and wildlife film and television', *Scope, an online journal of film studies* (NS), 1, Spring 2005, www.scope.nottingham.ac.uk, accessed August 2005.

7 Paul Faircloth, head of the production company Granada Wild, in *Broadcast*, 20 April 2001, p. 17, and Paul Sowerbutts, director of United Wildlife, in *Broadcast*, 6 October 2000, p. 21, both quoted in Cottle, 'Producing nature(s)', pp. 85–6.

8 Maggie Brown, 'I want to brighten and enlighten', *Guardian*, Media section, 24 October 2005, p. 10.

9 Jacquie Lawrence, commissioning editor, documentaries, Sky One, talking at 'Commissioning contemporary factual' panel at Sheffield International Documentary Festival, 14 October 2005.

10 www.skymedia.co.uk/pages/sponsorship-opportunities-skyone-lastchancetosave, accessed July 2005.

11 Quoted in Coward, 'Back to nature', pp. 6–7. *Pride* (broadcast on BBC1, 27 December 2004) is a feature-length scripted drama using footage of a family of lions, voiced by a cast of British stars including Kate Winslet, Helen Mirren and Sean Bean. It is thus rather like a live footage version of Disney's hugely successful animated film *The Lion King* (1994). The official *Pride* website describes the show as follows: 'A real pride of lions, filmed on the plains of Africa, become the characters in a magical and dramatic tale of love and survival in *Pride*, an ambitious new family film ... John Downer ... is one of the world's most prominent natural history film makers. He has teamed up with leading television writer Simon Nye *(Men Behaving Badly, How Do You Want Me, Beast)* to create the captivating live action tale. With the aid of computer manipulated images as well as some habituated lions, *Pride* depicts the almost human traits of real lions in a close community. Family, love and loyalty are tested in a conflict with another pride of marauding wanderers over ultimate control of the Pride lands. Simon Nye [comments] "*Pride* is a rip-roaring tale, a fusion of comedy, drama and natural history", www.bbc.co.uk/drama/pride/abouttheshow. shtml, accessed November 2005.

12 Quoted in Coward, 'Back to nature', pp. 6–7. *Deep Jungle* was broadcast in three one-hour programmes on ITV1 in the UK in 2005. It was an international co-production involving Granada Wild and Thirteen/WNET in New York, in association with National Geographic Channel International and France 5. Production information from www.int.granadamedia.com, accessed January 2006.

13 Quoted in Coward, 'Back to nature', p. 7.

14 Fothergill speaking at 'Planet Earth: an HD Masterclass' at Sheffield International Documentary Festival, 14 October 2005.

15   Quoted in Coward, 'Back to nature', p. 7. In UK documentary televi-
      sion Robert Thirkell has also popularised a new attention to storytelling.
      Following in the footsteps of celebrated Hollywood screenwriting
      gurus like Robert McKee, Thirkell, who was series editor on the hit
      series *Jamie's School Dinners*, promotes a seven-step model for 'the
      perfect documentary'. This is focused on 'the development of tradi-
      tional dramatic structure to allow transformation of character through
      time and conflict'. Sheffield International Documentary Festival, Oc-
      tober 2005, programme information, p. 30.
16   Quoted in Cottle, 'Producing nature(s)', p. 89.
17   Todd Gitlin, *Inside Prime Time* (New York, Pantheon Books, 1983,
      1985), p. 64.
18   *Springwatch with Bill Oddie*, BBC2, 30 May 2005.
19   John Ellis, *Visible Fictions: Cinema Television Video* (London, Routledge
      and Kegan Paul, 1982), Chapter 7, 'Broadcast TV as cultural form'.
20   Broadcast on 7 June 2005.
21   A US-based specialist channel, Animal Planet is one of several brands
      (including Discovery Channel) owned by Discovery Communications
      Inc., which promotes itself as 'the leading global real-world media
      and entertainment company', www.discovery.com. The BBC's Natu-
      ral History Unit has a co-production deal with Discovery that runs
      until 2012, and Discovery has been a significant partner in more 'up-
      market' BBC programming, including flagship series such as *Blue Planet*
      and *Planet Earth*. For an insight into some of the tensions resulting
      from the BBC's Joint Venture Partnership with Discovery, see Georgina
      Born, *Uncertain Vision: Birt, Dyke and the Reinvention of the BBC* (Lon-
      don, Secker and Warburg, 2004), pp. 171–2. Thanks to Ted Ulas for
      this reference.
22   The show quoted was broadcast on BBC1, 31 August 2005.
23   The series is not listed in Attenborough's profile carried on the BBC
      website www.bbc.co.uk/nature/programmes/who/david_attenborough.
      shtml, accessed November 2005. Helen Wheatley locates within
      Attenborough's established persona 'a number of the associated "vir-
      tues" of quality public service television', including 'reserve coupled
      with a "typically British" sense of eccentricity' and 'the whispery
      reverent timbre of his voice'. Wheatley, 'The limits of television?',
      pp. 328–9.
24   Gregg Mitman, *Reel Nature: America's Romance with Wildlife on Film*
      (Harvard University Press, Cambridge, MA, 1999), p. 206.
25   For further discussion of the audience research process, see method-
      ological appendix.
26   While the directive did not privilege television as a mode of consump-
      tion, the vast majority of correspondents wrote only about watching
      television, as I had expected they would. The full directive, details of

respondents, and questionnaires used in the other stages of research, are included in the methodological appendix.

27   In 2004, steps were taken to diversify the sample, by recruiting more men, younger people and more correspondents living outside the south of England.

28   For a discussion of how gender is effectively constituted and privileged as a relevant *a priori* analytical category via the archive's physical organisation of responses into distinct male and female groupings (in separate cardboard boxes), see Stanley, 'Women have servants and men never eat'.

29   For more on contextual factors in viewing scenarios, see Austin, *Hollywood Hype and Audiences*. On television and domestic contexts see, for instance, David Morley, *Family Television: Cultural Power and Domestic Leisure* (London, Comedia, 1986); Roger Silverstone, *Television and Everyday Life* (London, Routledge, 1994); Shaun Moores, *Satellite Television and Everyday Life: Articulating Technology* (Luton, John Libbey Media, 1996); David Gauntlett and Annette Hill, *TV Living: Television, Culture and Everyday Life* (London, Routledge, 1999).

30   John Ellis has described mainstream television's dominant mode of viewing as a relatively inattentive 'glance', which contrasts with the more intense 'gaze' of the spectator at the cinema. However, while the concept of the glance allows Ellis to consider television's use of sound to call attention back to the screen, it is too reductive to describe the diversity of ways in which people actually watch television with varying degrees of engagement and attention. Ellis, *Visible Fictions*, pp. 162–3. On how a 'media ensemble' of overlapping forms and technologies might be experienced in the domestic sphere, see Hermann Bausinger, 'Media, technology and daily life', *Media, Culture and Society*, 6:4, (1984), pp. 343–51.

31   Contextual study presents a huge, if not infinite, terrain for the researcher, whose attempts to map it can only ever be selective. This awareness should not be taken as grounds for abandoning such an approach, however, but rather as a reminder of the necessarily incomplete nature of any inquiry. On this topic, see Barbara Klinger, 'Film history, terminable and interminable: recovering the past in reception studies', *Screen*, 38:2 (1997), pp. 107–28.

32   In 2001, *Social Trends* recorded the proportion of households in the UK without a television at just 1 per cent. *Social Trends*, 31 (Norwich, The Stationery Office, 2001), p. 225.

33   Some very different examples of productive and self-reflexive thinking about negotiations of identity and the risks and opportunities that audience research presents to its participants might include: David Buckingham's work with young boys talking about television, Ellen Seiter's honest account of a 'troubling interview', Lyn Thomas's report

of focus group discussions of Inspector Morse, and my own research into teenage viewers of *Basic Instinct*. See David Buckingham, 'Boys' talk: television and the policing of masculinity', in Buckingham (ed.), *Reading Audiences: Young People and the Media* (Manchester, Manchester University Press, 1993), pp. 89–115; Seiter, 'Making distinctions in TV audience research'; Thomas, *Fans, Feminisms and 'Quality' Media*, Chapter 4, 'In love with Inspector Morse', pp. 75–102; Austin, *Hollywood, Hype and Audiences*, pp. 77–91.

34   This kind of apology for not enjoying cultural objects that have been validated as 'worthwhile' or 'elevating' is comparable to defensive admissions about consuming 'unworthy' or 'trashy' objects, sometimes phrased along the lines of 'I know it's rubbish but …'. An example of this process is viewers of reality television reproducing critical stigmatisations of the genre. See Annette Hill, *Reality TV: Audiences and Popular Factual Television* (Abingdon, Routledge, 2005), pp. 85–7.

35   Nichols, *Representing Reality*, p. 3.

36   See also this comment: 'My brother had just bought a 32″ Panasonic set and as I had only a 14″ one, I inherited it when he died a year ago – it is great for documentaries and scenic displays.' (Female, 83 years, widow, retired teacher) (T1411).

37   Tom Gunning, 'The cinema of attractions: early film, its spectator and the avant-garde', *Wide Angle*, 8:3–4 (1986), reprinted in Thomas Elsaesser with Adam Barker (eds), *Early Cinema: Space, Frame, Narrative* (London, BFI, 1990), pp. 57, 58. Discussing the decline in the dominance of the cinema of attractions in the US after 1907 or so, Gunning, Andre Gaudreault and many others have pointed to the growing historical significance of constructions of (fictional) character and narrative in providing the means to assemble disparate shots into longer forms, both motivating and ultimately harnessing the potentialities of movement and display, and so drawing audiences into filmic diegesis via their engagement with the processes of story. See, for instance, Andre Gaudreault, 'Film, narrative, narration: the cinema of the Lumiere brothers', *Iris*, 2:4 (1984), reprinted in Elsaesser with Barker (eds), *Early Cinema*, pp. 68–75, and several other articles in the same collection.

38   Gunning summarised in Miriam Hansen, 'Early cinema, late cinema: transformations of the public sphere', in Linda Williams (ed.), *Viewing Positions: Ways of Seeing Film* (New Brunswick, Rutgers University Press, 1995), p. 137.

39   Gunning, 'The cinema of attractions', p. 56.

40   A similar presentational aesthetic is evident in *Le Peuple Migratuer/ Winged Migration*, a surprise theatrical hit in France and the US, which presents spectacular sequences of (unspecified) bird behaviours filmed across several continents, only loosely connected by a minimal voice-

over narration offering generalities about seasonal change and the drive to survive. Ronald Fricke's *Baraka* (US, 1992) could come under the rubric of a nature- and humanity-focused cinema of attractions, as could the recent BBC production *Natural World Symphony* (broadcast on BBC4, 28 December 2005), which recalls *Baraka* in its use of a wordless montage of decontextualised images of the natural and human worlds, deploying timelapse sequences, rapid cutting, and an original score (by Nitin Sawney for the BBC, and various artists for *Baraka*). On *Baraka*, see Martin Roberts, '*Baraka:* World cinema and the global culture industry', *Cinema Journal*, 37:3 (1998), pp. 62–82.

41 Lorraine Daston and Gregg Mitman, 'The how and why of thinking with animals', in Daston and Mitman (eds), *Thinking with Animals: New Perspectives on Anthropomorphism* (New York, Columbia University Press, 2005), p. 12.

42 *Ibid.*, p. 13.

43 Dai Vaughan, 'Let there be Lumiere', *Sight and Sound*, Spring 1981, republished in Elsaesser with Barker (eds), *Early Cinema*, p. 66.

44 *Ibid.*, p. 65.

45 Wheatley, 'The limits of television?' p. 333.

46 *Ibid.*, p. 332.

47 *Ibid.*, p. 329. Wheatley borrows this term from Charlotte Brunsdon's analysis of discourses of quality in television, in her *Screen Tastes: Soap Opera to Satellite Dishes* (London and New York, Routledge, 1997).

48 Wheatley, 'The limits of television?', p. 327.

49 *Ibid.*, p 326.

50 As previously discussed, the Mass Observation Archive is skewed towards middle-class and middle-aged or older respondents, but my smaller samples mitigated this to a degree by tapping into younger viewers with a broader class mix. Annette Hill's recent research, based on a sample of 4,500 British televison viewers, reports that 73 per cent of middle-class viewers watch natural history documentaries at least sometimes, while the figure for working-class viewers is 64 per cent. Hill, 'Documentary modes of engagement', in Thomas Austin and Wilma de Jong (eds), *Rethinking Documentary* (Buckingham, Open University Press, forthcoming 2008).

51 Nor is a presentational aesthetic exclusive to this subgenre. It may also be found, for example, in 'reality television' compilations of amusing moments involving pets and children, or footage of endangerment, accidents and narrow escapes.

52 Sarita Siegel, 'Reflections on anthropomorphism in *The Disenchanted Forest*', in Lorraine Daston and Gregg Mitman (eds), *Thinking With Animals: New Perspectives on Anthropomorphism* (New York, Columbia University Press, 2005), p. 197.

53 Crowther goes on to speculate: 'For some children, [talking about the

'facts of life'] is as close as they get to human sex-talk with their parents ... If wildlife programmes do have this educational function, families, and women and girls in particular, could surely be better served by a more gynocentric focus. There is still widespread ignorance, secrecy and embarrassment within families surrounding human female biology. Indeed the whole natural history genre could be cast in a different educational mould and explore other topics – physiology, medical conditions, hormone activity, fertility, aging, and so on. But there is no "demand" for this.' Crowther, 'Towards a feminist critique of natural history programmes', in Penny Florence and Dee Reynolds (eds), *Feminist Subjects, Multimedia: Cultural Methodologies* (Manchester University Press, 1995), pp. 130, 141.

54 For a study of gendered (and classed and age-based) patterning in some emotional responses of cinema audiences, based on a Mass Observation study conducted in 1950, see Sue Harper and Vincent Porter, 'Moved to tears: weeping in the cinema in postwar Britain', *Screen*, 37:2 (1996), pp. 152–73. They note: 'Time and again, women reported that scenes of children, animals or loss would prompt them to tears. But men were moved by "realism" and scenes of patriotism and self-sacrifice.' *Ibid.*, p. 171.

55 This is true of audience responses to screen fictions, as well as to documentaries. On the former, see Austin, *Hollywood, Hype and Audiences*, pp. 139–41.

56 For further discussion of the coexistence of narrative and non-narrative elements in Hollywood's fiction cinema, see Thomas Austin, '"A never-ending flashback": time, space and narrative in Anne McGuire's *Strain Andromeda The*', *New Review of Film and Television*, 4:2 (2006), pp. 131–46.

57 David Morley, *Home Territories: Media, mobility and identity* (London, Routledge, 2000), p. 268n.

58 Gail Davies, 'Virtual animals in electronic zoos: the changing geographies of animal capture and display', in Chris Philo and Chris Wilbert (eds), *Animal Spaces, Beastly Places: New geographies of human – animal relations* (London, Routledge, 2000), pp. 247–8.

59 The harnessing of new imaging technologies to produce novel spectacle is deployed very differently in the BBC/Discovery/NHK series *Planet Earth*, the UK channel's first major documentary excursion into High Definition television. An innovative 'heli-gimbal' stabilising device supporting a tiny high definition camera on a helicopter delivers extensive rock-steady aerial footage of animals in remote landscapes, and allows for cutting and zooming between close-ups and extreme longshots. The device is foregrounded and celebrated in the '*Planet Earth* diaries' segment at the end of episode one, broadcast in the UK on 3 March, 2006.

60 *Life in the Undergrowth*, episode one, BBC 1, 23 November 2005.

61 In another example, Alastair Fothergill, executive producer of *Planet Earth*, promoted the $40 million project and sought distributors for a film spin-off in Cannes with a silent showreel that foregrounded spectacle, accompanied by a live commentary which centred on the new capabilities of the apparatus. His pitch emphasised the promise of new attractions for audiences, and offered another instance of the spectacularisation of nature in the context of technological innovation. Chapter headings provided by intertitles in the showreel repeatedly stressed the novelty of the images on display: New Locations; New Species, New Behaviours; New spectacle; New perspectives; New Speeds. Alastair Fothergill, 'Planet Earth: an HD Masterclass', Sheffield International Documentary Festival, 14 October 2005.

62 'Life in the Undergrowth', *Guardian*, The Guide, 26 November 2005, p. 81. Note that in this review display threatens to overwhelm argument, but the two are still considered to be in some kind of equilibrium, even if the former is particularly dominant.

63 Such proposals and attempts to guide the viewer are never simply guaranteed and their efficacy cannot be taken for granted.

64 Vocal narration in wildlife documentaries also recalls the activity of the 'lecturer' in early cinema, who would 'specify spatio-temporal connections, point out details, and provide dialogue and motivation for the characters' actions'. Miriam Hansen, *Babel and Babylon: Spectatorship in American Silent Film* (Cambridge, MA, Harvard University Press, 1991), p. 45. Hansen is writing here about lecturers clarifying early narrative films for their audiences. But, as she notes, lecturers were most commonly associated with 'genres like travelogues, scenics, topicals, and actualities'. *Ibid.*, p. 96. Such staples of early cinema can be seen to have fed into what we now call screen documentary.

65 John Corner, 'Visibility as truth and spectacle in TV documentary realism', in Ib Bondebjerg (ed.), *Moving Images, Culture and the Mind* (Luton, University of Luton Press, 2000), p. 145. That Corner's argument parallels that of Hansen is not surprising, as dominant conventions of form in both cinema and television have developed to accommodate diversity and coherence in some kind of equilibrium. Corner adds: 'The need to instantiate general points and to keep the account strongly visual required frequent resort to "nominal portrayal" – the use of filmed material to illustrate general classes of person, place, thing and action rather than specific actualities.' This point can also be applied to the many unnamed, 'typical' animals that appear in wildlife documentaries. *Ibid.* Corner is citing Noel Carroll, *Theorizing the Moving Image* (Cambridge, Cambridge University Press, 1996), p. 241.

66 Nichols, *Representing Reality*, p. 31.

67 Bill Nichols, *Blurred Boundaries: Questions of Meaning in Contemporary Culture* (Bloomington, Indiana University Press, 1994), p. ix.

68 See for instance, Michel Foucault, *The History of Sexuality, Volume 1: An Introduction*, trans. Robert Hurley (London, Penguin, 1979); *Power/Knowledge: Selected Interviews and Other Writings* (ed. Colin Gordon) (Brighton, Harvester, 1980).

69 Of course wildlife documentaries can be seen to incite another activity, that of tourism, or seeking direct experiences of animals and locations only previously accessed through the act of viewing. For more on direct and mediated experiences, see the next section.

70 In his critique of recent developments in natural history programming, Simon Cottle notes 'a general avoidance of "gloom and doom" series (such as those purportedly thought to have turned away audiences in the 1970s)'. Cottle, 'Producing nature(s)', p. 97.

71 John Berger, *About Looking* (New York, Vintage International, 1980, reprinted 1991), p. 16.

72 Michael J. Watts, 'Afterword: Enclosure', in Chris Philo and Chris Wilbert (eds), *Animal Spaces, Beastly Places: New Geographies of Human–Animal Relations* London and New York, Routledge, 2000), p. 293.

73 *Ibid.*, pp. 293–4.

74 This is not always the case, however. Some documentaries promise to take viewers 'behind the scenes' of wildlife television. For instance, in the case of *Life in the Undergrowth* and *Planet Earth*, each hour-long episode in the series included a ten-minute sequence offering 'making of' footage of film crews and technology. The end credits of *March of the Penguins* show footage of the film's crew, who are excluded from the main body of the film. On how zoo designs absent their 'means of production' through the use of concealed enclosure and security measures, including moats and other hidden barriers, see Davies, 'Virtual animals in electronic zoos'.

75 Cottle, 'Producing nature(s)', p. 97.

76 Nichols, *Representing Reality*, p. 271n.

77 For a thoughtful discussion of the issues around 'fakery' in documentary, see Brian Winston, *Lies, Damn Lies and Documentaries* (London, British Film Institute, 2000), pp. 9–39.

78 Jonathan Burt, *Animals in Film* (London, Reaktion Books, 2002), p. 30

79 *Ibid.*, p. 12.

80 On the shift towards new formats exploring animal-human interactions, see also Cottle, 'Producing nature(s)', pp. 94–6.

81 Mitman continues: 'In Africa, native peoples, once an entertaining spectacle of nature for America audiences, became in the 1950s wildlife's greatest threat … By embracing an aesthetic of pristine wilderness, nature films reinforced a [conservationist and tourist-oriented] management scheme that effectively divorced humans from

the natural landscape. In East Africa, the Maasai and their livestock, once active agents in a biologically productive system, were expelled when international environmental organizations sought to promote tourism as the future source of wealth.' Mitman, *Reel Nature*, pp. 189, 202.

82   John B. Thompson, *The Media and Modernity: A Social Theory of the Media* (Cambridge, Polity Press, 1995), p 207. Thanks to Charlotte Adcock for pointing me to this book.

83   Polly Toynbee, 'Why weep over rodeo horses when there are the orphans of Kosovo also available for our tears?' *Radio Times*, 4–10 July 1998, p. 10.

84   Burt, *Animals in Film*, p. 25.

85   Berger, 'Why look at animals?' p. 17, using concepts from Lukacs, *History and Class Consciousness*, no page given. Building on Berger's work, Akira Lippit has written: 'Modernity can be defined by the disappearance of wildlife from humanity's habitat and by the reappearance of the same in humanity's reflections on itself: in philosophy, psychoanalysis, and technological media such as telephone, film and radio ... Technology and ultimately cinema came to determine a vast mausoleum for animal being.' Akira Lippit, *Electric Animal: Toward a Rhetoric of Wildlife* (Minneapolis, University of Minnesota Press, 2000), pp. 25, 187, cited in Burt, *Animals in Film*, p. 27.

86   Berger, 'Why look at animals?' p. 17.

87   Werner Herzog takes up this challenge in his film *Grizzly Man* (US, 2005). For a discussion of the film, see Thomas Austin '"... to leave the confinements of his humanness": authorial voice and constructions of nature in Werner Herzog's *Grizzly Man*', forthcoming, 2008.

88   Although he makes no mention of the 'daydream' passage, Burt critiques Berger and others influenced by him, such as Akira Lippit, for what he sees as their sweeping and homogenising distrust of screen images of animals, and for simplifying modernity's complicated and ambiguous ways of thinking about animal welfare. He comments: 'Of course Berger and Lippit have plenty of grounds for pessimism given the recent history of human–animal relations that the rapid rates of species extinction and widespread animal cruelty reveals [sic]. But the central question here is whether they are correct to imply that the multiplication of the animal image is, ultimately, not just a symptom but a contributory factor to this process.' Burt, *Animals in Film*, pp. 27–9.

89   Mitman draws historical links between developments in animal photography and filming for the US market, internationally-oriented conservationist discourses and policies in the US, and the burgeoning tourist trade, selling Africa as a relatively depopulated Garden of Eden available for wealthy Americans to explore on 'photographic safari' in the 1950s. He writes: 'In reinforcing an aesthetic relationship in which

the links between humans and nature were established primarily through the eye, wildlife films accentuated a nature seen through the tourist's lens. The removal of animals as a source of produced goods [through human activities such as poaching or culling, for example] was critical to this transformation of nature into a recreational economy.' Mitman, *Reel Nature*, p. 195. Binyavanga Wainaina has parodied Western attitudes to Africa in tips on 'how to write about Africa'. These include: 'Treat animals as well rounded, complex characters. They speak ... and have names, ambitions and desires. They also have family values: see how lions teach their children? Elephants are caring, and are good feminists or dignified patriarchs. Elephants may attack people's property, destroy their crops, and even kill them. Always take the side of the elephant.' 'How to write about Africa in five easy steps', advert for *Granta* magazine in *Guardian*, Review, 28 January 2006, p. 24.

90   It is important to remain sensitive to how the specificities of local contexts and histories might shape such attitudes, without 'excusing' them. For an examination of how local factors have shaped the world views of elderly white residents of London's East End see Geoff Dench, Kate Gavron and Michael Young, *The New East End: Kinship, Race and Conflict* (London, Profile Books, 2006).

91   As Tim Healey and Karen Ross have noted, elderly people need to be taken seriously as media consumers within academic research. One recurring concern among older viewers is the relatively infrequent and often stereotyped representations of elderly people on television. Tim Healey and Karen Ross, 'Growing old invisibly: older viewers talk television', *Media Culture and Society*, 24 (2002), pp. 105–20.

92   Ben Highmore, 'Homework: routine, social aesthetics and the ambiguity of everyday life', *Cultural Studies*, 18: 2/3 (2004), p. 324.

93   *Ibid*. Highmore is referring to C. Nadia Seremetakis, 'The memory of the senses, part I: marks of the transitory', and 'The memory of the senses, part II: still acts', in Seremetakis (ed.), *The Senses Still: Perception and Memory as Material Culture in Modernity* (Chicago, University of Chicago Press, 1994), pp. 1–18, 3–43.

94   Edward O. Wilson, quoted in Scott McVay, 'Prelude: a Siamese connexion with a plurarilty of other mortals', in Stephen R. Kellert and Edward O. Wilson (eds), *The Biophilia Hypothesis* (Washington D.C./Covelo, CA, Island Press/Shearwater Books, 1993), pp. 4–5.

95   Gary Paul Nabhan and Sara St. Antoine, 'The loss of floral and faunal story: the extinction of experience', in Kellert and Wilson, *The Biophilia Hypothesis*, p. 242.

96   Robert Michael Pyle, 'Intimate relations and the extinction of experience', *Left Bank*, 2 (1992), p. 66, quoted in *Ibid*., p. 242.

97   See various works by David Buckingham on this topic, such as David

Buckingham, *Moving Images: Understanding Children's emotional responses to Television* (Manchester: Manchester University Press, 1996); *Children Talking Television: the Making of Television Literacy* (London: Falmer Press, 1993).

98 Quoted in Ros Coward, 'Wild Shots', *Guardian Weekend*, 6 December 1997, pp. 34–40.

99 Quoted in E. Jane Dickson, 'The Greatest show on earth', *Radio Times*, 4–10 March 2006, p. 15.

100 *Ibid*, p. 14.

101 A United Nations report, 'Global Biodiversity Outlook 2', released around the same time as the television series, painted a very different picture. The report warned that 'The direct causes of biodiversity loss – habitat change, over-exploitation, the introduction of invasive alien species, nutrient loading and climate change – show no sign of abating … Biodiversity is in decline at all levels and geographical scales'. David Adam, 'UN warns of worst mass extinctions for 65m years', *Guardian*, 21 March 2006, p. 17. In this context, *Planet Earth*'s representation of a planet untouched by human activity may be reassuring, but it is also misleading and alarmingly complacent. A revealing instance occurs in the episode on freshwater environments, which includes a sequence on Lake Malawi, celebrated for having more species of fish than any other lake on the planet. No mention is made of the neighbouring Lake Victoria, where the introduction of the non-indigenous Nile perch has almost wiped out native fish, as depicted in Hubert Sauper's film *Darwin's Nightmare* (Austria, Belgium, France, Canada, Finland, Sweden, 2004).

102 Burt, *Animals in Film*, pp. 47–8.

103 *Ibid*., p. 48.

104 For instance, a feature in the travel section of the *Guardian* newspaper timed to coincide with the broadcast of *Planet Earth* offered information on five trips to featured locations with the promise 'Here's how to experience the highlights yourself'. Chris Madigan, 'Natural thrillers', *Guardian*, 1 April 2006, Travel, p. 3.

105 Thompson, *The Media and Modernity*, p. 265.

7

Conclusion: documentary world views

In this concluding chapter I want to revisit an issue that has been raised intermittently throughout the book, and continues to appear in ongoing debates around screen documentary. This is the thorny question of the social and political potential of the mode, grounded in its promise to re-present something of the world to its viewers. Of course, it cannot be assumed that this potential is always and unproblematically realised. Furthermore, any attempt to explore the orientations towards the world proposed via documentary must attend not only to its capacity to invite and stimulate audiences' engagement with, understandings of, and respect for, the people (and animals and environments) on screen, but also to the ways in which it can mobilise practices of distinction, disgust and the denial of any possible points of connection.

I use the phrase 'world views' to describe documentary representations and their multiple possible consequences. The term is useful, firstly because it is both a reminder and a refusal of the claims to transparency implicit in the cliché 'window on the world'. These claims – and, significantly, associated audience investments – still cling to some notions of documentary. But 'world view' also draws on another usage in common speech, where the expression emphasises the value-laden nature of a given perspective. In this sense it stresses the inevitably mediated, constructed and partial quality of any and every documentary's images, words, arguments and proposals. It gestures not only to the impossibility of neutrality or objectivity but also to the understanding that any view presented is the consequence of decisions and choices, resulting in one (or more) out of a multiplicity of perspectives that could possibly have been offered.[1] Finally, 'world views' is a form of shorthand for my critical method, which tries to hold in balance three objects of study: texts, audiences and contexts (commercial and social, of both large and small scales). More specifically, it suggests both how audiences are offered particular positions or 'invitations to view' on given topics, events and people, and how their acts of viewing will be shaped by variable and contingent locations, dispositions, values, experiences and senses of self – and also how some of these may on occasions be revised as a consequence of watching a documentary.

Some useful tools for further thinking through these issues are provided by Elaine Scarry's article 'The difficulty of imagining other persons'.[2] Scarry considers the 'difficulty of picturing other persons in their full weight and solidity'. This issue of the 'imaginability' or 'picturability' of others is important, she argues, because 'the way we act towards "others" is shaped by the way we imagine others.'[3] Ultimately, Scarry is concerned with constitutional and legislative changes necessary to solve the problem of 'foreignness', with its many ramifications for the treatment of 'strangers', from 'street cruelty' to the arena of 'international arms'.[4] Such changes, she argues, would be more effective than relying on spontaneous, local 'generous imaginings' of other people, although the two processes could be mutually supporting.[5] But she suggests that in some instances art can facilitate 'the imaginative labor of knowing "the other"', overcoming the relative poverty of mental imagining to 'achieve the vivacity of the perceptual world'.[6]

Scarry's definition of art is certainly problematic: by this she tends to mean 'great' literature, poetry and theatre, although she does allow Fassbinder's *Berlin Alexanderplatz* into her canon.[7] In addition to the contingencies of taste, subjectivity and cultural capital passed off as objective assessment that underpin her discussion at this point, the general neglect of audiovisual forms is striking. Nevertheless, her work offers an important reminder of both the potential and the limitations of cultural imagining, in which documentary (overlooked by Scarry) plays an important part.

Of course, such consequences may also be encountered by viewers of fiction film and television, and it would be both sweeping and wrong to suggest that this kind of material is entirely divorced from the 'real world' or irrelevant to audiences' understandings of that world.[8] Moreover, the categories of screen fiction and documentary are fluid, shifting, and far from monolithic; each encompasses a wide array of material, and no watertight barrier exists between the two.[9] While the films analysed in this book, not to mention new television hybrids, from wildlife shows to so-called 'gamedocs',[10] borrow devices from fiction and entertainment forms, the rhetorics of documentary and reality television are deployed in a plethora of dramas, fiction films and 'mock-umentaries'.[11] Nevertheless, a sense of difference persists, even while there is no automatic consensus about the exact location of the lines of demarcation between fiction and documentary. In Bill Nichols's pithy phrase, 'documentary is a fiction (un)like any other'.[12]

Dai Vaughan has argued that a 'puritan conscience informs documentary'. He writes: 'It is not that fiction cannot tell The Truth, but rather that fiction cannot lie ... Our puritan conscience de-mands a mode in which untruth is a hazard, just as science de-mands that a statement be open to disproof; otherwise, life is no more than a warm bath of solipsism.'[13] In the era of *Big Brother*, Vaughan's notion of a common 'puritan conscience' may seem both overstated and anachronistic.[14] Furthermore, his remarks are freighted with assumptions about shared audience strategies and responses. However, I think his argument still needs to be taken seriously. The point is that, however 'truth' about the world 'out there' might be defined – and such definitions may vary widely – documentary as a mode retains a (complicated, mediated, never direct) relationship with 'truth' that can set it apart from fiction. The realisation of this kind of expectation or aspiration is not to be taken for granted. But that fact does not necessarily diminish the significance of documentary's potential.

How and why does this capability often remain unfulfilled? However similar or distinct from fiction formats documentary is conceived to be, there is nothing that elevates the mode above the methods and consequences of caricature or oversight. Scarry of-fers a reminder of the way in which cultural representations can reinforce negative attitudes to others, via either ignoring or ste-reotyping them. The twin problems of 'underexposure and over-exposure' result in invisibility on the one hand, monstrosity on the other.[15] These are the negative impacts that haunt any docu-mentary, even while it may have the potential to mobilise more 'generous imaginings'.

The phrasing of Scarry's term here raises another pertinent

issue by emphasising the comfortable position of privilege from which the imaginer may be invited to view the other, such that 'discussions of "the Other" … sometimes allow the fate of "the Other" to be contingent on the imaginer: now another person's fate will depend on whether we decide to be generous and wise, or instead narrow and intolerant'.[16] This 'paternal power'[17] is recognisable in some of the world views, propositions and conceptions of self offered by documentaries to their audiences. For instance, as discussed in Chapter 5, *Paradise Lost 2* represents on screen, and itself could be seen to constitute, an attempt to connect across regional and class divides. But these efforts coexist with the film's mobilisation of a classed gaze that is both sympathetic and condescendingly judgmental. The power imbalances that produce, at one extreme, paternalist concern for those screened, and, at the other, the managed thrills of the freakshow, may also affirm the viewing self, comfortable and secure in her/his sense of superiority.[18]

So what will watching documentary 'world views' result in, beyond the temporary engagements of the process of viewing? Sometimes nothing immediately evident or tangible, perhaps nothing accessible to the probings of audience research. Sometimes an affirmation of initial orientations or assumptions, simplistic or reliant on stereotypes though they may be (as evident in some of the responses to *Capturing the Friedmans* discussed in Chapter 4). Sometimes a refusal to open up to novel proposals or understandings, however forcefully or subtly they may be presented. But at times watching a documentary may contribute towards a shift in senses (both cognitive and emotional) of the world 'out there', and associated attitudes towards it. Viewing may even, on some occasions, precipitate a revision of understandings of self, of others and of the relations between the two (again traceable in some viewers' comments about *Capturing the Friedmans*). In these instances – however transient, ambiguous, or complicated by the dynamics of voyeurism or stereotyping some of them might be – may be seen the power of documentary to enlarge viewers' capacity for 'generous imaginings' of others, but also for confronting, re-imagining, and grappling with a new, less complacent sense of self.

Notes

1   This is not to suggest that all documentaries are unequivocal in their proposals. As some of the instances discussed in this book show, differing degrees of multivocality, polyvalence, ambiguity and inconsistency abound in documentary texts.

2   Elaine Scarry, 'The difficulty of imagining other persons', in Eugene Weiner (ed.), *Handbook of Inter-Ethnic Coexistence* (New York, Continuum, 1998), pp. 40–62.

3   *Ibid.*, p. 40.

4   *Ibid.*, p. 40.

5   *Ibid.*, pp. 55, 57–8.

6   *Ibid.*, pp. 45, 46.

7   *Ibid.*, p. 46.

8   For a discussion of how senses of self and others, including understandings of gender roles, are worked through via watching a fiction film, see Austin, *Hollywood, Hype and Audiences*, Chapter 3, 'Basic Instinct: woman on top?'.

9   Moreover, Philip Rosen emphasises similarities between documentary and fiction film when he argues that: 'If shots as indexical traces of past reality may be treated as documents in the broad sense, documentary can be treated as a conversion from the document. This conversion involves a synthesizing knowledge claim, by virtue of a sequence that sublates an undoubtable referential field of pastness into meaning ... mainstream [fiction] cinema also works through the sublation of document into sequence. The "document" here is the shot comprehended as an indexically traced record of a pre-existent, profilmic field. Such preexistents include actors' bodies ... performances, and studio or location settings.' He also suggests that, historically, 'in its own originary self-definitions, the documentary tradition shares the denigration of preclassical cinema [in particular, 'actualities'] with its putative other, mainstream fictional film making.' Rosen, *Change Mummified*, pp. 240–1, 243.

10   Corner, 'Performing the real', pp. 255–69.

11   On mock-documentaries, see Jane Roscoe and Craig Hight (2001) *Faking It: Mock-Documentary and the Subversion of Factuality* (Manchester, Manchester University Press, 2001) and Paul Ward, *Documentary: The Margins of Reality* (London, Wallflower Press, 2005), pp. 12–13, 69–72.

12   Nichols, Representing Reality, p. 109.

13   Vaughan, *For Documentary*, p. 198.

14   By contrast, in a recent analysis of *Big Brother*, Jon Dovey notes 'a generalised sense that public culture has lost any claims to seriousness that it may once have made and instead become the domain of

playfulness, games and pleasure'. In response to both Vaughan and
Dovey I would argue that the puritan and the playful intertwine and
overlap in often complicated ways within 'factual' television and film,
as well as in public culture more generally, and that neither one should
be overemphasised at the expense of the other. Dovey, 'It's only a
game show: Big Brother and the theatre of spontaneity', in Mathijs
and Jones (eds), *Big Brother International*, p. 235.

15 Scarry, 'The difficulty of imagining other persons', p. 48. Scarry makes
the point that the two techniques may be combined in a powerful
synergy. For instance, the absenting of Iraqi casualties from American
television screens during the first Gulf War was accompanied by the
'magnified, overexposed, sexually caricatured image of Saddam
Hussein'. Scarry's analysis here could equally apply to the second Gulf
War: 'As we watched missiles going into targets that appeared to have
no people within, it was as though either no one would be killed or
the Gruesome Tyrant alone would be killed.' *Ibid.*, p. 48.

16 *Ibid.*, p. 52.

17 *Ibid.*, p. 53

18 See also Myra Macdonald, 'Politicizing the personal: women's voices
in British television documentaries', in Cynthia Carter, Gill Branston
and Stuart Allan (eds), *News, Gender and Power* (London, Routledge,
1998).

Methodological appendix

Throughout this study I have combined textual and contextual investigations of documentary forms with qualitative audience research. Each of the various methods of data gathering and analysis employed in this research has its own advantages, weaknesses and consequences. I have directly sought expressions of response from filmgoers via questionnaires designed according to my research concerns and imperatives. I have also drawn on existing materials, such as web postings, whose production has been shaped by a number of influences, but not my own interventions. In between the two poles of these 'solicited' and 'found' viewer statements lies the Mass Observation Archive, a pre-existing forum to which I addressed a specific set of questions. Finally, I have examined my own responses to the two *Paradise Lost* documentaries, not in order to elevate myself as a viewer more worthy of attention than others quoted in this book, but rather to acknowledge and foreground my own speaking position, which has informed the whole project.

Whatever the particular audience research method in use at any moment, a number of points are pertinent. First, my own decisions and actions, both in research design and the selective interpretation of viewer responses, need to be acknowledged. It is vital that any researcher remain aware of her/his own interventions in producing audience statements as knowable data. This process will include gathering and organising data, often arranging individual respondents into larger groups, and according significance to chosen extracts. I have termed this discursive production of audiences and their activities 'audiencing'.[1]

The partial, incomplete and contextually shaped nature of any knowledges produced via audience research should also be recognised. I have already pointed to some examples of this in earlier chapters. But while the chain of decisions involved in audiencing requires self-reflexive examination, care should be taken to avoid losing sight of the purpose of the study and tipping over into critical paralysis and/or the assumption that somewhere over the horizon might lie a source of direct, unmediated access to the 'truth' of audience response. (This is not to argue for a relativist tolerance of any and all research methods as equally compromised or useful, however. It is still possible to make critical distinctions between successful and unsuccessful audience research.) Accordingly, in this book I have paid attention to some of my research choices and their implications while trying to avoid the defeatism born of excessive self-criticism. At the end of this appendix, I have listed questionnaires and relevant sample information for my case studies. In the next two sections, I consider procedures of data gathering and analysis in a little more detail.

Data gathering

The contingent and performative nature of statements from respondents needs to be confronted. These have inevitably been shaped in part by the various conditions of their production, whether the relevant context is a website forum, archive sample, or a questionnaire handed out at a particular cinema. Consequently, decisions about how to locate – and in some ways produce – an audience sample, and how to gather data from it, become significant.

For instance, Chapter 6, on watching wildlife documentaries on television made use of a questionnaire handed out to 27 sixth-formers of various ethnic and class backgrounds from an inner London college, who were taking a short residential course at the campus where I work. This step enabled me to widen the ethnic and social range of respondents discussed, beyond the largely white and often middle-class samples provided by my pilot study and the Mass Observation Archive. The particular social context of this research scenario, namely an educational setting in a university teaching room, and accompanying power relations between myself as an admissions tutor and researcher and the visiting sixth-formers, may well have encouraged demand characteristics whereby respondents try to give the 'right answers'. In an attempt to mitigate this, I tried to present the event as an exchange rather than a formal exercise, a chance to swap information (about the University, about viewing habits) that would be mutually beneficial. The success or otherwise of this strategy is ultimately up to the reader to decide, but it is important to register it (and my perception of the need for it) as one small part of the research process. The study also drew on the writings of Mass Observation Archive correspondents, who employed a range of modes of self-presentation, from the apologetic to those making bids for distinction. An awareness of context-specific and presentational elements such as those discussed here does not invalidate my analyses, but should pre-empt any empiricist claims of straightforwardly accessing some objective truth.

Data analysis and interpretation

On the whole, qualitative audience research tends to devote more attention to self-reflexive consideration of method than many other traditions under the wide rubrics of film studies and media studies. However, as Ann Gray has noted, this self-reflexivity tends to focus more on moments and scenarios of data gathering rather than on the (inevitably intertwined) processes of 'writing up':

> Many researchers are now writing about their role and position within the research process, and especially … in relation to 'field work' of various kinds. However, the ways in which researchers go about organising and analysing their data and research material are rarely discussed. This is strange because, arguably, this is one of the most creative parts of the process where the researcher puts their own unique stamp on the project through their interpretation and analysis.[2]

As constituted and made sense of through such necessary processes of interpretation, audience materials can be used to open up dialogues with established understandings and theories. Suggestive discoveries made through audience research may support, confirm or challenge the researcher's prior assumptions, at times demanding that new critical models be proposed. In this way, audience research has the potential to function as an engine powering innovations in critical thinking. The researcher may thus become invested in seeking confirmation of a certain premise or hypothesis, or in seeking material that challenges existing paradigms, or may oscillate between these two positions. In any case, it is crucial that the s/he is sufficiently open-minded to view surprise as a positive outcome, and if necessary, to take the trouble to rethink critical approaches and interpretations in response to any such shock thrown up by audience research. This is also an important way of showing respect for people being 'audienced' by the researcher.

Matt Hills's consideration of the contrasting possibilities of confirmation or surprise, developed via his application of Christopher Bollas's notion of the 'aleatory object' to the procedures of audience research, is of relevance here. Hills suggests that:

> the encounter of academic Self and respondent Other can itself be considered as an interplay between desire and surprise. That is, the researcher may still hear what he or she wants to, may focus on statements and behaviour that appear to fit into pre-existent theoretical frameworks, and may use such statements to support theoretical certainties and orthodoxies ... But certain moments ... may also give rise to material that is not felt to be theoretically prefigured ... To this extent, the ethnographic Other can act as a form of aleatory object for the researcher, where 'the individual uses things while knowing that the aleatory vector is so prominent that he will also be played upon by the object'.[3]

In Chapter 6 I considered the research process in terms of a series of risks and opportunities, when viewed from the perspective of respondents. The same is also true from the researcher's standpoint. Audience research carries the promise of new discoveries, in terms of both novel understandings or knowledges and the means by which to engage with existing theories and debates. However, these prizes are far from guaranteed. One of the disincentives associated with audience studies is the disappointment experienced (or merely feared) when a project leads to little that can be rendered 'useful' or productive. Of course, much of the researcher's (relatively invisible) labour is precisely in forging connections of various kinds between current understandings within the field and new audience data. It is this under-explored labour of 'making use' of audience research via critical interpretation that both Hills and Gray call attention to in the passages quoted above.

An understandable response to research disappointments is to want to draw a veil over them, rather than admit to mistakes or to a lack of progress or insight. In a rare exception to this general silence, Ellen Seiter writes of a 'troubling interview' at which she found it impossible to build any rapport with two men who were talking to her about their television viewing, or to gain material that she considered usable or relevant. Ultimately, Seiter recuperates this negative experience as the motor for a self-reflexive assessment of the interview as research process and of the power relations which structured it.[4] I cannot recuperate all my own problems and dead ends quite so effectively here. I have already written in this book about the difficulty of tracking down viewers who have refused to watch, or have never encountered, certain films and programmes. However, one or two other moments in the project have been of rather less utility. Nevertheless, I do still want to acknowledge them as a part of the larger story of this research project.

As in any audience study, I experienced moments of disappointment and thwarted expectations, as well as of surprise and excitement. The latter included the range and depth of responses discovered via the Mass Observation Archive, the *Capturing the Friedmans* website forum, and questionnaires returned by viewers of *Touching the Void*. For me, parts of the case study of audience responses to *Etre et avoir* were rather more problematic, however. I was hoping that this study would deliver more material on issues of class and taste than proved to be the case. In the event, I feel that the chapter works well as a discussion of generic expectations of the documentary mode, and as an initial inquiry into middle-class taste publics. Fortunately, as this was my first study in the project, I also had time to respond by designing and writing another inquiry (now Chapter 5) which made use of autoethnography to extend my consideration of issues of class and/in documentary.

Before moving on to details of the questionnaires used, and audience samples produced, in this study, I want to briefly return to one point raised above: the role of audience statements in catalysing critical inquiry. When audience research is written up, the final format may at times seem to imply that all research questions have been considered, read around, and refined before any engagement with the audience, who simply add the final, illustrative, pieces in the puzzle. This is not in fact the case in the current study (nor in my earlier work on audiences for Hollywood fiction films). Of course, in both cases I did have significant initial areas of interest, questions and avenues of inquiry which shaped, among other things, the choice of case study films and television programmes. But, at every subsequent step of the journey, audience responses raised, or newly inflected, such issues in ways that demanded further thought.

In the current study, these instances included discussions of the appeals of France among the *Etre et Avoir* sample, notions of a portable inspiration attested to by viewers of *Touching the Void*, engagements with the personal and the political raised on the *Capturing the Friedmans* website, and a range of attitudes towards mediated and first-hand encounters with the natural world displayed by correspondents in the Mass Observation Archive. The interpretation and analysis of this kind of material required looking further into such issues, reading more, and ultimately, working to accommodate these themes and issues into the structure of each chapter. This last activity may on occasions downplay the vicissitudes of research activity in order to stress the authority and coherence of the final argument presented. In this brief appendix I hope to have redressed the balance slightly by pointing to some of the halting steps taken on the way to producing such 'finished' audience research.

Etre et avoir questionnaire

QUESTIONNAIRE
PART ONE
*PLEASE ANSWER THE QUESTIONS ON THIS PAGE BEFORE READ-
ING THE REST OF THE QUESTIONNAIRE*

1   What were your responses to *Etre et avoir*?
    (please use another page if necessary)
2   Why did you go to see the film?
3   What did you know about the film before watching it? Where did this
    information come from?
4   What did you like best about the film?
5   What did you like least about the film?
6   How important to your enjoyment was the fact that the film is a
    documentary?
    Please give reasons for your answer.
7   How important to your enjoyment was the fact that the film is French?
    Please give reasons for your answer.
8   How would you describe the *differences* between this particular film and
    a typical fiction film?
9   How would you describe the *similarities* between this particular film
    and a typical fiction film?
10 How would you describe the ideal audience for the film?
11 Who did you identify with when watching the film, and why?
12 Did you notice anything about the film's *form* (over and above its *content*)?
    If so, what was your response to this element/s?
13 Are you a regular consumer of documentary films?
    If 'yes', please say why. If 'no', please say why not.
14 Please list the last three documentaries you watched.
15 How would you define a good documentary film?
16 How would you describe the *differences* between documentary film (in
    general) and fiction film (in general)?
17 How would you describe the *similarities* between documentary film (in
    general) and fiction film (in general)?
18 Are you a regular consumer of 'reality television'?
    If 'yes', please say why. If 'no', please say why not.
19 Please list the last three 'reality television' programmes you watched.

20 How would you define good 'reality television'?

21 Do you trust documentary films to tell the truth?
Please give reasons for your answer.

22 Do you trust 'reality tv' to tell the truth?
Please give reasons for your answer.

23 What are the last three fiction films that you watched (on tv, video or at the cinema)?

24 What are your three favourite programmes on tv?

25 What radio station/s do you listen to?

26 What are the last three books you read?

27 Please list your six favourite leisure pursuits in order.
Would you include going to the cinema or watching tv on your list?

28 Is there anything else you would like to say, about documentaries or any other issue raised by the questionnaire so far?

PART TWO

The following questions are entirely about you. I would be very grateful if you could answer them all. However, if you'd rather leave some blank, please do so.

29 First Name:
(please state 'Anonymous', if you wish)

30 Age:

31 Gender:

32 Nationality:

33 Race:

34 Occupation:

35 Education – please tick against relevant heading:

Secondary school – left at 16 (state)

Secondary school – left at 16 (private)

Secondary school – left at 18 (state)

Secondary school – left at 18 (private)

Further education – please give details:

Higher Education:

University degree (BA, BSc etc)

University degree (MA, MSc etc)

36 Do you speak French?

37 Contact details (these are optional):

Address:

Phone no:

Email address:

38 Would you be prepared to be interviewed for the second stage of the research project   = individually?   = in a group?

39 Would you be prepared to be quoted in any publication based on this research? (please tick)

Yes – by first name   Yes – anonymously
No

THANK YOU FOR YOUR TIME

Etre et avoir audience sample

Anon., (1), British, white, female, school counsellor, age 51
Anon., (2), no race or nationality given, male, student, age 30
Anon., (3), French, white, female, senior lecturer, age 44
Anon., (4), British, white, male, entertainment news editor, age 38
Anon., (5), British, white, female, secretary, age 59
Anon., (6), British, white, female, educational psychologist, age 35
Anon., (7), British, white, female, teacher/lecturer, age not given
Anon., (8), British, white, female, nurse, age 52
Anon., (9), British, white, female, teacher, age 45
Anon., (10), British, white, male, student, age 30
Anon., (11), British, white, female, learning and development facilitator, age 50
Anon., (12), British, white, female, occupational therapist, age 28
Anon., (13), British, white, male, teacher and psychotherapist, age 52
Anon., (14), Spanish, white, female, postgraduate student, age 26
Paul, British, white, male, teacher, age 31
Chris, British, white, male, teacher, age 44
Sophie, British, white, female, tacher, age 23
Caroline, British, white, female, student, age 34
Mark, British, white, male, book editor, age 39
John, English, white, male, instructor, age 60
Tim, British, white, male, teacher, age 46
Lynne, British, white, female,teacher, age 51
Kenneth, British, white, male, retired telecomms engineer, age 82

Mar, Spanish, white, female,research fellow in physics, age 36
Jon, British, white, male, teacher and psychotherapist, age 52
David, British, white, male, teacher, age 36
Bernard, British, white, male, chartered surveyor, age 52
Victoria, British, white, female,teacher, age 29
Haydn, British white, male, Access student, age 29
Cas, British, white, female, teacher, age 51
Anne, British, white, female, home tutor, age 55
Graham, British, white, male, teacher, age 57
Janet, British, white, female, university lecturer, age 52
Pascal, French, white, male, project engineer, age 30
Adrian, British, white, male, journalist, age 34
Roy, British, white, male, retired accountant, age 65

Touching the Void questionnaire

QUESTIONNAIRE
PART ONE
PLEASE ANSWER THE QUESTIONS ON THIS PAGE BEFORE READING THE REST OF THE QUESTIONNAIRE

1 What were your responses to *Touching the Void*?
   (please use another page if necessary)

2 Why did you go to see the film?

3 What did you know about the film before watching it? Where did this information come from?

4 What did you like best about the film?

5 What did you like least about the film?

6 Did *Touching the Void* remind you of any other films (or tv programmes)? Please give details

7 If you have read Joe Simpson' book, *Touching the Void*, how would you compare the book and the film? Do you prefer one over the other? If so why?

8 Do you think anything should have been done differently by the filmmakers?
   If so, please give details.

9 How important to your enjoyment was the fact that the film is a documentary?
   Please give reasons for your answer.

10 How important to your enjoyment was the fact that the film was based on Joe Simpson's book? Please give reasons for your answer.

11 Were any other factors important to your enjoyment of the film? Please give details.

12 Do you think this story would have worked as well, better, or less well, as a fiction film? Please give reasons for your answer

13 How would you describe the ideal audience for the film?

14 Who did you identify with when watching the film, and why?

15 The film combines interviews with re-enactments of the climb.
Do you think these two elements combined successfully or not?
Did you prefer one of these elements over the other?
(Please give reasons for your answer)

16 Do you think the film ran into any ethical or moral dilemmas or problems?
(Please give reasons for your answer)

17 Are you a regular consumer of documentary (on film, video or tv)?
If 'yes', please say why. If 'no', please say why not.

18 Please list the last three documentaries you watched.

19 How would you define a good documentary film?

20 Do you think documentaries are best suited to the cinema, video, or television, or all three? (Please give reasons for your answer)

21 Do you trust documentary films to tell the truth?
Please give reasons for your answer.

22 Do you have any experience of climbing yourself?
(If so, please give details)

23 Please list your six favourite leisure pursuits in order.
Would you include going to the cinema or watching tv on your list?

24 Is there anything else you would like to say, about *Touching the Void* or any other issue raised by the questionnaire so far?

PART TWO

The following questions are entirely about you. I would be very grateful if you could answer them all. However, if you'd rather leave some blank, please do so.

25 First Name: (please state 'Anonymous', if you wish)

26 Age:

27 Gender:

28 Nationality:

29 Race:

30 Occupation:

31 Education – please tick against relevant heading:

Secondary school (state)

Secondary school (private)

Further education – please give details:

Higher Education:

University degree (BA, BSc etc)

University degree (MA, MSc etc)

32 Contact details (these are optional):

Address:

Phone no:

Email address:

33 Would you be prepared to be interviewed for the second stage of the research project   = individually?   = in a group?

34 Would you be prepared to be quoted in any publication based on this research? (please tick)

Yes – by first name   Yes – anonymously

No

THANK YOU FOR YOUR TIME

Touching the Void audience sample

Anon. (1), white, British, male, playwright, age '50s', no climbing experience

Anon. (2), white, British, male, academic, age 45, with climbing experience

Anon. (3), white, British, male, accountant, age 40, no climbing experience

Anon. (4), no details given.

Anon. (5), no details given.

Anon. (6), no details given, some climbing experience

Anon. (7), white, British, female, housing officer, age 45, no climbing experience

Anon. (8), white, British, female, therapist, age 36, limited climbing experience

Anon. (9), white, British, female, yoga teacher, age 51, climbed briefly when younger

Anon. (10), white, British, female, doctor, age 40, mountain walking experience

Anon. (11), white, British, male, GP, age 40, some climbing experience

Anon. (12), white, Austrian, therapist, female, age 37, no climbing experience

Anon. (13), British, no race given, male, visual effects artist, age 49, lists walking as a hobby

Anon. (14), British, no race given, female, office worker, age 58, no climbing experience

Anon. (15), British, no race given, male, age 49, no climbing experience

Anon. (16), white, British, female, conference organiser, age 47, some climbing experience

Anon. (17 and 18), mother and son completed questionnaire together, white, British, female, teacher, age 54 and white, British, male, school student, age 16

Anon. (19), British, no race given, male, head of research group, age 54, 'limited' climbing experience

Anon. (20), British, no race given, female, unemployed, age 49, no climbing experience

Anon. (21), white, French, female costumier, age 32, no adult climbing experience

Ben, white, British, male, account director, age 34, no climbing experience

Claire, white, British, female, education officer, age 27, indoor climber (Brighton Explorers)

David, white, British, male, mountain guide, age 39

Jack, white, British, male, teacher, age 31, 'a little' climbing experience

Jane, British, no race given, female, public service manager, age 46, no climbing experience

Janet, white British, female, retired school teacher, age 60, some climbing experience

Jo, white, British, female, doctor, age 40, general mountain walking

Julia, white, British, female, environmental health officer, age 36, climbs 'a very small amount'

Kim, white, British, female, painter and decorator, age 46, some climbing experience 'as a learner'

Linda, white, British, female, administrator, age 52, non-climber

Martin, white, British, male, cabinet maker, age 27, some climbing experience

Peter, white, British, male, Ph.D. student/painter and decorator, age 37, hill walker

Peter, white, British male, clerical worker, age 38, 'low-level' climber

Phil, white, British, male, signalman, age 40, occasional climber (Brighton Explorers

Zoe, white, British, female, university administrator, age 60, non-climber

Mass Observation directive, summer 2005:

As usual, please start all three parts of your reply on a new sheet of paper with your M-O number, (NOT name), sex, age, marital status, the town or village where you live and your occupation or former occupation.

Remember not to identify yourself or other people inadvertently within your reply.

Part 1:
The Universe and Outer Space
...

Part 2:
Wildlife documentaries

Your viewing
What was the last wildlife documentary you watched? Was it a film/DVD/ video/TV programme? Why did you watch it? Where did you watch it? Whom did you watch it with? What did you think of it?

How often do you watch wildlife documentaries on DVD, VHS, TV?

Do you usually watch them on your own or with anyone else? Does anyone else in your family or house watch them?

Your opinion
What do you think of wildlife documentaries? Do they appeal to particular groups?

If you had to categorise them, how would you group them?

What makes an enjoyable wildlife documentary? And what makes a bad one? Please give examples.

Do you have a favourite show/presenter/channel for wildlife documentaries?

What do you think we learn from wildlife documentaries?

Part 3:
The General Election 2005
...

Respondents to part 2 of the directive:
(62 men, 108 women. Information on each respondent appears exactly as supplied)

Men:
A833 Male, 71, married, a son and daughter, Chelmsford, retired architect
A3153 Male, 42, married, Paddock Wood, Kent, Bank manager
B1426 Male age 70, married, living in Bracknell, retired quality engineer

now working part time as an activities tutor in a boarding school

B1442 Age 82, male married retired, served 43[?] years in aviation. During the war I held a commission in the RAF. Living in Spelthorne

B1509 Male aged 76, married, Oxford, retired chartered surveyor

B1654 Male pensioner (74), married and living with wife in Rugeley, Staffordshire. Former editorial manager with a weekly newspaper group publishing in Scotland

B1989 Male, aged 77, retired teacher, widower, living in Tunbridge Wells, Borough councillor (Liberal Democrat), former county councillor

B2240 Married male aged 84 Cathedral city in the south Retired senior business executive

B2969 54, male, lives in Hastings, married, retired

B3133 Sex – Male. Age – 21. Marital status – Single. Where I live – Prestwood, Buckinghamshire. Occupation – Computer Games Tester

B3227 Gender: male. Age: 38. Marital status: single. Home: Birmingham. Occupation: University Administrator

B3252 60 y-o social worker married male Stafford

C2256 Male age 56 married resident in Birmingham. Former secondary school teacher, retired 2002 as a result of ill health. Now doing some p[art time consultancy work for the Royal Meteorological Society and various voluntary activities.

C3006 Male 46 years divorced Gloucester local authority town planner

C3086 Male 31 Single Morpeth, Northumberland, Systems engineer

C3143 Male 47 married, Ipswich, management consultant

C3167 Male Single Aged 34 Stoke-on-Trent Warehouse operative

D1602 Male, 63, single, Wimbledon, retired newspaper executive

D3197 (no information given)

E2977 Male, age 23, single, living in Shropshire, working full-time in a factory making tiles

F2218 Anglo-Caledonian single male, aged 76, retired NHS supplies officer, resident in village of NE England.

F3174 Age 47 lecturer in History 6th form college Live in Wakefield Marital status: single

G2134 Male aged 86 retired civil servant Cheam widower

G2818 Male 50 single teacher Manchester

G3025 Male 42 married Cressbrook, Derbyshire, business analyst for a large, national communications company

G3126 Male aged 64 married Bedford French polisher

G3226 Age 57, married, retired police officer, now working part-time for the National Trust, resident in Swanage, Dorset

H3177 Male 61 Oldham married

H3216 Male married 46 Witham, Essex, primary school teacher

J3248 Male aged 58, Caerleon, Newport, South Wales, information and research manager

K3125 Male 49 Cheadle Staffs, Humanities teacher retired

L1504 Male 79 yoa married. Ottery St Mary [Devon], retired Administrator

M2854 Male 54 single Wisbech distance learning tutor

M 3118 (no details)

M3190 Male, 46, married, civil servant, living in east Boldon

M3217 Male, 36, single, Stamford, Lincolnshire, Screen printer/engrave/sign maker

N3031 Male age 55 married Solihull West Midlands Office Worker

P1278 (no details given)

P2034 Male, 78, ex school/music teacher Married Newark, Notts

P2915 Male 46 years old single Kingston Upon Thames teacher

P3135 Male 41 married Guisborough, Yorkshire, local government officer

P3209 Male age 65 married Welton, East Yorkshire, artist

R40 Married male retired builder East London

R470 Male, 71 years, retired LGV driver, widower, Basildon

R1418 Male aged 83, widower, retired decorator, Derby

R2065 Married retired 89 formerly administrator of the personal health services in London teaching district Mitcham Surrey

R2143 Male 83 years old married to the same wife for 57 years dwelling in Hythe, Hampshire, since retirement 18 years ago a retired chartered engineer ... working ... around the world.

R3032 Male, aged 63, married, Cardiff, retired civil servant

R3198 Aged 56, Caucasian male. Married with three 'children' all at University in England ... retired in 2004 as a business development director of a 'top three' pharmaceutical company ... B.Sc., Ph.D., D.Sc (Medicine) – all London University. Currently spending 2 weeks in Spain where we have a house.

S2083 Male age 74, married Kingston, Lewes, East Sussex, semi-retired part-time book-keeper

S2246 Age 82 Male Widower Northampton Retired engineer/teacher

S3035 I am a 58-year-old retired banker ... I took early retirement at the age of 50 and haven't regretted it for a moment. I am currently a part-time student studying for a BA in Landscape Studies at Sussex University ... I am married with two grown up daughters, and three grandchildren.

S3071 Male year of birth 1967 Aberdeen chartered surveyor

T3076 Male single 38 Melling, Liverpool Writer/PhD student/Digital TV tester

T3094 Male 34 married Macclesfield (Cheshire) analytical chemist

T3129 Male 36 single Great Somerford Wilts Army officer

V3091 Male 42 Cheltenham journalist

W565 male 78 years of age. Married. Herne Bay Kent Retired, Farmer

W1382 Male age 81 married retired technical writer Weston-super-Mare

W1893 b.1924. Male. Grew up in the Wirral ... Retired 1983 after 43
    years with the same company – as Seignior Production Manager in
    large food factory ... Lived in various locations in U.K. and Republic of
    Ireland. Now in Felixstowe. Have never voted Tory.

W3176 [Male] retired teacher widower, aged 64, living in Greenfield,
    Saddleworth

W3199 Sex: male, age: 16, marital status: single, occupation: student town:
    Barnstaple

Women:

A1292 grandmother p/t teacher Croydon 72 years

A1706 Female married ward clerk // artist Shoreham by Sea

A2801 I am female 39, single, living in York. Unable to work due to a long-
    term illness – I have had M.E. for nearly 17 years. Previously, I was
    training to be a solicitor.

B86 Female, 82, E. London, library asst., housewife

B89 Female aged 74 divorced Leighton Buzzard retired typist

B736 Female

B1771 Female age 69 married, Mitcham, Surrey, retired secretary

B2810 Female divorced 38 Todmorden

B3170 Male 23 single Wrexham administrator

B7867 Female, married, Barnstaple, retired secretary PA

B1180 Female 67 southcoast

B1215 Female 52 years, married + 2 children p/t recruitment advisor
    Plymouth

B1475 Female, 62, single, Chesterfield, retired auditor

B1898 Female, 73, married, Tunbridge Wells, formerly claims advisor,
    beauty consultant, etc. Now writing short stories.

B2154 Retired radiographer (therapy), single, female, aged 72. Small
    Cotswold town.

B2065 F married Staines Middx ex civil servant age 73 3 children 4 grand-
    children

B3019 Female, aged 38, single, living in the Isle of Man, civil servant,
    specialising in Government pension schemes

B3154 Female, 42 years old, married. Stoke on Trent. Money advisor.

B3185 Female, 38, married, Sheffield, Homemaker

B3220 Female, 38 years old, divorced, Kentallen, post office clerk

C41 Female 46 single Shetland single parent

C108 Female, 60 years, widow, RC, 3 stepsons, 1 son, retired, suburbs

C1191 Female age 50 divorced carer Limavady

C1786 Female age 55 married village in Bucks School secretary

C2053 Female, aged 51, married, chartered librarian, now a self-employed
    clerical worker, living in Attleborough.

C2078 Female 61 married Odiham

C2654 Female 62 married Birmingham retired adult education teacher

C2677 Female 53 married Lackock teaching assistant

C2888 Married female age 49 local government officer from Portslade, East Sussex

C1713 Female 56 yrs married Preston receptionist

C2091 Female 65 retired public librarian Eastbourne

C3038 Female 32 single London VT editor/videotape operator (television)

C3210 [no details]

D156 I am a married mum of three. I live in the south east of England. I was born in 1952, married in 1971, my children were born in 1972, 1976 and 1980. I am the manageress of a florist shop and I have 4 grandchildren...so far. D826 F aged 54, married, living in Bristol. Part-time social worker

D966 Female, aged 78, living in London, divorced/ Retired from work in a Citizens Advice Bureau, but still there as a volunteer receptionist; also a part-time minute taker at meetings.

D2585 Female – early 60s Nr Bristol – married 38 years 'children' now 37 and 34 (both still single!) 20 years work as Secretary in large aero-engine company Now P/T clerical at local hospital.

E124 Retired spinster headmistress, born 1924 East Lancs village was long term resident of Gtr Manchester town

E743 Female, born 1951 in Yorkshire. Married, living in Warrington, Cheshire. Part-time teacher of Special Needs in large comprehensive school. One husband, two adult children, two step; children, one cat.

F1560 Female, widow, retired, 84

F1589 F. born 1932 Nfk retd SRN 3 children family bizs [unreadable] firearms. Lives N Staffs

F3137 Female age 36, married, Mulbarton, Norfolk, researcher

G226 Married female age 64. Retired counsellor /therapist Living Fylde coast, N.W.England.

G1041 Female, 79, married, Purley, retired librarian

G3187 Female age 35 Southport Staff nurse

G3201 Female age 40, married, village Aberlemno Occupation: practice manager

H260 Married lady – age 75 – ex-shop manager Brentwood Essex

H266 Widow, 82, living happily in small Lincs town, many interests, USA, NWR Painting, writing, people, holidays, etc

H1703 58 year old female HR assistant married Derbyshire

H1705 Married female 54 Part time word processor operator/amateur artist St Helier, Jersey

H2410 Woman, aged 75, married ex Grammar school teacher, at present living in small North Yorkshire village

H2418 Female 53 single London reception/information worker

H2673 Female aged 65 widowed living London Docklands Working p/t Librarian

H2639 Female (married) aged 64 years library assistant (retired) housewife – Ipswich Suffolk

H2911 Female 40 years of age married Herstmonceux special needs assistant

I3189 Female 39 yrs, married

J1407 Widow, 80 London and LOW[?]

J2891 I am a 40 year old married woman with two children/ I have changed career from Occupational therapy to administration and have been doing volunteer work and courses to improve my skills. I am working part time temporarily in a HE College. I live in N Wales but I am not Welsh.

K798 54 year old married female; part-time student and writes, living Norfolk

L1625 F 83 single Grantham retired teacher

L1991 Female 68 years widow Brighton retired nurse/civil servant

L3253 Female 54 years married, Grimbsy housewife

M348 Writer, single, aged 75, SE England

M388 Female, 74, married retired lecturer live in Norfolk market town

N399 70 yr old mother grandmother, widow. Former nurse, former hospital clerical officer, living east London BSc Hons (Open) Dip H&SW. Retired due to ill health but now Author and writer.

M1201 Female 42 yo married Chester le Street housewife

M1395 Female, age 75 Divorced Cobham , Surrey formerly CAB adviser

M1571 Female age 74 married West Sussex village retired subpostmistress

M2164 F 78 widow retired biologist Essex village

M2290 Female, 76, married Glos village, ex journalist

M2629 F 77, married Bristol formerly tutor in adult education

M3055 Female 30 single London compliance manager

M3132 I am female, 42 (born August 1963), married and living in Linlithgow in the county of West Lothian in Scotland. I am a personal finance journalist and am also working on my first novel. I'm writing this on Friday, August 12, 2005.

M3147 Female 45 married husband, daughter 19, son 12, father in law, Conwy, shopkeeper

M3202 Married female Penymyndydd, Nr Chester 39 Snr prescribing support technician

N403 Female 68 years widow Pampisford[?] retired part time cleaner

N3212 Female, 29, married, Accrington, law librarian.

N3181 Female unmarried with long term partner 30 Leeds librarian

P1009 Female 65 married Aberystwyth

P1282 Female age 67 married, Lichfield Staffs, BA Humanities, retired, carer for two grandchildren

P1326 Female, married, aged 67, retired civil servant, living in a rural location near Bath with husband and dogs, with a large garden full of weeds and birds and wild creatures!

P1796 Female 59 part time consultant live in Dorset, married

P2138 Female born 1920s married Chorley, Lancs statistician (retired)

P2546 Woman, 80, married. Village near Hereford, retired social work manager

P2819 Female, age 40, married, from a country town, doing secretarial work.

P3213 Female married Dwygyfylchi

R860 Female married 1 son 57 yrs old South Cheshire retired hairdresser – lecturer – J.P. I still give talks with ladies groups

R1025 62 year old housewife, formerly book-keepr, living in Milton Keynes

R1227 F, 61, married, village near Exeter, primary school teacher.

R1468 F. 82. Rtd Eng Insp R.R Derby. Widow.

R1760 Female aged 75 widowed resident SW Essex retied civil servant

R2144 Female age 69 married, Birmingham resident, retired teacher

S1399 Female 56 married Tunbridge Wells no job

S2220 Fem. Widow German born/bred. Brit. Since 1947, in wee Scot. town, retired Headteacher

S2581 Aged 54 retired bursar Mirfield

S3179 Female 26 living with partner Stockport PA

S3188 Female 39 married Scunthorpe housewife

S3223 [no details]

T1411 Female 83 years widow retired teacher

T1843 Female caseworker separated, 56, Disley

T2543 Female, 71, single, retired library asst, Dudley west Mids.

W563 F retired m/o h/w tho' not Welsh lives in Welsh village and v happy here tho' alone.

W571 Female aged 67 married ex-sales assistant 1 daughter, 2 teenage grandsons. Cottingley, nr Bingley, West Yorkshire.

W632 Female/63/widow/Southwick W Sussex

W633 Female, married, 62. Journalist North-East England. One adult daughter, not living at home

W729 Age 48 female, married, supply teacher

W2107 F 64 divorced Ely museum asst

W2244 F married 76 years retired teacher/careers hamlet in small N town.

W2338 Retired female married teacher age 72 village near York

W3163 Female. 47. Co-habiting. Bacup, Lancashire. Wages clerk.

W3233 Female, 25, single, Woodhall Spa, part time sales assitant – full time student

Y2926 I am a married woman of 47, with 2 children, living in Horsham and working at the local Hospital

Notes

1 Austin, *Hollywood, Hype and Audiences*, p. 68.
2 Gray, *Research Practice for Cultural Studies*, p. 147. See also Ien Ang, 'Wanted: audiences. On the politics of empirical audience studies', in Ellen Seiter, Hans Borchers, Gabriele Kreutzner and Eva-Maria Warth (eds), *Remote Control: Television, Audiences and Cultural Power* (London, Routledge, 1989), p. 105: 'it is only through the interpretative framework constructed by the researcher that understandings of the "empirical" come about'.
3 Matt Hills, 'Patterns of surprise: the "aleatory object" in psychoanalytic ethnography and cyclical fandom', *American Behavioural Scientist*, 48:7 (2005), p. 808, quoting Christopher Bollas, *Being a Character: Psychoanalysis and Self Experience* (London, Routledge, 1993), p. 37.
4 Seiter, 'Making distinctions in tv audience research', pp. 61–84.

Select bibliography

.

Aldred, Nannette and Martin Ryle (eds.), *Teaching Culture: The Long Revolution in Cultural Studies* (Leicester, NIACE, 1999).

Altman, Rick, *Film/Genre* (London, British Film Institute, 1999).

Ang, Ien, 'Wanted: audiences. On the politics of empirical audience studies', in Ellen Seiter, Hans Borchers, Gabriele Kreutzner and Eva-Maria Warth (eds), *Remote Control: Television, Audiences and Cultural Power* (London, Routledge, 1989).

Arthur, Paul, 'Extreme makeover: the changing face of documentary', *Cineaste*, 30:3 (2005), 18–23.

——'On the virtues and limitations of collage', *Documentary Box*, 11 (1997), 3.

Aufderheide, Pat, 'The changing documentary marketplace', *Cineaste*, 30:3 (2005), 25–8.

Austin, Thomas, *Hollywood, Hype and Audiences: Selling and Watching Popular Film in the 1990s* (Manchester, Manchester University Press, 2002).

——'"To leave the confinements of his humanness": authorial voice and constructions of nature in Werner Herzog's *Grizzly Man*', in Austin and De Jong (eds), *Rethinking Documentary* (forthcoming, 2008).

——'"A never-ending flashback": time, space and narrative in Anne McGuire's *Strain Andromeda The*', *New Review of Film and Television*, 4:2 (2006), 131–46.

Bausinger, Hermann, 'Media, technology and daily life', *Media, Culture, Society*, 6:4 (1984), 343–51.

Bell, James, 'Memphis Blues', *Sight and Sound* (NS), 15:6 (July 2005), 87.

Berger, John, *About Looking* (New York, Vintage International, 1980, reprinted 1991).

Berrettini, Mark L., '"Danger! Danger! Danger!" or when animals might attack: adventure activism and wildlife film and television', *Scope* (NS), 1, (2005), online.

Biressi, Anita, 'Inside/out: private trauma and public knowledge in true crime documentary', *Screen*, 45:4 (2004), 401–12.

Bondebjerg, Ib, 'Public discourse private fascination: hybridization in "true-life-story" genres', *Media, Culture and Society*, 18 (1996), 27–45.

——(ed.), *Moving Images, Culture and the Mind* (Luton, University of Luton Press, 2000).

Bordwell, David, 'The art cinema as mode of film practice', *Film Criticism*, 4:1 (1979), 56–64.

Born, Georgina, *Uncertain Vision: Birt, Dyke and the Reinvention of the BBC* (London, Secker and Warburg, 2004).

Bourdieu, Pierre, *Distinction: A Social Critique of the Judgement of Taste* (London, Routledge, 1986).

Brunsdon, Charlotte, *The Feminist, the Housewife, and the Soap Opera* (Oxford, Oxford University Press, 2000).

——*Screen Tastes: Soap Opera to Satellite Dishes* (London and New York, Routledge, 1997).

Bruzzi, Stella, *New Documentary: A Critical Introduction* (London, Routledge, 2000).

Buckingham, David, 'Boys' talk: television and the policing of masculinity', in Buckingham (ed.), *Reading Audiences: Young People and the Media* (Manchester, Manchester University Press, 1993).

Burt, Jonathan, *Animals in Film* (London, Reaktion Books, 2002).

Butler, Tim and Mike Savage (eds), *Social Change and the Middle Classes* (London, UCL Press, 1995).

Chanan, Michael, 'On documentary: the Zapruder quotient', *Filmwaves*, 4 (nd), www.mchanan.dial.pipex.com/zapruder.htm.

Clover, Carol, 'Judging audiences: the case of the trial movie', in Christine Gledhill and Linda Williams (eds), *Reinventing Film Studies* (London, Arnold, 2000).

Collins, Jim, 'Genericity in the nineties: eclectic irony and the new sincerity', in Jim Collins, Hilary Radner and Ava Preacher Collins (eds), *Film Theory Goes to the Movies* (New York and London, AFI/Routledge, 1993).

'Commissioning contemporary factual', panel at Sheffield International Documentary Festival, 14 October 2005.

Corner, John, *The Art of Record: A Critical Introduction to Documentary* (Manchester, Manchester University Press, 1996).

——'Documentary values', in Anne Jerslev (ed.), *Realism and 'Reality' in Film and Media* (Copenhagen, Museum Tusculanum Press, University of Copenhagen, Northern Lights Film and Media Studies Yearbook, 2002).

——'Performing the real: documentary diversions', *Television and New Media*, 3:3 (2002), 255–69.

——'Visibility as truth and spectacle in TV documentary realism', in Ib Bondebjerg (ed.), *Moving Images, Culture and the Mind* (Luton, University of Luton Press, 2000).

——'Meaning, genre and context: the problematics of "public knowledge" in the new audience studies', in James Curran and Michael Gurevitch (eds), *Mass Media and Society* (London, Edward Arnold, 1991).

Corner, John, Kay Richardson and Natalie Fenton, *Nuclear Reactions: Form and Response in Public Issue Television* (Luton, John Libbey, 1990).

Cottle, Simon, 'Producing nature(s): on the changing production ecology of natural history TV', *Media, Culture and Society*, 26:1 (2004), 81–101.

Cousins, Mark 'What's up doc?', *Sight and Sound* (NS), 14: 2 (2004), 5.

Coward, Ros, 'Back to Nature', *Guardian*, 9 May 2005, G2, 6.

——'Wild Shots', *The Guardian Weekend*, 6 December 1997, 34–40.

Crowther, Beverley, 'Towards a feminist critique of natural history programmes', in Penny Florence and Dee Reynolds (eds), *Feminist Subjects, Multimedia: Cultural Methodologies* (Manchester, Manchester University Press, 1995).

Cruz, Jon and Justin Lewis (eds), *Viewing, Reading, Listening: Audiences and Cultural Reception* (Boulder, CO, Westview Press, 1994).

Daston, Lorraine and Gregg Mitman, 'The how and why of thinking with animals', in Daston and Mitman (eds), *Thinking with Animals: New Perspectives on Anthropomorphism* (New York, Columbia University Press, 2005).

Davies, Gail, 'Virtual animals in electronic zoos: the changing geographies of animal capture and display', in Chris Philo and Chris Wilbert (eds), *Animal Spaces, Beastly Places: New Geographies of Human–Animal Relations* (London, Routledge, 2000).

Dench, Geoff, Kate Gavron and Michael Young, *The New East End: Kinship, Race and Conflict* (London, Profile Books, 2006).

Dickson, E. Jane, 'The greatest show on earth', *Radio Times*, 4–10 March 2006, 12–16.

Dovey, Jon, 'It's only a game show: *Big Brother* and the theatre of spontaneity', in Ernest Mathijs and Janet Jones (eds), *Big Brother International: Format, Critics and Publics* (London, Wallflower Press, 2004).

Dyer, Richard, *White* (London, Routledge, 1997).

Dyja, Eddie, (ed.), *BFI Film Handbook 2005* (London, British Film Institute, 2004).

Ehrenreich, Barbara, *Fear of Falling: The Inner Life of the Middle Class* (New York, Harper Perennial, 1990).

Ellis, John, *Seeing Things: Television in the Age of Uncertainty* (London and New York, I.B. Tauris, 2000).

——*Visible Fictions: Cinema Television Video* (London, Routledge & Kegan Paul, 1982).

Faden, Eric, *Media Stylo 4: The Documentary's New Politics* (DVD, 2005).

Falcon, Richard, 'Back to basics', *Sight and Sound* (NS), 13:7 (2003), 29.

——'White ladder', *Sight and Sound* (NS), 14:1 (2004), 34–5.

Felski, Rita, 'Nothing to declare: identity, shame, and the lower middle class', *PMLA*, 115:1 (2000), 33–45.

Finch, Lynette, *The Classing Gaze* (London, Allen and Unwin, 1993).

Foucault, Michel, *Power/Knowledge: Selected Interviews and Other Writings* (ed. Colin Gordon) (Brighton, Harvester, 1980).

——*The History of Sexuality, Volume 1: An Introduction*, trans. Robert Hurley (London, Penguin, 1979).

Gabriel, John, *Whitewash: Racialized Politics and the Media* (London, Routledge, 1998).

Gant, Charles, 'Does truth pay?', *Sight and Sound*, 15:9 (September 2005), 8.

Gaudreault, Andre, 'Film, narrative, narration: the cinema of the Lumiere brothers', *Iris*, 2:4 (1984), reprinted in Thomas Elsaesser with Adam Barker (eds), *Early Cinema: Space, Frame, Narrative* (London, BFI, 1990).

Gauntlett, David and Annette Hill, *TV Living: Television, Culture and Everyday Life* (London, Routledge, 1999).

Gauthier, Guy, *Un Siecle de Documentaire Francais* (Paris, Armand Colin, 2004).

Gitlin, Todd, *Inside Prime Time* (New York, Pantheon Books, 1983, 1985).

Gledhill, Christine (ed.), *Home is Where the Heart Is: Studies in Melodrama and the Woman's Film* (London, BFI, 1987).

Grant, Barry Keith and Jeannette Sloniowski (eds), *Documenting the Documentary: Close Readings of Documentary Film and Video* (Detroit, Wayne State University Press, 1998).

Gray, Ann, *Research Practice for Cultural Studies* (London, Sage, 2003).

——'Audience and reception research in retrospect: the trouble with audiences', in Pertti Alasuutari (ed.), *Rethinking the Media Audience* (London: Sage, 1999).

Gripsrud, Jostein, '"High culture" revisited', *Cultural Studies*, 3:2 (1989), 194–207.

Gunning, Tom, 'The cinema of attractions: early film, its spectator and the avant-garde', *Wide Angle*, 8:3–4 (1986), reprinted in Thomas Elsaesser with Adam Barker (eds), *Early Cinema: Space, Frame, Narrative* (London, BFI, 1990).

Hansen, Miriam, *Babel and Babylon: Spectatorship in American Silent Film* (Cambridge, MA, Harvard University Press, 1991).

——'Early cinema, late cinema: transformations of the public sphere', in Linda Williams (ed.), *Viewing Positions: Ways of Seeing Film* (New Brunswick, Rutgers University Press, 1995).

Harding, Sandra (ed.), *Feminism and Methodology* (Milton Keynes, Open University Press, 1987).

Harper, Sue and Vincent, Porter, 'Moved to tears: weeping in the cinema in postwar Britain', *Screen*, 37:2 (1996), 152–73.

Hastrup, Kirsten, *A Passage to Anthropology: Between Experience and Theory* (London and New York, Routledge, 1995).

Healey, Tim and Karen Ross, 'Growing old invisibly: older viewers talk television', *Media Culture and Society*, 24 (2002), 105–20.

Highmore, Ben, 'Homework: routine, social aesthetics and the ambiguity of everyday life', *Cultural Studies*, 18:2/3 (2004), 306–27.

Hill, Annette, *Reality TV: Audiences and Popular Factual Television* (Abingdon, Routledge, 2005).

——'*Big Brother*: the real audience', *Television and New Media*, 3:3 (2002),

323–40.

Hills, Matt, *Fan Cultures* (London, Routledge, 2002).

——'Patterns of surprise: the "aleatory object" in psychoanalytic ethnography and cyclical fandom', *American Behavioural Scientist*, 48:7 (2005), 801–21.

James, David E., 'Introduction: Is there class in this text?', in David E. James and Rick Berg (eds), *The Hidden Foundation: Cinema and the Question of Class* (Minneapolis, University of Minnesota Press, 1996).

Keighron, Peter, 'What's up doc?', *Sight and Sound* (NS), 3:10 (1993), 24–5.

Kellner, Douglas, 'Poltergeists, gender and class in the age of Reagan and Bush', in David E. James and Rick Berg (eds), *The Hidden Foundation: Cinema and the Question of Class* (Minneapolis, University of Minnesota Press, 1996).

Kleinhans, Chuck, 'Class in action', in David E. James and Rick Berg (eds), *The Hidden Foundation: Cinema and the Question of Class* (Minneapolis, University of Minnesota Press, 1996).

Klinger, Barbara, 'Film history, terminable and interminable: recovering the past in reception studies', *Screen*, 38:2 (1997), 107–28.

Kuhn, Annette, *Family Secrets: Acts of Memory and Imagination* (London, Verso, 1995).

Lacey, Joanne, 'Discursive mothers and academic fandom: class, generation and the production of theory', in Sally R. Munt (ed.), *Cultural Studies and the Working Class: Subject to Change* (London, Cassell, 2000).

Lippit, Akira, *Electric Animal: Toward a Rhetoric of Wildlife* (Minneapolis, University of Minnesota Press, 2000).

Livingstone, Sonia, 'Audience research at the crossroads: the "implied audience" in media and cultural theory', *European Journal of Cultural Studies*, 1:2 (1998), 193–217.

Lockwood, David, 'Marking out the middle class(es)', in Tim Butler and Mike Savage (eds), *Social Change and the Middle Classes* (London, UCL Press, 1995).

Macdonald, Myra, 'Politicizing the personal: women's voices in British television documentaries', in Cynthia Carter, Gill Branston and Stuart Allan (eds), *News, Gender and Power* (London, Routledge, 1998).

McGown, Alistair D. (ed.), *BFI Television Handbook 2005* (London, British Film Institute, 2004).

McVay, Scott, 'Prelude: a Siamese connexion with a plurality of other mortals', in Stephen R. Kellert and Edward O. Wilson (eds), *The Biophilia Hypothesis* (Washington DC/Covelo, CA, Island Press/Shearwater Books, 1993).

Mathijs, Ernest and Janet Jones (eds), *Big Brother International: Format, Critics and Publics* (London, Wallflower Press, 2004).

Mepham, John, 'Television fictions: quality and truth telling', *Radical Philosophy*, 57 (1991), 20–7.

Messenger Davies, Maire and Roberta Pearson, 'Stardom and distinction: Patrick Stewart as an agent of cultural mobility: a study of theatre and film audiences in New York City', in Thomas Austin and Martin Barker (eds), *Contemporary Hollywood Stardom* (London, Arnold, 2003).

Minh-ha, Trinh T., 'The totalizing quest of meaning', in Michael Renov (ed.), *Theorizing Documentary* (New York, Routledge, 1993).

Mitman, Gregg, *Reel Nature: America's Romance with Wildlife on Film* (Harvard University Press, Cambridge, MA, 1999).

Moores, Shaun, *Satellite Television and Everyday Life: Articulating Technology* (Luton, John Libbey Media, 1996).

Moran, Joe, 'Childhood, class and memory in the *Seven Up* films', *Screen*, 43:4 (2002), 387–402.

Morley, David, *Family Television: Cultural Power and Domestic Leisure* (London, Comedia, 1986).

——*Home Territories: Media, mobility and identity* (London, Routledge, 2000).

Murdock, Graham, 'Reconstructing the ruined tower: contemporary communications and questions of class', in James Curran and Michael Gurevitch (eds), *Mass Media and Society* (3rd edn, London, Arnold, 2000).

Nabhan, Gary Paul and Sara St. Antoine, 'The loss of floral and faunal story: the extinction of experience', in Stephen R. Kellert and Edward O. Wilson (eds), *The Biophilia Hypothesis* (Washington DC/Covelo, CA, Island Press/Shearwater Books, 1993).

Neale, Steve, *Genre and Hollywood* (London, Routledge, 2000).

——'Melo talk: on the meaning and use of the term "melodrama" in the American trade press', *Velvet Light Trap*, 32 (1993), 66–89.

Nichols, Bill, *Blurred Boundaries: Questions of Meaning in Contemporary Culture*, (Bloomington, Indiana University Press, 1994).

——*Representing Reality: Issues and Concepts in Documentary* (Bloomington, Indiana University Press, 1991).

Paget, Derek, *No Other Way to Tell It: Dramadoc/Docudrama on Television* (Manchester, Manchester University Press, 1998).

Peterson, Richard A. and Roger M. Kern, 'Changing highbrow taste: from snob to omnivore', *American Sociological Review*, 61:3 (1996), 900–7.

'Planet Earth: an HD Masterclass', Sheffield International Documentary Festival, 14 October 2005.

Plantinga, Carl, *Rhetoric and Representation in Nonfiction Film* (Cambridge, Cambridge University Press, 1997).

——'Moving pictures and the rhetoric of non-fiction: two approaches', in David Bordwell and Noell Carroll (eds), *Post-Theory: Reconstructing Film Studies*, (Madison, University of Wisconsin Press, 1996).

Powrie, Phil, 'Unfamiliar places: "heterospection" and recent French films on children', *Screen*, 46:3 (2005), 341–52.

Press, Andrea, *Women Watching Television: Gender, Class and Generation in the American Television Experience* (Philadelphia, University of Pennsylvania Press, 1991).

Press, Andrea and Elizabeth Cole, 'Women like us: working-class women respond to television representations of abortion', in Jon Cruz and

Justin Lewis (eds), *Viewing Reading, Listening: Audiences and Cultural Reception* (Boulder, CO, Westview Press, 1994).

Reay, Diane, 'Children's urban landscapes: configurations of class and space', in Sally R. Munt (ed.), *Cultural Studies and the Working Class: Subject to Change* (London, Cassell, 2000).

'Reflections upon the encoding/decoding model: an interview with Stuart Hall', in Jon Cruz and Justin Lewis (eds), *Viewing, Reading, Listening: Audiences and Cultural Reception* (Boulder, CO, Westview Press, 1994).

Renov, Michael, *The Subject of Documentary* (Minneapolis, University of Minnesota Press, 2004).

'The rise of the cinema documentary', panel at Sheffield International Documentary Festival, 14 October 2005.

Roberts, Martin, '*Baraka:* World cinema and the global culture industry', *Cinema Journal*, 37:3 (1998), 62–82.

Roscoe, Jane and Craig Hight, *Faking It: Mock-documentary and the Subversion of Factuality* (Manchester, Manchester University Press, 2001).

Rosen, Philip, *Change Mummified: Cinema, Historicity, Theory* (Minneapolis, University of Minnesota Press, 2001).

Rotha, Paul, *The Documentary Film* (2nd edn, London, Faber, 1952).

Savage, Mike, James Barlow, Peter Dickens and Tony Fielding, *Property, Bureaucracy and Culture: Middle-Class Formation in Contemporary Britain* (London, Routledge, 1992).

Scarry, Elaine, 'The difficulty of imagining other persons', in Eugene Weiner (ed.), *Handbook of Inter-Ethnic Coexistence* (New York, Continuum, 1998).

'Science or art: commissioning specialist factual', panel at Sheffield International Documentary Festival, 13 October, 2005.

Seiter, Ellen, *Television and New Media Audiences* (Oxford, Oxford University Press, 1999).

——'Making distinctions in tv audience research: case study of a troubling interview', *Cultural Studies*, 4:1 (1990), 61–84.

Seremetakis, C. Nadia, 'The memory of the senses, part I: marks of the transitory', and 'The memory of the senses, part II: still acts', in Seremetakis (ed.), *The Senses Still: Perception and Memory as Material Culture in Modernity* (Chicago, University of Chicago Press, 1994).

Shaller, Deborah, 'Capturing the Friedmans', *Scope* (NS), 1 (2005), www.nottingham. ac.uk/film/journal/.

Siegel, Sarita, 'Reflections on anthropomorphism in *The Disenchanted Forest*', in Lorraine Daston and Gregg Mitman (eds), *Thinking With Animals: New Perspectives on Anthropomorphism* (New York, Columbia University Press, 2005).

Silvergate, Harvey A. and Carl Takei, 'Mistrial: the *Capturing the Friedmans* DVD sheds new light on the case', *Slate*, posted 27 February 2004, http://slate.msn.com/id/2096296/.

Silverstone, Roger, *Television and Everyday Life* (London, Routledge, 1994).

Simpson, Joe, *Touching the Void* (London, Vintage, 2003).

Skeggs, Beverley, *Class, Self, Culture* (London, Routledge, 2004).

——*Formations of Class and Gender: Becoming Respectable* (London, Sage, 1997).

Smith, Adam, 'Reel life drama', *Empire* (May 2004), 117–22.

Smith, Katherine M. Clegg, '"Electronic eavesdropping": the ethical issues involved in conducting a virtual ethnography', in Mark D. Johns, Shing-Ling Sarina Chen and G. Jon Hall (eds), *Online Social Research: Methods, Issues and Ethics* (New York, Peter Lang, 2004).

Smith, Murray, *Engaging Characters: Fiction, Emotion and the Cinema* (Oxford, Clarendon Press, 1995).

Smith, Paul, *Clint Eastwood: A Cultural Production* (London, UCL Press, 1993).

Social Trends, 31 (Norwich, The Stationery Office, 2001).

Stanley, Liz 'Women have servants and men never eat: issues in reading gender, using the case study of Mass-Observation's 1937 day diaries', *Women's History Review*, 4:1 (1995), 85–102.

Steedman, Carolyn, *Landscape for a Good Woman: A Story of Two Lives* (London, Virago, 1986).

Thomas, Lyn, *Fans, Feminisms and 'Quality' Media* (London, Routledge, 2002).

Thompson, John B., *The Media and Modernity: A Social Theory of the Media* (Cambridge: Polity Press, 1995).

Vaughan, Dai, *For Documentary: Twelve Essays* (Berkeley, CA, University of California Press, 1999).

——'Let there be Lumiere', *Sight and Sound* (Spring 1981), republished in Thomas Elsaesser with Adam Barker (eds), *Early Cinema: Space, Frame, Narrative* (London, BFI, 1990).

Vicente, Ana, 'Exhibition of documentary films in Europe', unpublished paper, 2004.

Vogler, Christian, *The Writer's Journey: Mythic Structure for Storytellers and Screenwriters* (2nd edn, London, Pan Books, 1999).

Walkerdine, Valerie, 'Video replay: families, films and fantasy', in Victor Burgin, James Donald and Cora Kaplan (eds), *Formations of Fantasy* (London, Methuen, 1986).

Ward, Paul, *Documentary: The Margins of Reality* (London, Wallflower Press, 2005).

Watts, Michael J., 'Afterword: enclosure', in Chris Philo and Chris Wilbert (eds), *New Geographies of Human–Animal Relations* (London and New York, Routledge, 2000).

Wheatley, Helen, 'The limits of television? Natural history programming and the transformation of public service broadcasting', *European Journal of Cultural Studies*, 7:3 (2004), 325–39.

Willemen, Paul, 'Looking at the male', *Framework*, 15–17 (1981), 16.

Winston, Brian, *Claiming the Real: The Documentary Film Revisited* (London, British Film Institute, 1995).

——*Lies, Damn Lies and Documentaries* (London, British Film Institute, 2000).

Wray, Matt and Annalee Newitz (eds), *White Trash: Race and Class in America*

(New York and London, Routledge, 1997).

Wyatt, Justin, *High Concept: Movies and Marketing in Hollywood* (Austin, University of Texas Press, 1994).

——'The formation of the "major independent": Miramax, New Line and the New Hollywood', in Steve Neale and Murray Smith (eds), *Contemporary Hollywood Cinema* (London, Routledge, 1998).

Zimmermann, Patricia R., *Reel Families: A Social History of Amateur Film* (Bloomington, IN, Indiana University Press, 1995).

van Zoonen, Liesbet, 'A Tyranny of intimacy? women, femininity and television news', in Peter Dahlgren and Colin Sparks (eds), *Communication and Citizenship* (London, Routledge, 1991).

Index

Note: 'n.' after a page reference indicates the number of a note on that page.

Africa 161, 174n.81, 175n.89
Africa's Elephant Kingdom 122
Animal Crime Scene 8, 128–9
Animal Planet 123, 128, 168n.21
anthropomorphism 140
Arthur, Paul 5, 12
Attenborough, David 128, 144–5, 168n.23
audience research methods 1–2, 34, 56n.10, 60, 85, 129–31, 133–6, 184–204
Aufderheide, Pat 20

Bang! Bang! In Da Manor 24
BBC (British Broadcasting Corporation) 22–5, 124, 164, 168n.21
Berger, John 151, 159–61
Berlinger, Joe 113, 114
Big Brother 15, 49, 180
Big Cat Diary 126, 153
biophilia 162
Biressi, Anita 93
Blair Witch Project, The 14
Blue Planet, The 125, 138–9
Bondebjerg, Ib 67–8
Bordwell, David 97
Bourdieu, Pierre 110

Bowling for Columbine 12, 14, 19
Broomfield, Nick 14, 15
Bruzzi, Stella 2, 88
Burt, Jonathan 152, 159, 164–6
Bus 174 14

Capturing the Friedmans 7, 8, 18, 20, 84–108, 181
Channel 4 22, 27n.12, 61
class 7, 34–5, 49, 51, 55n.3, 58n.40, 109–21, 130, 139, 171n.50, 181, 188
Clover, Carol 96
Cohen, Danny 22–3
Collins, Jim 44–5
Corner, John 2, 4, 41, 102, 146
Corporation, The 20
Cottle, Simon 21, 122–3, 152
Cousins, Mark 8, 15, 21
Coward, Ros 23
Crocodile Hunter 123
Crowther, Barbara 140
Czech Dream 13

Darwin's Nightmare 177n.101
Daston, Lorraine 138
Davidson, Martin 23
Davies, Gail 143

Deep Jungle 125
Discovery Channel 21–2, 154, 164, 168n.21
Disenchanted Forest, The 140
distribution 16–17
documentary 'boom' 8, 12–33,
DVD/s 20, 85–6

Ellis, John 24, 127, 169n.30
epistephilia 40–2, 54, 142, 146–9, 156
ethics 52–4, 75–8, 92–4, 104n.6,
Etre et avoir 6, 7, 8, 13, 16, 17–18, 20, 34–59
exhibition 17, 19

Faden, Eric 14, 17, 19, 21
Fahrenheit 9/11 17, 19
Felperin, Leslie 85
Felski, Rita 111
Fiske, John 111
Fog of War 12
Fothergill, Alastair 23, 24, 125–6, 164, 173n.61
Foucault, Michel 93, 150
Francophilia 49–51
Fraser, Nick 25

Galapagos 122
Gauthier, Guy 36
gender 72, 74, 118, 121n.30, 127, 132, 135, 140, 149, 169n.28
Gitlin, Todd 126
global warming 23, 164–5
Gray, Ann 35, 186–7
Gripsrud, Jostein 110
Gunning, Tom 137

Hankin, Richard 97
Hastrup, Kirsten 3
Herzog, Werner 69, 175n.87
Highmore, Ben 162
Hill, Annette 45
Hills, Matt 187

Holland, Luke 25–6
Hollywood cinema 15–16
Hoop Dreams 14

Irwin, Steve 123
ITV (Independent Television) 22, 125

James, David E. 111
Jarecki, Andrew 15, 86, 91, 95–6, 98, 102

Keighron, Peter 89
Kellner, Douglas 112
Klein, Richard, 124
Kleinhans, Chuck 111–12,
Kracauer, Siegfried 88

Last Chance to Save 124
Life in the Undergrowth 8, 144–6
Life on Earth 165
Lydon, John 153–4

Macdonald, Kevin 15, 16, 61, 63–4, 77–8
Macdonald, Myra 101
Mad Hot Ballroom 16
March of the Penguins 13, 18, 122, 153
marketing 5, 16–20, 30n.33, 38, 61–2, 90
Mass Observation Archive 129–30, 133, 184, 188
Mendez, Sean 24
Mepham, John 72, 80
Mitman, Gregg 129, 138, 153
Moore, Michael 14, 17, 19
Morley, David 143
Morris, Errol 14

Nichols, Bill 2, 15, 26, 40, 42–3, 52–4, 71, 75–6, 100, 113, 135, 146, 148, 152, 180
nostalgia 161–2

One Day in September 61, 63

Paget, Derek 79
Paradise Lost: The Child Murders at Robin Hood Hills 112–18, 181
Paradise Lost 2: Revelations 112, 115–18, 181
performance 52–3, 112, 115
Philibert, Nicholas 16, 49, 52,
Planet Earth 23, 125, 153, 164, 173n.61, 177n.101
Plantinga, Carl 61

reality television 15–16, 34, 47–9, 68
reconstruction 63–4, 76
Renov, Michael 2, 10n.9
Roger and Me 14

Savage, Mike 34, 110, 119n.9
Scarry, Elaine 179–81
Scholey, Keith 126
Seiter, Ellen 188
Seremetakis, C. Nadia 162
Shooting People 20
Skeggs, Beverley 10n.12, 51, 113
Sky One 124
Smith, Murray 73–4
Smith, Paul 69
spectacle 136–8, 145, 156
Spellbound 12, 16, 18, 20
Springwatch With Bill Oddie 126, 153
Spurlock, Morgan 17
Super Size Me 17

Tarnation 16

television 4, 7, 15, 20, 21–6, 45, 122–77, 180
Thin Blue Line, The 14
Thompson, John B. 154, 166
Touching the Void 6, 7, 8, 13, 16, 18, 20, 60–83
touristic gaze 156, 159, 174n.81, 175n.89
Toynbee, Polly 159
Trials of Life, The 129
truth claims 43–8, 88–9, 93, 96, 98, 100, 180

Vaughan, Dai 5, 65–6, 104, 138, 180
video 14, 84, 86–7, 89, 94, 96
Vogler, Christian 88

Walkerdine, Valerie 71
Watts, Michael 151
website/s 20, 22, 60, 77, 84–6, 90–1, 153
Wheatley, Helen 138–9
'white trash' 3, 113, 115–16
Wife Swap 15
wildlife documentaries 122–77
Willemen, Paul 69
Winged Migration 12, 13, 18, 19, 153
Winston, Brian 2, 3, 8, 21–2, 23, 49, 113
'world views' 178–8, 181
Wyatt, Justin 17

Zapruder, Abraham 88–9
Zimmermann, Patricia 94
van Zoonen, Liesbet 93